Jewish Families in Shtetl Kaushany, Bessarabia

Genealogy, History, Culture, Life and Death

by Yefim A. Kogan

JewishGen
מרכז עולמי לגנאלוגיה יהודית
The Global Home for Jewish Genealogy

A Publication of JewishGen
Edmond J. Safra Plaza, 36 Battery Place, New York, NY 10280
646.494.2972 | info@JewishGen.org | www.jewishgen.org

JewishGen is the Genealogical Research Division of the
Museum of Jewish Heritage – A Living Memorial to the Holocaust

MUSEUM OF
JEWISH HERITAGE
A LIVING MEMORIAL
TO THE HOLOCAUST

Library of Congress Control Number (LCCN): 2024951751

ISBN: 978-1-962054-19-5 (Hardcover: 220 pages, alk. paper)

About JewishGen.org

JewishGen, is a Genealogical Research Division of the Museum of Jewish Heritage - A Living Memorial to the Holocaust, serves as the global home for Jewish genealogy.

Featuring unparalleled access to 30+ million records, it offers unique search tools, along with opportunities for researchers to connect with others who share similar interests. Award winning resources such as the Family Finder, Discussion Groups, and ViewMate, are relied upon by thousands each day.

In addition, JewishGen's extensive informational, educational and historical offerings, such as the Jewish Communities Database, Yizkor Book translations, InfoFiles, Family Tree of the Jewish People, and KehilaLinks, provide critical insights, first-hand accounts, and context about Jewish communal and familial life throughout the world.

Offered as a free resource, JewishGen.org has facilitated thousands of family connections and success stories, and is currently engaged in an intensive expansion effort that will bring many more records, tools, and resources to its collections.

Please visit https://www.jewishgen.org/ to learn more.

Vice President for JewishGen: Avraham Groll

About JewishGen Press

JewishGen Press (formerly the Yizkor Books-in-Print Project) is the publishing division of JewishGen.org, and provides a venue for the publication of non-fiction books pertaining to Jewish genealogy, history, culture, and heritage.

In addition to the Yizkor Book category, publications in the Other Non-Fiction category include Shoah memoirs and research, genealogical research, collections of genealogical and historical materials, biographies, diaries and letters, studies of Jewish experience and cultural life in the past, academic theses, and other books of interest to the Jewish community.

Please visit https://www.jewishgen.org/Yizkor/ybip.html to learn more.

Director of JewishGen Press: Joel Alpert
Managing Editor – Peter Harris
Publications Manager - Susan Rosin

Cover Photo Credits

Cover designed by Irv Osterer

Kaushany map initially rendered by Khinka Kogan, Lev Bruter, and edited by Yefim Kogan.

Kaushany map redrawn by Irv Osterer.

Eleven photos are from Yefim Kogan's collection. Seven photos were donated by Kaushaners or their descendants to publish in this book.

Front Cover:

Top Row (Left to right):
Peisah and Hova Kogan, Peisakh Arkhimovich, Pincus Bruter
Second Row:
Elka Kogan
Third Row (Left to right):
Yosef Liebowitz, Khinka Kogan (Spivak) with her brother Izya Spivak, Ann Wise Shafter

Back Cover:

Top Row (left to right):
Zolman Kogan, Irikhem Kogan, Haim Haimovich, Meer Kogan, Motl Natanzon
Second Row:
Sheiva Srulevich with granddaughter Fanya Spivak (Haimovich)
Third Row (Left to right):
Eti Garshtein, Ershl Spivak, Shabsa Kogan
Fourth Row (Left to right):
Iosef-der-Roiter Kogan, Iosef Srulevich

Geo Political Information

Map of Moldova, showing the location of **Căușeni (Kaushany)**

Căuşeni

Căuşeni, Moldova is located at 46°39' N 29°25' E and 36 miles SE of Chişinău

	Town	District	Province	Country
Before WWI (c. 1900):	Novyye Kaushany	Bendery	Bessarabia	Russian Empire
Between the wars (c. 1930):	Căuşenii-Noi	Tighina	Basarabia	Romania
After WWII (c. 1950):	Kaushany			Soviet Union
Today (c. 2000):	Căuşeni			Moldova

Alternate Names for the Town:

Căuşeni [Mold], Kaushany [Rus], Căuşenii-Noi [Rom], Koshany [Yid], Novyye Kaushany [Rus], Novyye Keushani, Novo Kaushani, Noui Căuşanii, Kaushani-Noui, Kaushani, Căuşani-Novi, Căuşanii-Noui, Causani Noui, Kausany

Nearby Jewish Communities:

Copanca 11 miles ENE
Bender 13 miles N
Lisne, Ukraine 13 miles SSW
Slobozia 15 miles ENE
Tiraspol 17 miles NE
Lambrivka, Ukraine 24 miles SSW
Răzeni 26 miles WNW
Olăneşti 26 miles ESE
Petrovca 28 miles NW

Jewish Population: 1,675 (in 1897), 1,870 (in 1930)

Yefim Kogan

Yefim Kogan was born in Kishinev, Moldova. After he emigrated from the Soviet Union in 1989, he did extensive genealogical and historical research. In 2012 he received Master of Jewish Liberal Studies Degree from Hebrew College, Boston with focus in Jewish Cultural History. He was active in Jewish Genealogical Society of Greater Boston. Yefim taught classes on Jewish Genealogy for the local Jewish and Russian-Jewish communities of Brookline and Boston. He also presented at the Jewish Genealogical Societies of Boston, Montreal, Toronto, Santa Cruz, and Sarasota.

In 2011 Yefim Kogan organized Bessarabia Special Interest Group, developed its website www.jewishgen.org/bessarabia , and worked on multiple projects. Two of the most important projects are: (1) the Bessarabia Revision List project, where already more than 320,000 are translated, and (2) the Bessarabia Cemetery project, where there are about 80 Jewish cemeteries in the region and many tombstones were photographed, and 76,000 were indexed.

Yefim developed KehilaLinks websites for the towns in Moldova: Kaushany, Dubossary and Kamenka, and in Ukraine: Tarutino and Lyublin. Websites can be accessed at
https://www.jewishgen.org/bessarabia/GEO_townlist.asp?action=KL

Since 2009 Yefim Kogan has presented at the IAJGS International conferences on multiple important topics. Below are selected titles of his presentations:
History of Jews in Bessarabia (Moldova) in the 15th to 19th Centuries (Philadelphia, 2009), *Estate and other categories of Jews in Bessarabia, Russia in the 19th century* (Paris 2012), *Kishinev – my native town: History of Jews and Genealogy* (Boston, 2013),
The Jewish Surnames in Bessarabia/Moldova (Jerusalem, 2015),
When, Why and Where did the Jews arrive to Bessarabia/Moldova (Seattle, 2016),
Why Jews from the Former Soviet Union Often Called Russians? (Cleveland, 2019),
Laws for Jews in Russian Empire (London, 2023),
Kishinev Pogrom of 1903, Who Were the Jews Killed? (Fort Wayne, 2025).
Information about all presentations can be found at
https://www.jewishgen.org/bessarabia/PTM_ArticleList.asp?attid=16&ord=D

In December of 2022, Yefim organized and participated in the international virtual *Bessarabia Winter Symposium - History, Genealogy, Culture*. During the three-day symposium, seventeen lectures and seminars were conducted by genealogists, historians, musicians from Ukraine, Moldova, Germany, France, Brazil, and USA. Slides and recordings can be found at
https://www.jewishgen.org/bessarabia/PTM_Article.asp?id=219

Jewish Families in Shtetl Kaushany, Bessarabia

Genealogy, History, Culture, Life and Death

Yefim A. Kogan

July 2025

Jewish Life in Bessarabia Through the Lens of the Shtetl Kaushany

Yefim A. Kogan

Kaushany, 1950s

Submitted in partial fulfillment of the
requirements of the Masters of Jewish Liberal Studies degree
at Hebrew College

May 2012

This book is dedicated to my dear mother and father.

My mother, Khinka Kogan (Spivak) (ז״ל), of blessed memory,

was born in Bessarabia and lived her last 32 years in Tzur-Shalom, Israel.

She inspired me and my whole family with great stories about her ancestors,

friends and many residents of the shtetl Kaushany.

My father, Buma (Abram) Kogan (ז״ל), of blessed memory,

who drew our genealogical tree many years ago,

and helped me to understand what family all is about.

I also dedicate this work to

all Jews of Kaushany.

Adviser: Dr. Barry Mesch, Provost and Stone/Teplow Families' Professor of Jewish Thought at Hebrew College

Table of Contents

CHAPTER 5.   MEMOIRS, STORIES FROM KAUSHANERS AND THEIR DESCENDANTS 62

APPENDICES 106

Chapter 0. Introduction to the second edition

The idea to update the Kaushany book came not from me, but from many people who read the original book, contacted me and have a lot to add. Original book was published on several web sites on the internet in the USA and Israel. I received messages from people who used to live in Kaushany or their parents and grandparents who lived there.

Here are several issues people found in the first edition.
- Not all families were listed in the Appendix. *I only wrote about families my mother and other relatives remembered.*

- There is a photo in the book from June 29, 1940, where Jews are greeting the Red Army. *My mother told me about one person on a truck – Aron Dvoirin, we knew him very well. The other person appeared to be Yankel Goldshtein. It is great that Yankel's daughter Raisa read the book, and I fixed that gap.*

- I named the Chapter IV "Instead of Conclusion: The end of the Jewish Community in Kaushany", *I was wrong, that was not an end of the Jewish Community. I knew little about Jews who lived in Kaushany after the war. In addition to families returned to Kaushany after evacuation or service in the army, there were many Jewish families arrived to Kaushany to work in 1950s, 1960s as teachers, doctors, etc. I am very glad to correspond with Nona Shpolyanskaya (Geisman) who taught me about Jewish life in Kaushany after the war. She wrote a memoir "Not the End of Jewish life in Kaushany", see in Chapter 4, Instead of Conclusion: The end or decline of the Jewish Community in Kaushany*

- Many new records were found at the archives and translated by JewishGen Bessarabia volunteers. *I want to thank all of them.*

- A new chapter was added to the book: Chapter 5. Memoirs, stories from Kaushaners and their descendants. *As I wrote above many people sent me stories and memoirs. I also add stories from my Family Book written by my mother, uncle, and relatives. I want to thank for their stories, additional information and help*

Sima Barash,	*Mara Berger,*
Claude Bruter,	*Tsilya Dunaevskaya,*
Dora Itskovich,	*Lynne Jacobs,*
Jeff Katz,	*Faina Klyuzman,*
Aleksander Kogan,	*Chloe Kogan,*
Julia Maksimova,	*Luba Marmorstein,*
Ronni Otake,	*Raisa Rozenkrants,*
Dmitry Rubinshtein,	*Nona Shpolyanskaya (Geisman),*
Mila Teper,	*Dina Vainman,*
Yasha Volodarskiy,	*Alexander Zeltser.*

Here are people, residents of Kaushany, who passed away, and we have their stories. May their memory be a blessing
Asya Geisman (Imas) ל"ז,
Usher Geisman ל"ז,
Khinka Kogan (Spivak) ל"ז,
Rosa Kogan ל"ז,
Izya Spivak ל"ז.

Chapter 1. Introduction

Very little, if anything, is written about *mestechko*, the small towns or townlets in Eastern Europe with fewer than two thousand Jewish residents. There is almost nothing about such places in Jewish scholarship. If lucky, one may find that Jews lived there in a certain year, and that a synagogue or a burial society was created in another year. For some small towns, there might be a line about Nazi atrocities. There are some exceptions, for example an 800-page book *There Once Was a World. A 900-Year Chronicle of the Shtetl of Eishyshok,* written by Yaffa Eliach[1].

Many Yizkor Books were written in the 1950s about the larger towns, with stories about Jewish life from the beginning of the 20th century throughout World War II. Most of them were published in Israel by societies connected to a town or a region[2]. These books are great testimonies to Jewish life in Eastern Europe. One of the major Jewish genealogical sources, JewishGen.org[3], affiliated with the Museum of Jewish Heritage, has thousands of volunteers creating a memorial for the Jews who once lived all across Europe. A section of JewishGen, KehilaLinks[4], includes websites for many towns, sometimes very small communities in Ukraine, Lithuania, Moldova, Hungary, and other countries. All these websites were developed by volunteers with connections to these places; they usually include a history of the town, a history of the Jews in that town, old town photos and maps, memoirs of the residents, testimonials from the survivors of the Holocaust, reports of recent visits to these places, discoveries of cemeteries, or synagogues hidden close by and more.

I have a special interest in the Bessarabia[5] region because I was born in Kishinev[6], which was once the capital of Bessarabia oblast and gubernia[7]. My parents, grandparents, and great grandparents were all born and lived in Bessarabia. In my 2006 Hebrew College course "Through Their Eyes" with Professor Jay Berkovitz, I engaged in a study of Jewish life in the whole region of Bessarabia/Moldova. My final paper for the course was "A geo-historical and cultural overview of Jewish life in Bessarabia/Moldavia region up to the beginning of the 19th century."

In addition, I have an interest in following my own Jewish heritage. Because of the political situation of the 1940's to 1980's in the Soviet Union, I had been unable to pursue that interest when living in Kishinev and in Moscow. Only after emigration from the Soviet Union in 1989 was I able to study Jewish subjects and be involved in historical and genealogical Jewish research.

Why Kaushany?

My mother and father, their parents and grandparents back six generations lived in the shtetl Kaushany, in the district of Bendery[8], before the Great Patriotic War[9] of 1941; my father was born there.

---

[1] Eliach, 1998 Eliach, Y. (1998). *There once was a world. A 900-Year Chronicle of the Shtetl of Eishyshok.* Boston, New York, London: Little Brown and Company.

[2] Many of the Yizkor Books are available online at NY Public Library: http://yizkor.nypl.org.

[3] http://www.jewishgen.org

[4] http://kehilalinks.jewishgen.org

[5] Bessarabia is a region between Rivers Prut, Dniester, Danube and the Black Sea. The name originally applied only to the southern part of the territory, and only in 19c under Russian rule the whole region was named Bessarabia.

[6] Capital of Moldova, the republic of the Soviet Union, and currently the capital of Republic of Moldova. A large part of Bessarabia was included after WWII into the Republic of Moldova, and southern and northern parts became part of the Ukraine.

[7] Oblast, gubernia - province in Russian Empire.

[8] A major town on Dniester River, now it is part of Transnistria, the self-proclaimed region.

[9] The name used in the U.S.S.R for the War between the Soviet Union and Germany, 1941-1945.

I am able to trace my relatives in Kaushany back to 1835, at which time it was in Bessarabia, in the Russian Empire. My ancestors probably lived there long before that, when it was under Tatar rule as part of the Ottoman Empire. Both my paternal and maternal ancestors lived, married, and raised children in this town, as well as in some other small towns in southern Bessarabia. I remember traveling to Kaushany with my parents as a child in the 1960s, when they went to visit the cemetery. At that time, the cemetery had already been partially destroyed. I remember a very dusty central square with a church in the middle. Later I found that this church divided Kaushany in two parts with the Jews living on one side and the Christians on the other[10].

Kaushany website at JewishGen KehilaLinks project

In 2008 I developed a web site: http://kehilalinks.jewishgen.org/Causeni/Kaushany.htm which was a first attempt to create a memorial to the Jews who lived in the shtetl Kaushany. There are only a dozen websites for the towns and shtetlakh in Bessarabia that have been created so far and that process continues. According to the Bessarabia Special Interest Group, Jews lived in about 700 large and small towns and shtetlakh in Bessarabia, and in numerous villages.

At the Kaushany website I have included historical information about the place, the genealogical data found in the Family History Library in Salt Lake City, Yad Vashem in Jerusalem, and many other sources. There is also a section at the site for reminiscences of my mother, uncle, and other residents of Kaushany. The memoirs are, in fact, the jewel of the site. Together with photographs and genealogical records, they help reconstruct the texture of Jewish life in Kaushany before the WWII.

Since 2008 many discoveries have been made. Recently the Map of the Jewish Quarters of Kaushany was upgraded with new information and recollections from Kaushany residents of the 1930s. I have also found Video Testimonies of Holocaust Survivors at the University of Southern California Shoah Foundation Institute for Visual History and Education. All six of the video testimonies from people born in Kaushany are now presented at the site.

Sources of information used in the research

- 19th and beginning of 20th centuries vital records from the Moldova State Archives digitized by the LDS church and transcribed from Russian and Hebrew/Yiddish and Romanian by JewishGen.
- Revision lists (census, family lists, others) from 1835 and 1869 from the Moldova State Archives, digitized by the LDS church and transcribed from Russian by a group of translators.
- The Romanian Business directory of 1924-25, translated and transcribed from Romanian.
- Memoirs about life in the 1930s in Kaushany from residents who now live in Israel, France and the USA.
- Documents related to Jewish life recently found by local residents of Kaushany and translated from Romanian.
- Fragments of gravestones / matsevot found recently in and around the town of Kaushany.
- Video Testimonies of Holocaust Survivors from Kaushany.[11]

---

[10] See on the Map of a Jewish Quarter of Kaushany 1930s' in Chapter III.
[11] University of Southern California Shoah Foundation Institute for Visual History and Education, https://vha.usc.edu/home .

How to write and pronounce Kaushany in different languages?

I am accustomed to the Russian and Yiddish pronunciation and writing of Kaushany – Каушаны, and – קאושאן (Kaushon). Some Jews also used Koshany, Kaveshon, Kaushen'. The modern Moldovan name of the town is Căuşeni with Romanian diacritic marks below and above the letters. On the German maps the town is Causanii, Causanii Noui or Kauszany, Nw. Kauszany, N. Kauschanii; while French maps show – Nvo Kauchany. The place sometimes was named Новые Каушаны (New Kaushany). Residents told me that "New" was usually used for the Jewish part of Kaushany. The Business Directory of 1924 in fact has Kaushany and New Kaushany separately, and almost all listed businesses were in New Kaushany and owned by the Jews.

Where Kaushany is on the map?

The shtetl Kaushany is located in the district (judeţul-Romanian, uezd-Russian) of Tighina (currently Bendery) in the southeast of the Republic of Moldova. The Republic of Moldova is a country located between the Ukraine and Romania, not far from the Black Sea.

From the World Atlas (www.worldatlas.com)
The Republic of Moldova is in the center
of Europe.

Kaushany is in the southeast corner of
the Republic of Moldova.

Kaushany is 13-15 miles from Bendery (Tighina) and 17 miles from Tiraspol, on the left bank of the River Dniester. The distance from Kaushany to the capital of the Republic of Moldova Kishinev (Chisinau) is 44 miles. On Google it is 57 miles.

11

N.Kauschanii (Kaushany) on a German map of 1856, obtained from the Library of Congress.

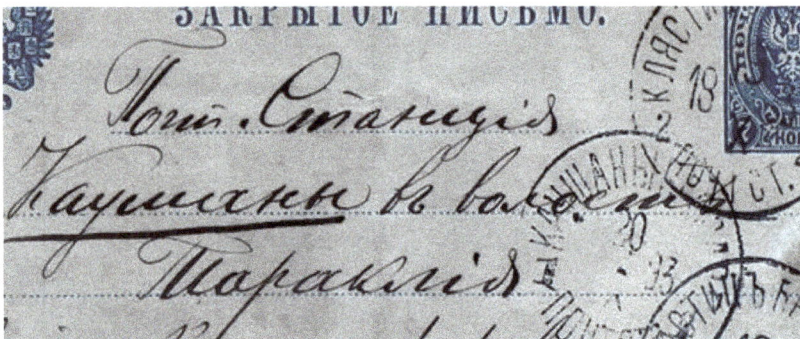

Kaushany was also a Postal Station in Bessarabia gubernia, located on a railroad from Kishinev-Bendery to Reni on Danube River. See above a postcard of 1893, written in Russian:
Postal Station Kaushany in volost' (subdistrict) Tarakliya. On the stamp - Kaushany, 1893.

Каушаны (Kaushany) on a Russian map of 1907, obtained from the Library of Congress.

Nvo Kauchany (Kaushany) on a French map of 1916[12].

From Political Map of Moldova, 1993, University of Texas at Austin

[12] *Map of the Carpathians, Roumania and Part of Balkans.* (1916). Albany, NY: Cartographer G. Peltier.

Getting help from Moldovans and Ukrainians local residents

Several years ago, I was contacted by two local residents of Kaushany, Vova Cheban and Sergey Daniliuck, who found the Kaushany website at JewishGen.org. They both were very interested and surprised to read about Jewish life in their own town, about which they were ignorant.

Vova Cheban told me the story of how he found out that Jews used to live in Kaushany. He and several friends were working in Romania in the beginning of the 1990s, buying and selling goods. One winter, probably in 1994, they worked in the town of Kovasny, a resort with mineral waters in the Carpathian Mountains. He writes that "One imposing man came to us to ask where we are from. Romanians often asked us questions, and we reluctantly answered. It appeared that he was from Kaushany before the war. After that we started to ask him questions. He told us that just before the Soviets came in June of 1940, he studied in Bendery, and his family owned a windmill, a blacksmith shop and also a tavern in Kaushany. The family was so afraid of the Soviets that he was sent immediately across the border to Romania, and from then on, he has never been back to Kaushany. At that time, he lived in Bucharest with his family. He also added that his family tavern was one of seven on the same block on the main street, and the other six were owned by Jews! He asked us if there are still Jews living in Kaushany? There were many Jews in town before…"

Sergey Daniliuck wrote to me that he is studying the history of Kaushany and the surrounding areas. He was very interested in the material from the website. He added that unfortunately the Jewish cemetery and most of the buildings from before the war have disappeared and he probably lives in a place where Jews used to live. He was willing to help me obtain pieces of information from the local museum and from other organizations. At the end of that letter, he wrote – "History should not be forgotten".

For the past two years I have received many emails from Vova and Sergey. They are full of new facts and photographs, excerpts from books, maps, and copies of documents about Jewish life in the town. Sergey photographed several remaining fragments of Jewish gravestones he was able to find.

Acknowledgements

I would like to thank all people who helped me and my family to come and settle in Boston and be able to study Judaism. I am extremely grateful to my good friend Barbara Palant of Lexington, who organized my first Jewish course, Songs of Shabbat with Cantor Charles Osborn, and many classes after that. I express my sincere gratitude to professors and students of Me'ah and Hebrew College for providing me with support during all years of study. I would like to specially thank Dr. Barry Mesch for being patient and very helpful, for devoting his expertise and time to mentor and challenge me at his courses and at final thesis.

I am greatly thankful to my dear wife Dr. Galina Dobrynina-Kogan for her support, encouragement, and always believing in me. I also want to thank my younger son David Kogan for translating many stories in that book.

Chapter 2. Kaushany before 1918

This chapter reviews the general history of Kaushany before 1918, the powers who governed the region since known times, the history of the Jews in the region and in the town and known genealogy about Jewish Kaushany.

Up to the 16th century

Based on what is known about the general history of Kaushany, it was a "selische" – a village or a small town which existed from the 9-10th century at the current location at the intersection of the Upper Trojan Wall[13] and river Botna. During the 14th century, the descendants of Daco-Romans, the Romanians, established two states, the principalities of Walachia and Moldavia[14]. Moldavia was created by people who left the northern part of Transylvania (Maramures) during the 14th century. They unified the people living in Moldavia and organized the territory into a state.

Flag of the Principality of Moldavia, 14-19 century

Kaushany was governed by different ruling powers from the 14th to 16th centuries; in general, it was under the Principality of Moldavia[15].

Because Bessarabia was conveniently located on a trade route from the Black Sea ports to Poland and the Baltic Sea, merchants, including Jews, frequently visited the land.

The earliest reference to the Jews in Bessarabia dates from the 14th century. There is evidence that there was an uninterrupted Jewish presence in the Moldavian and Walachian Principalities for centuries before the 14th century emigration into the area. "… Jews partly came from Palestine or were of Byzantine or Khazar origin and since the immigration from other European lands had not yet started, where else could they have come from"[16]. A document from 1574 established the fact of the Jewish presence in Moldavia during the reign of Prince Roman 1 (1391-1394) and Alexander Bun (Alexander the Good) (1401-1433)[17]. A number of Jewish communities in southern Bessarabia had been in existence since the 15th century. In the 16th-17th centuries there was a rabbinical court functioning in Akkerman (Cetatea Alba)[18], which is less than 60 miles from Kaushany. There were also Jewish communities from the 16th century in Kiliya and Izmail, both towns on the Danube River in Bessarabia. Jewish sources like

---

[13] The Upper Trajan's Wall is a fortification located in the modern Republic of Moldova, stretches 75 miles from Dniester River at the Teleneshty district to the Prut River. It is most likely of the Roman origin or of third/forth century Germanic origin.

[14] "Moldavia" is the spelling used in Russian and English to designate what the local people know as Moldova.

[15] At some time, it was under the Tatar rule of the Golden Horde. In the 15th century southern Bessarabia was occupied by the Ottoman Empire, but the inner land was given to Nogai Horde Tatars.

[16] Schulsohn, S. J. (n.d.). *Immigration and Settlement of the Jews in Bukovina.* New York: http://www.jewishgen.org/yizkor/bukowinabook/buk1_001.html.

[17] Broghauz, & Efron. (1908-1913). *Jewish Encyclopedia.* St. Petersburg, Russia.

[18] *The YIVO Encyclopedia of Jews in Eastern Europe, Bessarabia.* (n.d.). New York: YIVO, Bessarabia.

the Encyclopedia Judaica[19] mention that "A number of tombstones in the ancient Jewish cemetery in Kaushany, thought to date from the 16th century, indicate that there may have been Jews living in the place in this period"[20]. Unfortunately, this is impossible to confirm because two Jewish cemeteries were destroyed in Kaushany, one in 1930s and another in 1970-80s. There are very few reminders of the existing cemeteries in Kaushany[21].

From the 16th century to 1812

In 1538, the Principality of Moldavia was defeated by the army of Suleyman the Magnificent, and for almost three hundred years it was a vassal state of the Ottoman Empire. Moldova was never incorporated into the Ottoman Empire, and no Turks settled in the country, except in the fortified towns on the borders. For a long time, it had a special status, paying an annual tribute of gold and horses, and was ruled by the Moldovan princes, the gospodars[22].

Flag of the Ottoman Empire 1453-1844

Moldavia and the town of Kaushany, 1648

Excerpt from the Historical Atlas of Central Europe

(Magocsi & Matthews, 1993).

Bessarabia is on the map between the rivers Prut and Dniester and the Black Sea.

The southern part of Bessarabia, seen on the map above, was part of the Silistre Eyalets (province) of the Ottoman Empire. The Kaushany region was part of that territory under direct Ottoman control or Tatar rule, and Kaushany became a residence of Tatar Khan. The Tatars themselves paid tribute to the Ottoman Empire.

---

[19] Ed. Michael Berenbaum and Fred Skolnik. (2007). *Encyclopaedia Judaica*. Detroit: Macmillan.
[20] Ed. Michael Berenbaum and Fred Skolnik, 2007. Kaushany, Eliyahu Feldman.
[21] See section Jewish Cemetery, in Chapter III.
[22] Gospodar or hospodar is a term of Slavonic origin, meaning "lord" or "master". The term was used for the rulers of Wallachia and Moldavia from the 15th century to 1866.

The most famous Moldovan[23] of the 18th century was the Prince of Moldavia, Demetrius Kantemir. He was a writer, a political leader, and a scientist. He led ten thousand Moldovans on the Russian side in their fight against the Turks. After the Turks were victorious, Kantemir fled and settled in Russia. Peter the Great awarded him the title of Prince of the Russian Empire. Demetrius Kantemir wrote Descriptio Antiqui et Hodierni Status Moldaviae[24] the first and the most complete description of the Moldovan geography, history, government, and daily life.

In the first chapter which is about geography, Kantemir wrote about Ancient and Modern Moldavia: "Nogai Horde (Nogai Tatars) were divided in 2 branches: Orak-ogly and Orumbet-ogly. These two branches preserved carefully their tribal traditions. As their ancestors did, these nomad people live in the steppe, and they do not have towns, except Kaushany on the river Botna... "[25].

In the 16th century, Jewish immigration to Moldavia came from Galicia, Poland and Germany. They were mostly of Ashkenazi descent but some Sephardic merchants from Constantinople also began to reside in Bessarabia. Kantemir's work also included a description of the life of Jews: their rights, occupations, and relations with their neighbors. Kantemir described the town of Kiliya in the southern part of Bessarabia, where Jews used to live and trade from the 15th century. He says that Kiliya was a small but famous port where ships from as far as Egypt and Venice would be anchored. Kantemir described Kiliya as a cosmopolitan town with Turks, Jews, Christians, and Armenians living together peacefully. In the political section, the Jews were mentioned among other peoples living in Moldavia. According to the author, Jews were allowed to build wooden synagogues but not stone structures. Jews were citizens of the nation but paid an annual tax that was higher than other citizens. Jews were engaged exclusively in commerce and tavern keeping. The author reported that "…foreign traders, Turks, Jews and Armenians keep all commerce in their hands because the Moldavians are not enterprising and show no initiative"[26].

In 1579, Moldovan Prince Peter Schiopul (Peter the Lame) expelled the Jews from Moldavia on the grounds that they were ruining the merchants and had a total monopoly on the Moldavian commerce. 50 years later, new Moldavian princes invited the Jews back from Galicia, Poland. To attract Jews to the area they declared the expulsion ordered by Peter the Lame null and void. There is no evidence that any expulsion occurred in southern Bessarabia which was directly ruled by Turks.

From the 15-16th centuries the Jews lived in Bessarabian towns, including a town which is only 13 miles from Kaushany – Bendery (Tighina). It is likely that the Jews appeared in Kaushany at that time. I. Pilat in a book on the history of the Jews in Moldova, writes "In 1709 a priest Mikhail Epezhan in his report on a trip from Bendery to Constantinople describes Kaushany as little town, with a lot of Jews, but under the Turkish rule"[27]. The implication here is that the Jews were present earlier in Kaushany, at least at the last quarter of the 17th century. By 1760 there were 641 Jews living in Kaushany. At that time the town was a summer residence of Nogai / Budjak Tatar Khan[28]. The Nogai / Budjak people are Turkic ethnic group. These descendants of the Tatar-Mongol Golden horde ruled in

---

[23] Terms Moldovan and Moldavian have the same meaning. First used in Moldavia, Romania and the second – in Russia, Europe.

[24] Kantemir, D. (1714, Latin, 1973, Russian). *Descriptio Moldaviae (Biblioteka Academiae Mosqvitanae Scientiarum.* Kishinev.

[25] Kantemir, 1714, Latin, 1973, Russian, p.34.

[26] Kantemir, 1714, Latin, 1973, Russian, p.64.

[27] Pilat, I. (1990). *Iz istorii evreev v Moldove (From the History of Jews in Moldova).* Kishinev: Society of Jewish culture, p. 9.

[28] Khan – the title for a sovereign or military ruler, widely used by medieval nomadic Tataro-Mongol tribes.

the southern part of Bessarabia until the end of the 18th century. Catherine the Great of Russia resettled Nogais from Bessarabia and other southern parts of the current Ukraine into the Caucasus.

Russia did not rule Bessarabia yet, but the Russian Army was involved in many Russo-Turkish Wars on that territory. Kaushany was the headquarters of Commander Prince Potemkin of Taurida in 1789, before the victorious battle for the fortress of Bendery. The famous cavalry of Mikhail Kutuzov defeated 3,000 soldiers of the Budjak Tatar army in this area.

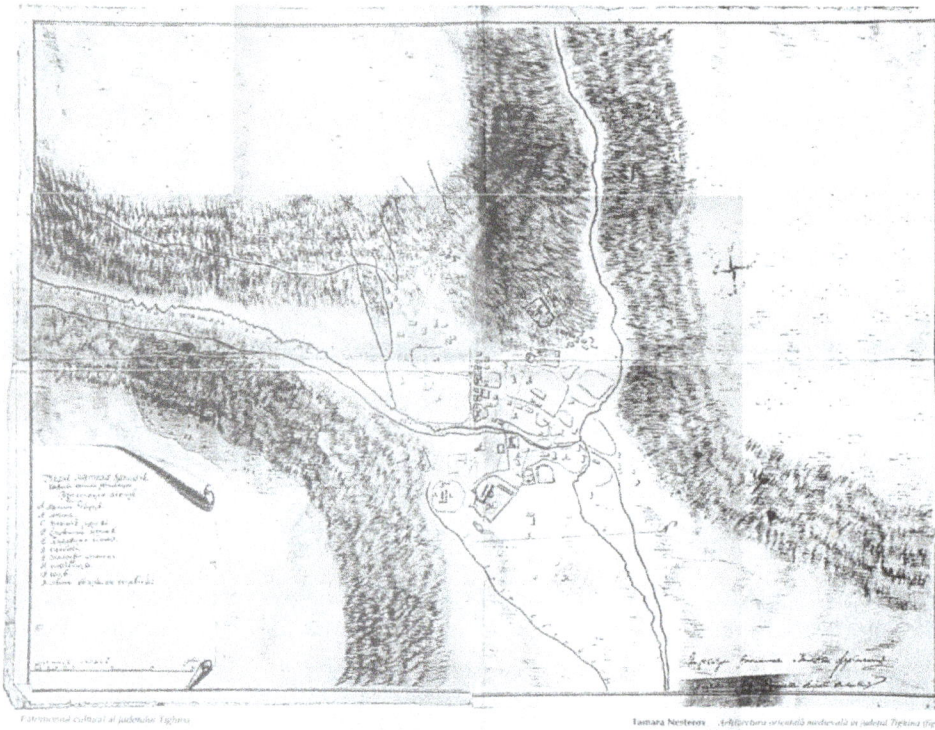

1789
Kaushany, summer residence of Tatar's Khan (Nesterov, 2002)

The map legend is written in Russian, and the description of the map was reproduced in Kishinev, Moldova in 2002, in a book 'Patrimoniul Cultural al Judetului Tighina, written in Romanian by the historian Tamara Nesterov. She writes that 'the map and also a panoramic plan of Khan's palace were executed in 1789 after the conquest of the area by the Russian armies". Describing the legend, Tamara Nesterov added that 'right near to the west, there was a Jewish School (on the map's legend it says 'zhidovskaya shkola')[29]. This gives evidence to the number of 641 Jews living in Kaushany in 1760, referred to above, but it also signifies that the Jews were of Ashkenazic descent, from Polish lands.

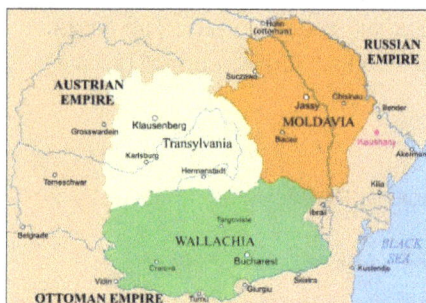

Sephardic Jews or Jews from Hungary would not use 'zhidovskaya', because 'zhid" is a Jew in the Polish language, and only later acquired a pejorative connotation.
More information about Kaushany find in an article by Igor Sapoznikov.[30]

1793-1812, Wikipedia map

---

[29] Nesterov, T. (2002). *Patrimonial cultural al judetului Tighina.* Kishinev, p. 104.
[30] Igor Sapoznikov (2016). *Causeni in the second half of the XVIIIc*

Simon Dubnov made an important observation of Jews in the Danube Principalities, and how they lived there in the middle of the 18th century: "Newcomers from neighboring Ukraine and Galicia colonized this sparsely populated Danube region, where in the second half of the 18th century the princes invited the Jews and Armenians to settle. Jewish settlements were purely Ukrainian in character. Jews lived in towns, in smaller villages and as tenants of landlords. In both principalities[31] the number of the Jews at the end of the 18th century was not less than thirty thousand. The majority of the Jews lived in larger towns like Jassy and in the smaller villages of Moldavia close to the Ukraine. Only a few thousand Jews lived in Walachia. The early Hasidim found refuge in the remote corners of Moldavia escaping from Haidamaks[32] and Galician poverty. Moldavia benefited economically and culturally from its close neighbors Podolia and Volynia once those territories were incorporated into Russia after the second division of Poland (1793) …"[33].

The Russian period, 1812 – 1918

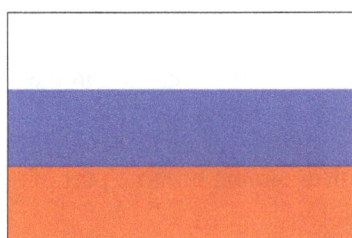

Flag of Russian Empire

In the aftermath of the Russo-Turkish War of 1806-1812, the whole region between the rivers Prut, Dniester, Danube, and the Black Sea was ceded by the Ottoman Empire to Russia at the Treaty of the Peace of Bucharest[34].

Central Europe, 1815

Excerpt from the Historical Atlas of Central Europe (Magocsi & Matthews, 1993).

Province of Bessarabia, part of the Russian Empire, 1815

---

[31] Moldavia and Walachia.

[32] Paramilitary bands in the 18th century Ukraine.

[33] Dubnov, S. (2002, reprint). *Newest History of the Jews,* vol.1, p.48-49.

[34] The Treaty of Bucharest between the Ottoman Empire and the Russian Empire was signed on 28 May 1812, in Bucharest, at the end of the Russo-Turkish War, 1806-1812.

The larger part of the added land had been in the Principality of Moldavia, and the southern part and the northern area around Khotin was under direct Ottoman rule. The territory gained by Russia included 5 cities (towns with fortresses): Akkerman, Soroki, Bendery, Khotin and Izmail, 15 market towns, and 500-600 villages, with a total population of 500,000, according to the official Russian Census of 1816. Several sources state that about 20,000 Jews or 5,000 families lived in Bessarabia at that time. Many Jews engaged in commerce, liquor distilling, and small industries.

The first laws concerning the Jews in Bessarabia were issued by the Russian government in 1818. "Regulations of establishing Bessarabia district" required Jews to join one of three estates, or classes: merchants, petty bourgeois (townsmen, middle class), or farmers. The "Regulations" stated that "…privilegias (privileges) given to Jews by Moldavian Princes (gospodars), will be kept in their entirety", while the existent Russian legislation concerning the Jews did not apply, since Bessarabia had autonomous status. The regulations even authorized the Bessarabian Jews to reside in the villages and engage in leasing activities and inn keeping, in contradiction to the Russian "Jewish Statute" of 1804. The Jews could even buy a piece of empty land for farming. Because of this regional autonomy, the Jews of Bessarabia were spared several of the most severe anti-Jewish decrees issued in the first half of the 19th century. At the same time the Jews were required to get hereditary surnames[35]. The main restriction the Jews as well as the Roma (Gypsies), had at that time in Bessarabia was that they could not hold government jobs. Exceptions were given to medical doctors. Because of these privileges many Jews from Galicia, and the Ukraine started to move to Bessarabia, especially when Bessarabia became part of the Pale of Settlement in 1835[36].

In 1817 there were 53 Jewish families in Kaushany, which comprised around 300-400 people. In 1827 there were 950 Jews, this was 36% of the total population[37].

Jewish agricultural colonies

Jewish agricultural colonies appeared in Bessarabia after a new "Status of Jews" law was approved on April 13, 1835. The principal goal of the laws was to organize the Jews under the new regulations and allow them some activities and not allow others. According to the new status, Jews could freely cross over into the farmer class without any restrictions. The new farmers could settle on crown, purchased, or leased land. Crown lands were set aside for Jews for an unlimited time for their sole use upon payment of taxes. In addition, in areas without much free crown land, Jews were permitted to lease or buy lands from private owners that they could select themselves. In this event, by investing their capital, they joined the rural community and became owners or renters of the land.

Seventeen Jewish agricultural colonies were established in Bessarabia, and one colony was in the Bendery district, not far from Kaushany. The Jews were involved in agriculture even outside of the agricultural colonies. From the statistical information of 1853 in Kaushany and in the shtetl Chimishliya, Bendery district 119 Jewish families worked in agriculture. Their estate/status was "gosudarstvennye krestiane" - state peasants or state farmers. Also, in the same year over 80 families of the Jewish farmers in Kaushany were granted landholdings by the state and were reclassified as "state farmers". Due to the difficult economic conditions, they were permitted to return in 1864 to the category of townsmen (Middle Class). Yet a number of Jews in Kaushany continued their work in agriculture, among them were cattle and sheep farmers: in 1849 two Jewish farmers owned approximately one thousand head of cattle and three thousand sheep and goats.

---

[35] The Moldavia Principality/Romania and the Ottoman Empire did not require surnames until later 19th century.
[36] According to the "Status of Jews" law, 1835, Nicholas I.
[37] Broghauz & Efron, 1908-1913, Bessarabia.

In the 19th and early 20th centuries the main areas of economic activity of Jews in Kaushany were wine, grain, and crafts. In 1899 the government rejected a request by 50 Jews to acquire land for farming.

In Kaushany there was one Jewish school, and two Jewish libraries. By 1910, there was an elementary boy's Jewish school, and in 1912, the Jewish Savings and Loan Society. By 1914, Jews owned taverns, 12 shops (including all three fabric shops), the only pharmacy. Among the Jews were 3 lumbermen[38].

According to the First All Russia 1897 Census 1675 Jews lived in the town from a total population of 3729 (44.9% from the total population). In 1912 there were about 800 Jewish families which represented a substantial increase.

Jewish genealogy of the 19th and 20th centuries, Kaushany

Many kinds of Jewish records were found for the Kaushany Jews. Most of them are from the Moldova State Archives in Kishinev, the Republic of Moldova and some records were microfilmed by the Family History Library at the LDS Church[39]. Finally, the records were digitized and translated into English by JewishGen, Bessarabia group[40]. Birth, death and marriage records were found for several years in the second half of the 19th century and beginning of the 20th century[41]. There are also records from several 'Revizskaya Skazka' - Revision lists[42], sometimes called census or family list. The enumerated individuals/families were subject to taxation and identified men for draft into the army. These records were written in Russian. Most likely the first Revision list was taken in Bessarabia in 1824, the 7th Revision[43], although not extant, is mentioned in the next 8th Revision list from 1835.

JewishGen has already translated and uploaded for its members almost 300,000 Revision list records for Bessarabia, but the total number of existing records is about 400,000-500,000 or more.

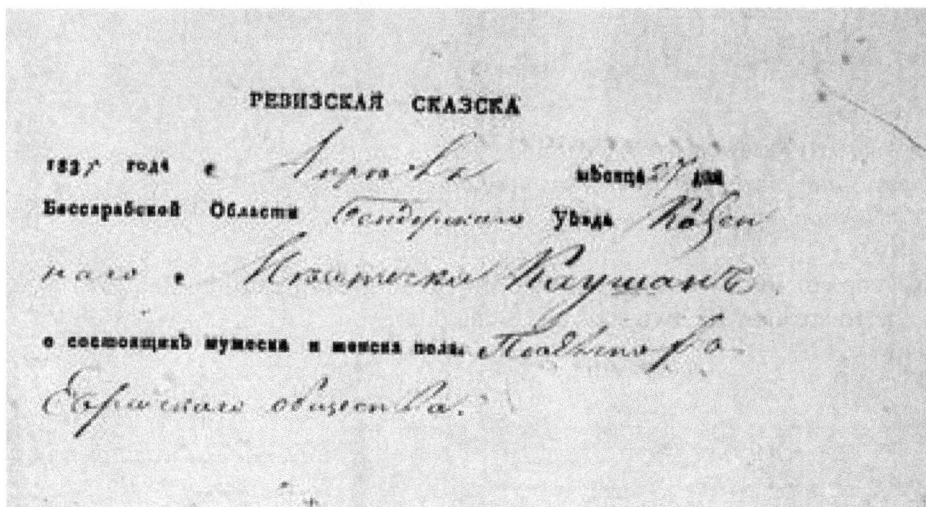

The Title page from the 8th Revision of 1835 of Kaushany, Bendery uezd (district) for Jewish Society

April 27, 1835

---

[38] Broghauz & Efron, 1908-1913.
[39] https://www.familysearch.org
[40] http://www.jewishgen.org/bessarabia
[41] http://www.jewishgen.org/databases/Romania/KishinevVRs.htm
[42] http://www.jewishgen.org/databases/Romania/BessarabiaRevisionLists.htm
[43] The 7th Revision was taken from 1815- 1825, and probably was not held in Bessarabia, because it became part of Russian Empire only in 1812, and the laws of Russia were first introduced in Bessarabia only in 1818.

Last page of 1835 Revision.

This Revision list was done by 4 trusted people from Kaushany Jewish Kahal and signed and stamped by them on August 28, 1835.

The Title page from the 9th Revision of 1848 of Kaushany

The Title page from the 9th Revision of 1848 of Kaushany.

Translation from Russian
Revizskaya Skazka (Revision list, Census)
Bessarabia Oblast, Bendery Uezd State 'mestechko'[44] of Kaushany about male and female dwellers from the Jewish society, November 10, 1848.

Excerpt from the 9th Revision of 1848 about the family of my great-great-great-grandfather Mendel Spivak born in 1815. Listed are his wife, two sons and a daughter.
(see translation of this page below).

Revision list was taken in November of 1848, Bessarabia oblast, town from Bendery district, the government 'mestechko' Kaushany.

---

[44] A little town.

Translation of the Revision list of 1848.

Registration #	Surname	Given Name	Father	Relationship to Head of Household	Sex	Age	Age at Last Revision	Comments
59	Spivak	Mendel	Shulim	Head of Household	M	33	20	
59	Spivak	Iosko	Mendel	Son	M	9		Born in 1840
59	Spivak	Shulim	Mendel	Son	M	1		Born in 1848
59	Spivak	Malka		Wife	F	31		
59	Spivak	Khaya	Mendel	Daughter	F	9		Born in 1840

Statistics of the Jewish residents of Kaushany

in 1835, 1848 and 1854 from Revision and other lists:

Revision	Year	Number of Jews present	Number of families	Total records, including who died, married or left town since prior Revision
8th	1835-36	374	101	374
9th	1848	520	104	638
10th	1854	523	94	615

Cheder List

	1857	25	1 class	

Additional Revision

	1859	15	2	

Removed from Farmers List and re-listed as Middle Class.

	1869	77	6	

Birth records found for Kaushany for four years in the 19th century: 1866, 1876, 1878 and 1887, and death records for 1884. These records were written in Russian and Yiddish (Hebrew). Birth records statistics from 1866, 1876, 1878, 1887, 1897, 1899, 1902, 1903, 1911, 1914:

	Total	Male	Female	Father				
				Foreign Citizen	Registered in other Russian gub.	Registered in other town in Bessarabia	In military	Registered in Kaushany
1866	51	32	19	3: 2-Moldova[45] 1-Turkey	5: 2-Podolia 2-Kherson 1-Grodno	28: 10-Kishinev 11-Bendery 5-Akkerman 1-Ataki 1-Khotin		15-Kaushany
1870	46	27	19	3: 3-Moldova	8: 3-Podolia 3-Kherson 1-Volyn 1-Minsk	34: 24-Bendery 2-Akkerman 5-Kishinev 1-Rashkov 2-Soroki		
1876	57	27	30	4: Moldova	5: 4-Podolia 1-Kherson	26: 8-Kishinev 15-Bendery 3-Akkerman	2: 1-in reserve	20-Kaushany society
1878	68	37	31	9: 5-Moldova 1-Holland 3-Turkey	6: 3-Kherson 1-Taurida 2-Kiev	32: 15-Kishinev 12-Bendery 4-Akkerman 1-Brichany	1	20-Kaushany society
1887	72	40	32	10: 6-Turkey 4-Moldova	13: 6-Kherson 1-Kiev 1-Taurida 2-Podolia 1-Volyn 1-Minsk 1-Mogilev	30: 2-Akkerman 15-Bendery 12-Kishinev 1-Orgeev	1	17 – Kaushany society _____ 1-Pharmacist
1897	65	35	30	3: 3-Romania	14: 1-Kiev 1-Volyn 5-Kherson 6-Podolia 1-Chernigov	16: 12-Kishinev 2-Soroki 1-Teleneshty 1-Akkerman		
1899	65	30	35	2: 2-Romania	14: 7-Kherson 7-Podolia	19: 10-Kishinev 1-Soroki 1-Khotin 3-Akkerman 4-Bendery		
1902	73	36	37	2: 2-Romania	12: 3-Podolia 6-Kherson	54: 2-Akkerman 38-Bendery		

[45] Moldova here is the Principality of Moldavia and from 1877 it was part of an independent Romania state.

	Total	Male	Female	Foreign Citizen	Registered in other Russian gub.	Registered in other town in Bessarabia	In military	Registered in Kaushany
					3-Volyn	14-Kishinev 1-Orgeev 1-Rezina		
1903	70	37	33	1: 1-Romania	7: 1-Kovel 1-Kherson 4-Podolia 1-Volyn	50: 1-Rashkov 1-Izmail 28-Bendery 18-Kishinev 1-Soroki 1-Akkerman		
1914	59	29	30		13: 1-Grodno 4-Podolia 2-Volyn 1-Minsk 3-Kherson 1-Vilno 1-Kovno	44: 3-Akkerman 26-Bendery 11-Kishinev 3-Orgeev 1-Soroki		
Total	**626**	**330**	**296**	**37:** 18-Moldova 10-Turkey 1-Holand 8-Romania	**94:** 35-Podolia 37-Kherson 2-Grodno 2-Taurida 9-Volyn 1-Minsk 1-Mogilev 4-Kiev 1-Chernigov 1-Kovel 1-Kovno	**326:** 115-Kishinev 26-Akkerman 1-Ataki 2-Khotin 173-Bendery 1-Brichany 2-Orgeev 1-Teleneshty 1-Rezina 1-Izmail 2-Rashkov 2-Soroki	**4:** 1-in reserve 3-active	**72-Kaushany** 1-Pharmacist

Almost all Jews were part of the Middle Class (Townsmen, Petty Bourgeois).

Death records from 1884:

	Total	Male	Female	Father				
				Foreign Citizen	Registered in other Russian gub.	Registered in other town in Bessarabia	In military	Registered in Kaushany
1884	**31**	**15**	**16**	**4:** 1-Moldova 1-Turkey 2-Austria	**2:** 1-Warsaw 1-Kherson	**18:** 8-Kishinev 4-Bendery 4-Akkerman 1-Rezina 1-Izmail		**7-Kaushany**

People died from following diseases:

Disease	Count		Age	Count
Diphtheria	11		0-5	19
Typhus	5		6-10	-
Diarrhea	3		11-20	2
Seizures	5		21-40	4

Consumption – 2   41+   6
Brain Inflammation – 1
Giving Birth – 1
Dropsy – 1
Old Age – 2

There is also an Additional Revision for a family of 14 people, farmers moving out of Kaushany in 1855 to another shtetl of Chimishliya in Bendery district. The last Revision found is of 1869 with 6 families, total of 77 Jews in Kaushany which were removed from farmers estate and re-classified as townsmen (Middle Class).

The Jews in the Russian Empire in 1906 and 1907 were entitled to vote for Duma representatives, the Russian Parliament. For Kaushany in this Russia Voter's list[46] there were 101 voters in 1906 and 199 voters in 1907. In order to vote in these elections, a person had to be male, over 24 years old, and for those who lived in small towns, be included in one of the categories: landowner, land manager (managed the land on the behalf of the owner), tenant/lessee (leases the land from the owner), clergyman, owner of immovable property (building, real estate, mills, etc.).

Jewish population of Kaushany, the combined numbers from all periods

	Families	Jews	Total residents	%	Male	Female	Source
1760		641					Encyclopedia
1817	53						Encyclopedia
1827		950		36%			Wikipedia
1848	104	520			245	275	Records
1854	97	523			251	272	Records
1897		1675	3728	45%			Russian Census
1912	800						Wikipedia
1930		1870		35.1%			Encyclopedia
1946	3						Encyclopedia
1991		6					Wikipedia
2004		6					Wikipedia

Some of the numbers in this table need further confirmation and possibly a few may not be accurate. For example, 950 Jews seems very high in 1827, especially for 20 years after, there were only 520 Jews. The last number is from the Revision list. It is possible though that not all Jews were listed in

---

[46] http://www.jewishgen.org/databases/Romania/BessarabiaDuma.htm

that Revision. The other questionable number is for the year 1912 – 800 families. In 1897, the number of Jews was only 1675, which is approximately 400 families or less. It is questionable that the number of families could have doubled in 15 years, especially when the Jews started to emigrate from Bessarabia to the West.

There were Jews involved in Public Life in Bessarabia. Gurfinkel, Itsko son of Meer was a Physician in Bendery Zemskoy Committee, we know that from records of 1897 to 1902:

Jews Involved In Public Life In Bessarabia

Name	Father	Gender	Organisation / Department / Occupation / Rank / Title	City / Uezd / Gubernia/ Region	Year / Source / Page	Note
GURFINKEL, Itsko-Meer		M	Benderi Zemskoy Committee Physician	Novie Kaushani Benderi Bessarabia	1897 Bessarabia Calendar 62	
GURFINKEL, Itsko	Meer	M	Benderi Zemskoy Committee Reserve Physician	Kaushani Benderi Bessarabia	1900 Bessarabia Calendar 68	
GURFINKEL, Itsko	Meer	M	Benderi Zemskoy Committee Physician	Kaushani Benderi Bessarabia	1902 Bessarabia Calendar 63	

Table header note: Searching for Town (phonetically like) : KAUSHANY — 3 matching records found. Run on Wed, 10 Jul 2024 14:16:54 -0400

There is an easy way to find all records for the town of Kaushany at www.jewishgen.org, You can search by town Kaushany in Bessarabia, and you find many records from different Business directories, Revision lists, Vital records, Holocaust database, and more.

Chapter 3. 1918-1940, Jewish life in the shtetl Kaushany

Democratic Republic of Moldova, 1917-1918

World War I brought a rise of nationalism and a political and cultural awareness to many nations living in the multinational Empire that was Russia. Following the Russian Revolutions of 1917, Bessarabia elected its own parliament, Sfatul Ţării[47] in October-November of 1917. At this parliament of 150 members, 14 were Jews. It proclaimed the Moldavian Democratic Republic on December 15th, 1917, and formed its government on December 21st with nine members, seven Moldavians, one Ukrainian, and one Jew[48].

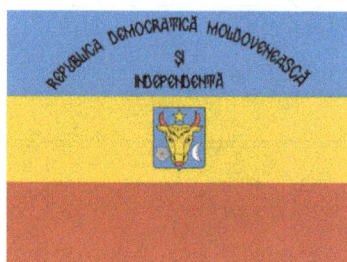

Flag of Democratic Republic of Moldova

1918

The republic did not last long. On January 18th the Bolshevik[49] troops occupied Kishinev, and the members of the parliament asked for help from Romania. On January 26th, the Romanian government sent the Romanian Army, and the Bolshevik troops retreated. On February 6th, 1918, the parliament proclaimed Bessarabian independence from Russia. On April 9th, 1918, Sfatul Ţării voted for the Bessarabia's union with Romania, and Romania soon approved this union. Jews were absent or refrained from voting for the union[50].

Some Jews from Kaushany served in the Russian army in World War I, and later most likely participated in the Moldova independence process.

Under Romanian rule

Romania, Bessarabia Region
From April 9, 1918 – June 28, 1940

The Romanian period in the history of Bessarabia has several specific features. First, there is little genealogical data available. Only recently we started to receive records from the 1920s. The other major feature is that a lot is known about life in Kaushany from people who lived there and who wrote memoirs and stories. My mother, Khinka Kogan (Spivak), gave me great insights into Jewish life in that town where she lived before the Great Patriotic War that genealogical data most likely cannot do. In her

---

[47] Country Counsel (from Romanian).
[48] Mitrasca, M. (2002) *Moldova: A Romanian province under Russian rule*, NY, p.34.
[49] Bolshevik troops – Red Army, later became Soviet Union army
[50] List of people voted for or against the Union - http://en.wikipedia.org/wiki/Sfatul_%C8%9A%C4%83rii

89 years she remembers and clearly describes everybody in the Gymnasium photo of 1937! She remembers not only 18 Jewish students on the photo, but also 3 teachers and 3 Moldovan pupils who studied with her. She also has a vivid memory of her great grandmother Sheiva Srulevich born in 1837[51] and with the genealogical successful research we have now a photo of that woman with her granddaughter, who is my grandmother. Because of such memories I was able to compose a comprehensive list of residents of Kaushany from the end of the 19th century to the 1940s[52]. In addition to the oral memoirs and stories which now are part of our Family Book[53] and Kaushany KehilaLinks website at JewishGen, I used many other sources available, including documents found by residents of Kaushany in 2010 and records at the Moldovan Archives in Kishinev.

Below is a map based on the current Google map of 2012 with the location of the Jewish Quarters as well as a place where TWO demolished Jewish cemeteries stood[54] and a place of Mass Killings of Jews.

On the next page is the map of the Jewish Quarters, which was created mostly from the memory of my mother Khinka Kogan (Spivak).

---

[51] See about Srulevich family in Chapter II.
[52] Appendix A.
[53] Kogan, Family Album, Volumes 1, 2. Sixth edition, 2009.
[54] See in section Jewish Cemeteries in this Chapter.

The map of the Jewish Quarters of Kaushany, 1930s

Khinka Kogan, Lev Bruter
edited by Yefim Kogan

Kaushany

Bendery district, Romania, 1930s

Jewish Quarters

Road to Voontirovka

Town Hall

Market

Road to the hospital, to Rail station and to town Bendery

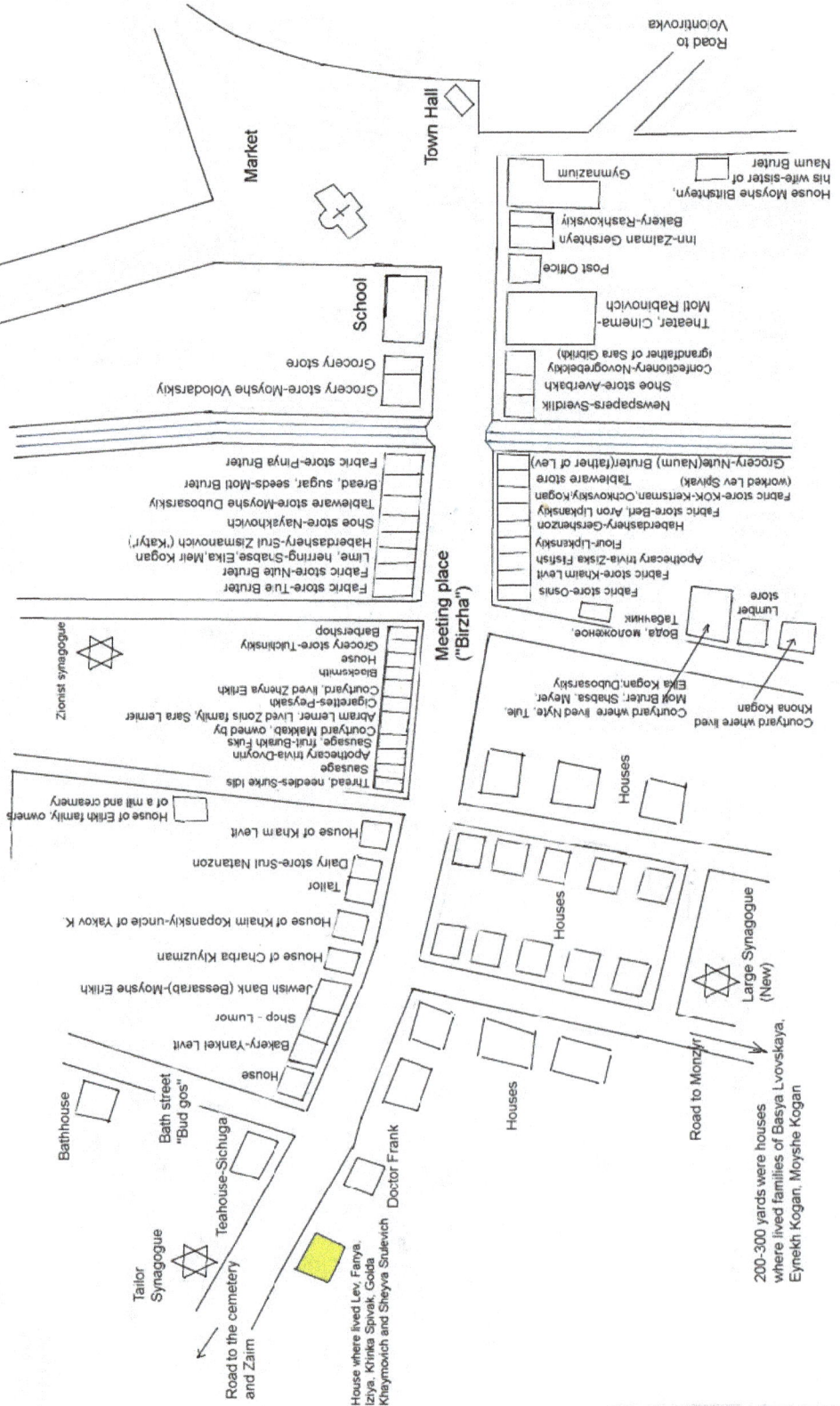

School

Grocery store

Grocery store-Moyshe Volodarskiy

Gymnazium

House Moyshe Birshteyn, his wife-sister of Naum Bruter

Inn-Zalman Gershteyn

Bakery-Rashkovskiy

Post Office

Theater, Cinema- Motl Rabinovich

Confectionery-Novogrebelsky (grandfather of Sara Glbrlkh)

Shoe store-Averbakh

Newspapers-Sverdlik

Fabric store-Pinya Bruter

Bread, sugar, seeds-Motl Bruter

Tableware store-Moyshe Dubosarskiy

Shoe store-Nayakhovich

Haberdashery-Srul Zismanovich ("Katyr")

Lime, herring-Shabse,Eika, Meir Kogan

Fabric store-Nute Bruter

Fabric store-Tule Bruter

Grocery-Nute(Naum) Bruter (father of Lev)

Tableware store (worked Lev Spivak)

Fabric store-KOK-Kertsman,Ochkovskiy,Kogan

Haberdashery-Gershenzon

Fabric store-Berl, Aron Lipkanskiy

Flour-Lipkanskiy

Apothecary trivia-Ziska Fitsish

Fabric store-Khaim Levit

Fabric store-Osnis

Вода, моложеное,

Табачник

Lumber store

Courtyard where lived Nyte, Tule, Moll Bruter; Shabse, Meyer, Elka Kogan,Dubosarskiy

Courtyard where lived Khona Kogan

Zionist synagogue

Grocery store-Tulchinskiy

Barbershop

House

Blacksmith

Courtyard, lived Zhenya Erlikh

Cigarettes-Peysakh

Abram Lerner, Lived Zonis family, Sara Lerner

Courtyard Makkab, owned by

Sausage, fruit-Burakh Fuks

Apothecary trivia-Dvoyrin

Thread, needles-Surke Idls

House of Erlikh family, owners of a mill and creamery

House of Khaim Levit

Dairy store-Srul Natanzon

Tailor

House of Khaim Kopanskiy-uncle of Yakov K.

House of Charba Klyuzman

Jewish Bank (Bessarab)-Moyshe Erlikh

Shop - Lumor

Bakery-Yankel Levit

House

Houses

Houses

Houses

Large Synagogue (New)

Road to Monzyr

Bathhouse

Bath street "Bud gos"

Teahouse-Sichuga

Tailor Synagogue

Road to the cemetery and Zaim

Doctor Frank

House where lived Lev, Fanya, Izlya, Khinka Spivak, Golda Khaymovich and Sheyva Srulevich

200-300 yards were houses where lived families of Basya Lvovskaya, Eynekh Kogan, Moyshe Kogan

Meeting place ("Birzha")

Life in Kaushany

Kaushany was divided in two parts – Old Kaushany, where Moldovans, Romanians, Gypsies, and others lived, and the New Kaushany with mostly Jewish population. In 1930, 1870 Jews, which was 35% of the total population, lived in Kaushany.

My relatives do not remember any big conflicts between nationalities, nor any anti-Semitic incidents, until 1937-38. They recall that it was not a single case of the desecration of the synagogues and the cemeteries while they lived in the town. My uncle says that nobody took seriously the conflicts at the Market between Jews and Moldovans. When a Moldovan would say: «Ты жидуля, что хочешь всё даром?» - "You, zhidulya (from zhid[55]) want all for free?" it was seen as almost charming addressing a Jew.

Kaushany was intersected by several roads to Bendery, Volontirovka-Reni, Chimishliya-Kishinev, Talmaz-Chadyr Lunga[56]. They were mostly dirt roads, and no one could come to the school without boots or galoshes. Galoshes were traditional Jewish shoes at these years in Kaushany. At the end of the 1930s the roads started to be covered with stones and some of them with asphalt with small sidewalks and with drainage for the rainy weather. The courtyards with houses and apartments stood alongside these roads. All houses were one-story[57], many were built with plans for future expansion in order to have an apartment for their children when they grew up. Thus, the courtyard usually included an extended family. Many families rented their apartments. Here is a description of one such courtyard where my mother lived with her large family[58]. In front of the courtyard was the house of my great grandfather Shloime Spivak. They had 3 rooms, a corridor and a kitchen. Near their house grew four beautiful trees, and a large bench stood under them. My mother and uncle loved to sit there with their friends. At the windows of the house there were wooden shutters that were closed and locked at night with hooks. Into the courtyard led a small wicket and a gate. The other house where my grandparents and mother with her brothers lived stood on a dais. They had 2 rooms, a corridor and a kitchen.

Grandfather's brother Yankel lived in a third house and the fourth was for rent. On one side of the courtyard were small sheds, where they kept wood and corncobs for heating flats in the winter. Just to note, that Kaushany did not have electricity until 1939, and they used kerosene lamps for lighting and stoves for cooking. In every Jewish courtyard was a cellar for storing vegetables, fruits, and barrels of good Moldovan wine. My great grandfather sold the grain, so their yard had a large barn, where the grain was dried before shipping to customers.

Friday

Friday was a very happy day. The Jews who worked for others received their salaries. Also on Friday, the Jews went to the hairdresser. It was like a ritual - everyone went to his barber; of course, they sat in a line, got the latest news and listened to stories. Finally, after a haircut and shave all the happy people returned to their homes to celebrate Shabbat. My uncle recalls that "Friday was a hard day in a Jewish family. My grandmother would get up very early, bake bread, cook dinner, clean the house and then, having washed herself, wait for the grandfather to come home from the synagogue. The grandfather Shloime was a "Gobe" - Gabbai in the largest synagogue in Kaushany. He was deeply religious and, like

---

[55] A derogatory term for a Jewish person. In many Slavic languages it meant a Jew.
[56] See the map of the Jewish Quarters of Kaushany, 1930s in this Chapter.
[57] Several houses were with two stories according to Land and Property documents, Kaushany, 1940-41, Archive of Republic of Moldova, Kishinev.
[58] See at the Kaushany Jewish Quarters map in yellow.

many Jews at that time, wore a beautiful beard. Almost all the Jews went to a synagogue on the Sabbath. Even those who did not attend regularly attended synagogue at the Jewish holidays"[59].

Religious life, synagogues, rabbonim

There were six synagogues in the town of Kaushany in 1930s: The Large (main), Zionistishe (Zionist's), Shnaydershe (Tailor's), Old, Shustershe (Shoemaker's) and Khasidishe (Hasidic). Before 1928 the "official government Rabbi" was Isroel Geller, and after 1928 up to the beginning of the war - Iosif Yatom. Iosif was a son of Reb Motel, a Rabbi in Peschenka, Ukraine and in Bendery, Bessarabia. A brother of Reb Iosif, who made aliyah in 1934, writes in the Bendery Yizkor Book following: "One of R. Motel's sons, R. Iosif Yatom, became a Rabbi in Kaushany when he returned from Russia. The regulations in Romania stipulated that in order to graduate from high school one had to pass final examinations in Romanian. Rabbi Iosif studied at the Schwartzman High School[60] for one year. According to Iosif there were several adults at that time that had returned from Russia and had to study in Romanian. R. Iosif Yatom was an outstanding orator and spoke on behalf of Mizrahi."[61]

Many Jews had their designated seats in the synagogues. My mother wrote that her "…dad and grandfather went to Shnaydershe shul. It was not that they were tailors… it's just that it was right across the street from us. My mom knew the prayer book well and was able to translate. On holidays, she read in the synagogue among the women. The synagogues weren't large, or particularly richly appointed, but they all had Torah scrolls, and were always clean. Of course, women sat separately from the men. Before every holiday, the attendees would donate what they could for the needs of their synagogue"[62]

On my father's side, my grandmother's father was Shabsa Kogan (my grandparents had the same surnames, and possibly were related). Shabsa was a merchant and a Rabbi. This is how our family tradition paints him, but we do not know where he was a Rabbi. Most likely he preached in one of the Kaushany synagogues. There is also a story about the photo on the left. My uncle, Sarin, Shabsa's grandson, was an artist and painted a portrait of his grandfather, using this photo, but when he immigrated to the US in 1970s, the Soviet authorities did not allow him to bring the portrait with him, and he left it to me.

Shabsa Kogan, 1910s

The story was repeated when my family immigrated to the US in the late 80s, and the portrait was donated to the Jewish Organization in Moscow. I hope in the future to find the portrait.

Shabsa's father – Irikhem

---

[59] Kogan, Family Album, Volumes 1, 2. Sixth edition, 2009, p.209-210.
[60] Schwartzman Hebrew High School in Bendery, Bessarabia.
[61] Tamari, M. (1975). *Kehilat Benderi: sefer zikaron.* Tel-Aviv, p.397-398.
[62] Kogan, Family Album, Volumes 1, 2. Sixth edition, 2009, p.156-157.

Irikhem (1842 – 1908, Dubossary) was a melamed in Tomashpol, in April 1866 was a Rabbi in Ismail, he was expelled. In July 1866 in Kishinev, was one a main Rabbi in town, lived in 1871 in Gancheshty, 1872 – in Kaushany, where he was in Beit Din[63]. From August 1886 was in Dubossary, served as a town Rabbi.

Scholar works of Reb Irikhem see at http://forum.otzar.org/viewtopic.php?f=19&t=25526

His parents: mother - Esther, father - Rabbi Shabtai, son of Aaron, who was also a great Jewish sage. Rabbi Irikhem comes from families of great Jewish Rabbis and therefore all his descendants are a continuation of this chain of world-famous Torah scholars. The genealogy of Rabbi Irikhem refers to the descendants of the Shakh (**Hebrew**: ש"ך) - Rabbi Shabtai ben Meir HaKohen. Read more about Rabbi Irikhem in Appendix F. *An article about Irikhem from Dubossary Memorial Book (Hebrew, English).*

House in Kaushany, which is to this day called "Synagogue", even though no synagogues have existed in Kaushany at least for 60 years.
Photo - courtesy of Sergey Daniliuck, Kaushany 2010

In the Shnaidershe shul the cantor was Syoma Kleyman. His pleasant and resonant voice touched the hearts of worshipers, especially when he sang Kol Nidre on Yom Kippur. Sometimes on holidays the synagogue was so full that the boys had to listen to the cantor on the street. Many Jews wore talleysim on the street before and after the prayers. Iosif Batsian was a great singer and khazan in one of the synagogues and after the war he sang in Kishinev. Iosif Talmatskiy also was a khazan and very nicely sang in the synagogue during the holidays.

Sholom Blank was a melamed in cheder in 1920s, but later the cheder was closed and another melamed, Khaymale taught writing and reading in Yiddish to young boys and girls at home. Shloime Spivak was a gabbai and Usher Feigin was a shamesh[64] in the Shnaidershe shul, and he was responsible for the order in the synagogue.

In the town was established a Khevra-Kadisha[65], Talmud-Torah, Mikve[66], and a Jewish nursing home, a Jewish Women Society "Damen Verein" to help poor women[67], a Society to produce Matza for all Jews in the town.

---

[63] A beth din is a rabbinical court of Judaism

[64] Gabbai or Shamesh - a person who assists in the running of a synagogue or its religious services.

[65] Khevra-Kadisha, literally means Holy Society, are the group of Jewish people who care for the deceased to prepare them for burial.

[66] A mikvah (מִקְוֶה, also spelled mikveh) is a pool of water, in which Jewish people immerse to affect purity.

[67] See section: Documents found about the Jewish affairs.

Religious personnel in Kaushany in the 19th and the 20th centuries

	Given Name	Last Name	Years of service	Comments
Rabbi	Mordko	Liberman	1860s, 1870s	was Official Government Rabbi
	Mordko	Rabinovitch	1870s, 1880s	was Official Government Rabbi
	Isroel	Geller	up to 1928	was Official Government Rabbi
	Iosif	Yatom	1928-1940	
	Shabsa	Kogan	?	
	Irikhem	Kogan	1872	was in Beit Din
Cantor	Syoma	Kleyman	1930s	In Shnaidershe shul
	Iosif	Batsian	1930s	
	?	Talmatskiy	1930s	
Gabbi or Shamesh	Shloime	Spivak	1930s	In Shnaidershe shul
	Usher	Feigin	1930s	In Shnaidershe shul
Moel	Itska	Kitsis	1860s	
	Iosl	Goldfarb	1870s, 1880s	
	M.	Goldfarb	1910s	
	Gersh	Rabinovich	1860s	
	Geinikh	Rabinovich	1860s	
	Mordko	Liberman	1860s	
	Duvid	Liberman	1860s	
	Oizer	Karasik	1860s	
	Gershko	Khakham	1860s	
	Yankel-Shamshen	Flisfish	1870s, 1880s	
	Fishl	Kaliski	1870s, 1880s	
	Gersh	Reizenraikh		
Melamed in cheder	Shlomo	Blank	1920s	
	Shimon	Shesterman	1850s	

Jewish cemeteries

There were two Jewish cemeteries in Kaushany and both cemeteries were destroyed:
Old Jewish Cemetery
New Jewish Cemetery

See Kaushany map above with location of Jewish Quarters from 1930s, two Jewish cemeteries demolished and place where Jews were murdered in 1941-1944 at the section Under Romanian rule.

The Old Jewish Cemetery had tombstones from 1500s up to beginning of 20th century. It was destroyed in 1920-30s.

Photo of Old Kaushany Jewish cemetery

Found in Moscow Archive

1910-1920s

More information about this cemetery, including article about old graves at the cemetery, list of 31 Jews buried in Old Kaushany Jewish cemetery from Death records of 1884, you can find at the cemetery report at
https://www.jewishgen.org/Bessarabia/files/cemetery/Kaushany/KaushanyOldJewishCemetery.pdf

The New Jewish Cemetery was established at the end of 19th – beginning of 20th century on the road to Zaim. This is the cemetery my parents, many relatives and residents of Kaushany remembered. My grandmother, her parents and many relatives were buried there. The cemetery was destroyed in the 1970 - 1980 and houses were built in that place. Some families moved graves of their loved once to Bendery or Kishinev Jewish cemeteries.

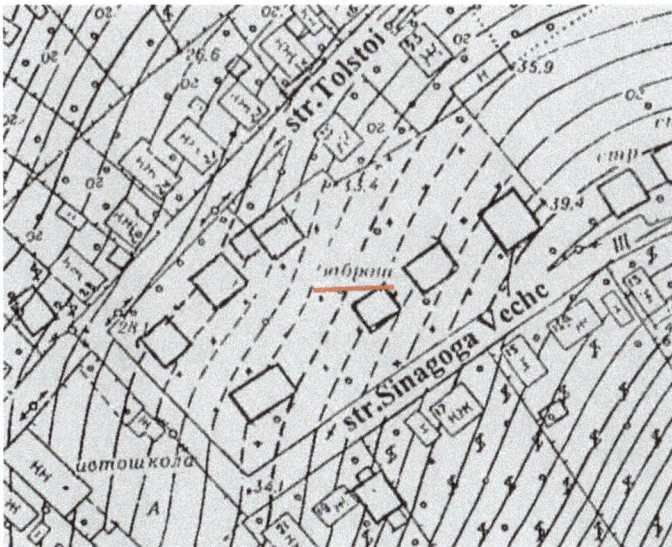

From the topographical map of 1982.

This is the place where the cemetery once stood. The square area is bordered with str. Sinagoga Veche (Old Synagogue Street), and str. Tolstoi (Tolstoy Street). Inside the quarter it is written in Russian "Заброшено" – Abandoned.

With the help of Sergey Daniliuck FIVE pieces of gravestones from the New Jewish cemetery were found and photographed.

Here lies
an important old woman

Yenta-Riza
[daughter of Reb] Eliezer-
Yehuda

The first piece was found in the local museum. As Sergey told me, nobody knew what that was, and how to read it, or even if it is Jewish.

The second piece was found by children, and I believe it was brought to the museum too.

…wife of Reb Meyer Dov

[…]akur

[Kisl]ev 5692 (1932),
Second day
Died

The third piece was found in an abandoned church, and this is where it is located now.

Woman
Daughter of Moshe
ש יטכה...

(Name יטכה is Yudes, according to "A Dictionary of Ashkenzic Given Names", Alexander Beider).

The fourth piece was found in the forest not far from Kaushany.

Mariyasin
Avraham ben Israel

Killed Erev Shavuot, 5682
His memory will never leave us.

Mariyasin
Abram, son of Srul.
Tragically died 2-Jun-1922.

The fifth piece

Natanzon
Ma?

Died 18 February 1928

Dear, too soon you left us.

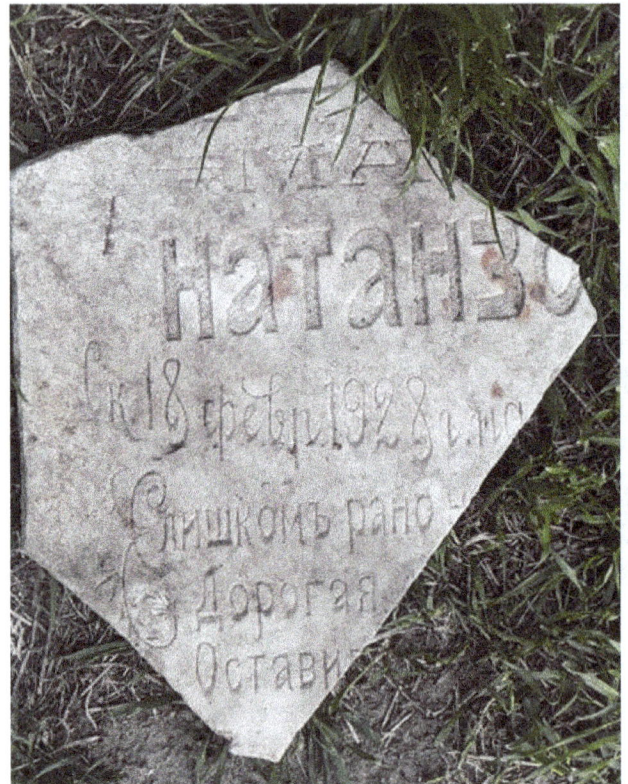

I still believe that the gravestones cannot disappear completely. They might be broken, moved or buried, but people will find them, and I hope that many will be moved to a place close to where the cemetery once stood or to a place where a Monument to Jews be erected.

More information about this cemetery, including photos, and list of 50 Jews buried in New Kaushany cemetery received from relatives and friends of deceased, and Jews who were killed in Kaushany in 1941 see at
https://www.jewishgen.org/Bessarabia/files/cemetery/Kaushany/KaushanyNewJewishCemetery.pdf

Zionist organizations

In Kaushany, there were three Zionist organizations - Betar[68], Maccabee[69], and Gordonia[70]. Betar was a right-wing organization and some Jews in Kaushany called it "fascists," because they thought that the government (Israel) had to be taken through battle. Maccabee was largely a sports organization. They also studied Yiddish, had different sport sections, and art activities. And once every two months, they had a dance party. One time, a woman from Palestine came to Kaushany; she collected money for the country, and it was a party in her honor. My mother remembers that she got two Yiddish poems to learn,

---

[68] The Betar movement is a Revisionist Zionist youth movement founder in 1923 in Riga, Latvia, by Vladimir Ze'ev Jabotinsky.
[69] Jewish Sport and Zionist organization. In Russia, first Maccabi society was founded in Odessa in 1913.
[70] Gordonia was a Zionist youth movement. Its doctrines were based on the beliefs of Aaron David Gordon. i.e. the salvation of Eretz Yisrael and the Jewish People through manual labor and the revival of the Hebrew language.

but she didn't know Yiddish back then, and so organizers wrote the text for her in Romanian, she memorized it and recited it with a good "Jewish" accent. The visitor wanted to meet my mother's parents and asked them how their daughter learned Yiddish so well. But when she realized that my mom did not know the language, she was very surprised and suggested she learn Yiddish.

Sunday – Market Day

Sunday was a market day. The market was huge. Most sellers were Romanians, Moldovans and Gypsies, and the buyers: the Jews. Trade was very lively. The Jewish men worked hard that day in the shops, workshops, at the market. Every woman went to buy chickens, meat, vegetables and fruits. Jews artisans waited for their customers to deliver products manufactured by them - suits and dresses, footwear, wood and metal, photos, and many others. My uncle recalls: "It was especially interesting to watch how a Jewish woman chose a fat chicken for her holiday yukh (chicken soup). Tax collectors and the police also browsed the rows of the market and observed that there were no scandals. In this crowd, Jewish boys tried to buy something like fruits and nuts, which they needed for the games. On market day, people generally came with money and were not averse to visit a tavern and drink a glass of a good wine at the end of the day".

All state agencies: the court, town-hall - town officials, post office was closed on Sundays.

Businesses, occupations, professions

The business directory tells incredible stories about people and life in the town. If one can believe in statistics, in 1930, New Kaushany had population of about 1,870 Jews and Old Kaushany, about 2,800 non-Jews. When I asked relatives how many Jews used to live in Kaushany before the war, the numbers were much larger: from 3,000-5,000.

The businesses were all concentrated in New Kaushany where Jews used to live. A total of 175 businesses[71] were recorded in the directory and only 10 were owned by non-Jews. Also, it was a strangely large number of specific businesses, for example: they had 26 grocery stores! It was probably because most of the stores were very small and had sold combinations of odd products, like at one of the stores they sold only herring and "izvest"- lime - a sort of whitening to paint the ceilings and walls. Another store sold sugar, bread and sunflower seeds. There were also an unproportionally large number of taverns and inns – 29! Some of the taverns and inns were on the roads between towns or even located in other villages around Kaushany. There were also 16 fabric stores! At first it was hard to explain why in the world they needed that many and also how they could survive in the competition, until mother explained it to me. The town did not have any stores to buy ready to wear coats, suits, dresses, and the only way they could get something new is by buying fabric and going to a schneider – tailor. The richer people also went to the town of Bendery or even Kishinev to get modern clothes.

From the Business Directory it appeared that the only three windmills and a water mill were owned by non-Jews, but Jews owned six steam mills.

In addition to owning businesses the Jews were employed by others in shops, taverns, mills, and banks. Many Jews were clerks in shops, and taverns, or worked as cashiers and accountants. There was a relative, Moyshe Kogan, who studied in Odessa and became an accountant with a "government rights" license. After getting his license, he returned to Kaushany and became an accountant for five mills.

---

[71] See Business Directory Records from 1924-1925 in the Appendix C.

The poor people tried to get into some business too. They borrowed some money, bye some products, grain, and sold them at the market for a little bit. See below about such merchant Shloime Spivak.

I found out about a fabric store, located in the center of the town, from my relatives. It was called "Societății KOK" – „Society (company) K-O-K", where K-O-K were the first letters of the surnames of the owners of this company: Kogan, Opachevsky and Kertsman. The store was fairly roomy, with two wide entrance doors. At the circumference of the shelves was a large variety of fabric and other textiles. You could buy fabric for a dress, suit, raincoat or overcoat. They sold silk and wool, one-color and multicolor fabrics. There were signs everywhere in Romanian. Eight or nine clerks worked there, all Jews. Among them were Avrum Blitshteyn, Jacob Ochakovsky, Milya Pressman. On the market day in the crowded store were 30-40 customers. My grandfather Lev Spivak was an accountant in this shop, and he sat on the dais and watched the trade. The clerk received the order, the material was measured, he wrote out what and how much material was cut off, and Lev calculated the sum and took the money. Thus, Lev, shop owners and clerks worked all day, making sure there was no loss or theft, which sometimes happened. At the end of the day, Lev totaled the balance, the money was put into the bank and before closing the store on Friday, the profits were calculated, and payments were given to clerks and the store was sealed. On Saturday in the town, all shops were closed.

There was a hospital in the town where the doctors were Jews, and other medical personnel were Moldovans and Jews. Usually, the doctor was called to the house, but they also had offices for the reception of patients. The payments for doctors' visits and medicines were very high and not every Jew could afford a doctor's appointment.

Documents found about the Jewish affairs

Two years ago, Sergey Daniliuck[72] found two documents in the local ethnographic museum: one was the statute of a Jewish Women Society "Damen Ferein" from 1923; the other document, minutes from a meeting with county and town officials about a dispute between the town and a Jewish family from 1934. Both documents with translation are presented in Appendix A and B in full.

The purpose of the Jewish Women Society[73] was to help poor women in health care, medicine, and food. If necessary, the Society would hospitalize the sick in a local hospital. In order to fulfill the obligations, the society employed a doctor, who was available at the request of the Society to visit and treat the sick. All the expenditures were disbursed from the funds of the Society. The funds were made up of registration fees, dues, donations and special events. Every member of the Society paid 20 lei registration fee and monthly fee of 10 lei, payable a month ahead. Also, money came from donations made by members of the Society or Private; from collections which the society organized in many weddings in Kaushany or other towns, and from spectacular evening balls, benefit soirées, concerts, readings and other events organized by the Society. The status of the Society shows that the organization was very well structured, with several ways to collect money, bookkeeping, registering members, and even an Executive Committee who made the decisions to help the poor.

Another document[74] was official minutes taken from a meeting about a dispute between the town and the Jewish families who built a wooden booth which, according to Tighina County inspectors, was obstructing the road construction with sidewalks. It is also clear from this formal written document that the Jewish families built the wooden booth on their private land, not violating any laws or regulations.

_____

[72] A current Kaushany resident, who is helping to re-discover Jewish past.
[73] Statute of a Women's Society 1923, Appendix A.
[74] Dispute Meeting, 1934, Appendix B.

The family refused to tear down the structure, and the town and the county were considering an expropriation of this piece of land. No further information is available on the matter, and it is possible that we will not know the outcome of this case.

I got a sample of the Land document from the National Archive of Republic of Moldova. It is from the 1930s, from Kaushany. You can find in Appendix H the copy of the first page of the original document in Romanian with translation. You can get an idea of how people lived in Kaushany, what houses they have.

In 2024 our Bessarabia group started to work on Bessarabia Court documents, and we have inventory of such records, including court cases for Kaushany residents. Here are several court cases:

1891. The case of issuing a permit to the Bendery tradesman Khaikin G. to perform prayers in prayer house No. 1 in Kaushany, Bendery district. 1891-1893

1910. The case of the dissemination of the charter of the "Society for Benefiting Poor Jews of the Kaushany." The charter is attached. 01/14/1910-02/28/1910

1917. The case is on the consideration of the petition of a resident Talis of the Kaushany, Bendery district for issuing him a permit to open an illusion. 1917

1941. Property evacuated Jewish population. 1941

Inventories of available court cases are going to be transcribed and available at the JewishGen Bessarabia database in 2025.

Customs, weddings

Typically, at Jewish wedding all mishpokha (family) from close relatives to the most distant one gathered. For example, there were 15-20 families with the surname Spivak in Kaushany and, apparently, all were relatives. At the wedding 100 to 200 people could gather. It took usually two to three weeks to prepare for such a celebration. Women baked cakes, baklava and more sweets. Usually, the wedding was in the courtyards, sometimes in homes. Guests arrived dressed well and the klezmer musicians played with a flourish. All the guests came with gifts, and neatly wrapped flowers. The wedding ceremony itself began with the Rebbe, when the couple went under Chuppah. The Rebbe read the prayer; the couple went around. Then the Rebbe presented the parents of bride and groom. After the official part, the guests ate all kinds of tasty food, drank good wine, and danced.

Here is a story about the wedding of my grandfather's sister Esther, a very beautiful and interesting girl. She was proud, and none of her many suitors pleased her. There was one, whose last name was also Spivak, who was forced to leave Kaushany because of her. Time passed, she didn't get married and got close to 30 years old. So, through a shotchen – matchmaker, she was introduced to a man from the township of Petrovka, 35 km away. But he wanted a dowry. Ester's father had a house on the street, and three apartments on his property, so he promised the fiancé one of the apartments, and 20,000 lei. Esther's brother, my grandfather borrowed 10,000 lei, but that was all he could get, and they still needed 10,000 to proceed.

One day before the engagement, a letter arrived from my grandmother's uncle in China. In the letter were 10 dollars, and since one dollar was 500 lei, which made 5,000 lei, and the money immediately was offered for the dowry. The engagement day arrived, Esther was dressed up, but the fiancé was not coming... they were 5,000 lei short. Esther said: "I feel something is happening. You know, if I go and take off this dress, then that's it - I'm not putting it back on!" The fiancé was some distant relative of the owner of the store where my grandfather worked, and my grandfather went to the owner and asked him for a loan of 5,000 lei, or to be a guarantor. The owner agreed; all the guests got together, and the deed was finally done. Esther with the fiancé later got married in Kishinev and lived happily in his town Petrovka. In a year, she gave birth to her son Monia. That's the story that happened in my family, and many similar stories happened to girls who had no dowry.

Poor and Rich

The economic situation of the Jews during the period between the World Wars was unstable. In 1922 Romanian Red Cross opened in Kaushany an eatery for up to 80 poor children[75]. Some of the families were better off, others not so well.

A very large clan of Bruter families with five sons of a Rashkov townsman moved to Kaushany sometime in the 1870s to get married, and the sons were born from 1872 to 1896. The families owned two grocery shops and two fabric stores. A grandson of one of the brothers, Claude Bruter, writes that according to his father, grandfather acquired a huge area of land from a Russian nobleman. He added that you should be very cautious in interpreting such stories. What was really meant by 'huge area of land?' In any case, the family was definitely not poor, and some of them were very rich. They could send several of their sons to study in France. Some owned land, wineries, and buildings.

There were total of 72 families[76] with surname Kogan with 204 people, in the List of families[77] which lived in Kaushany, Bendery district in the 1920-1930s[78]. Their wealth was very different from each other. Several families owned stores. As explained in the previous chapter, a large estate was divided by Berl Kogan in the 1910s into four parts for his sons' families. Not all Kogans in Kaushany were related, or possibly had a very distant relationship.

The surname Kogan originated from the priestly Kohanim, but according to the family legend the children of Berl were not Kohanim. The story is that Berl's father Moyshe, who was born in c.1820, sometime in the middle of the 19th century changed the surname to Kogan. The reason given was that he or his son did not want to go to the Tsarist Army.

There were many families with the surname Spivak, and most of them were related. When one hears a family story it is not clear if the family is rich or poor. My great grandfather Shloime owned a courtyard with 3 houses, described above, but still at the end of 1930s in order to survive, he would borrow money every market day to buy and sell grain. It is possible that he was rich some time ago, but not in the late 1930s. Here is an episode from my mother's school years, which tells a lot how "rich" they were. My mother was in the second year (1936-37) in a Gymnasium, and she was selected for a dance or a performance presentation. For that she needed a blue folding skirt and a white blouse. She told her parents, and they replied that they would do this for her, but they could not buy her any other new clothes for some time. So, she wore a same sarafan (sundress) in the morning, they called tirolka, and in the evening went for a walk in this new blue skirt for the whole summer... This is how they lived.

227 families owned land and property in Kaushany according to the Land and Property documents from 1940-1941[79]. This is from about 1000 families living in the place by the end of the

---

[75] Wikipedia in Russian.

[76] Families counted by heads of household, and an old alone widow or widower were counted as a family.

[77] See Appendix I.

[78] See in Appendix A.

[79] (1940-1941). *Land and Property documents*. Kishinev: Moldova Republic Archive, Photocopies from originals.

1930s. The value of the properties varied from 2,000 lei (at some point in 1930s 1 dollar was equal to 500 lei!) to 200,000 lei. A place for a house and a yard of 80 square meters, which is less than 9*9 meters, costs 2,000 lei. One of the most expensive places with a value of 200,000 owned by Zelik Kalitskiy, a winemaker, consisted of following: 1 stone house with two floors consisting of 12 rooms, 4 kitchens, 1 storage area, all covered by shingles, 2 large stone cellars, 1 shed covered with shingles, 1 fountain, 1 additional house covered with shingles with 2 rooms, 1 kitchen, 8 large barrels, 5 large presses, and 1 large yard[80].

Emigrants from Kaushany

Many people emigrated from Kaushany in the 1930s. Some of them went to the US, China, several families went to Palestine (Israel) as Khalutsim. Also, a few families sent their children to study in Europe, and most of them did not come back.

Srul Srulevich, one of Sheiva's (Sheiva is my great-great-grandmother) 12 children left for Shanghai, China in 1918. In the previous chapter (Kaushany before 1918) I described the immigration of three other children of Sheiva to America in 1904-1905. Sometime in the middle of the 1930s, my grandparents found out about Srul in Shanghai, and they started to correspond, and Srul also included some dollars in the letters.

Boris Bruter came to France in 1936 to study chemistry at Ecole de Chimie de Strasbourg. Several other people moved to France, and one was studying medicine in Belgium, who later returned to Kishinev after the war and worked in the hospital. Before the War a number of families immigrated to the US, Australia, and a few young Jews moved to Palestine in the 1930s, including one of my mom's cousins.

Jews also migrated to other towns in Bessarabia, or sometimes to Romania proper in order to find work, to study for a professional certificate or a college diploma. Some moved to Jassy, Bucharest, Bendery and Kishinev. My grandfather, an accountant, at some point moved from Kaushany to Tarutino, then to Galatz, and back to Kaushany, and that was just to get a job.

Education

Most of the Jewish families preferred the State Romanian schools for their children. Only 50 students studied in Talmud-Torah[81]. In Kaushany in this period were two schools, an elementary and a secondary, and a gymnasium, but the gymnasium was closed at the end of 1939. The education was in Romanian. In every classroom on a prominent place was a sign "Speak only Romanian!". My uncle remembers how they were afraid of a Romanian teacher. Although the students were mostly Jewish, they tried not to speak Yiddish, so as not to be sent to a corner, stay on their knees or get hit with a stick on the hands. Uncle writes: "In school teachers taught us calligraphy, arithmetic, drawing, labor lessons, where I remember we made small stools, and did different things with our hands. In good weather, the teacher took the whole class outdoors, where we talked about the surrounding terrain and vegetation. Typically, classes lasted 45 minutes, and during recess we would run out into the yard, playing games. Boys and girls studied in schools together. I also for some time went to cheder, where we studied Yiddish, reading and writing, and Jewish History".

---

[80] Land and Property documents, 1940-1941, p.11.
[81] Religious school for boys in the Jewish world.

In the Gymnasium students have studied mathematics, native language (Romanian), history, and geography, physics, religion, and foreign languages: French, German and Latin. My mother recalls: "The director of the school was Chernenko, a very dour man - I don't remember him ever smiling - but fair. All the students were afraid of him. We were allowed to be around until 8 o'clock in the evening, and when the director came out to check on us, word of it would spread instantly, we'd hear "the director is coming" and would be gone like the wind, going home. From 2nd grade of secondary school (*1935-36*), we got a new director, Lipkan, a more sociable man, who maintained a good relationship with the students"[82].

About 80% of the students in the Gymnasium were Jewish. Jews studied religion with a Rabbi by the name Usim. He was intelligent, but slovenly, so the students sometimes made fun of him.

1937, Gymnasium

Kaushany

From left to right: Gorovets (a girl from Kalarash), Sara Natanzon, Riva (Ruchl) Dubosarskaya, Riva (Ruchl) Garshtein, Sheiva Kertsman, Belka Blitshtein, Valya Pipla *(director's sister)*, Golda ('Koka') Bruter, Leizer Maryasin, Sorokopur *(son of the Gymnasium secretary)*, Lungu.
Second row: Basya Lvovskaya (died in Holocaust), Khinka Spivak, Sara Gibrich (died in Holocaust), Tsukman *(physics teacher)*, Lipkan *(director)*, Sorokopur *(the secretary)*, Leva Bruter, Nema Kogan (died on the front of WWII).
Third row: Udel Blitshtein (died in Holocaust), Riva Maryasin, Tsilya Letichever, Nona Galigorsky, Buma (Abram) Kogan.

In the above photo more than half of the students are my parents' relatives or good friends. Many Moldovan children did not go to the secondary school at all, especially girls. Parents thought that it is enough for a girl to have 3 or 4 classes. Before 1937 the schools and Gymnasium were public, but in 1937 the Gymnasium became partly private. Many parents could not afford to pay the high cost. In 1938, the director of Gymnasium was a fascist, but not for long, because the school closed, many students went to schools in some other towns or townships. My mother studied in a place called Volontirovka, and father and his sister went to Bendery Commercial School. Right around Purim, the fascists were overthrown – the Soviets put forth an ultimatum that if Romania did not get rid of the fascist party, the Soviet Union would move into Bessarabia.

---

[82] Kogan, Family Album, Volumes 1, 2. Sixth edition, 2009.

Subjects which were taught in Romanian gymnasium, from memoirs of Khinka Kogan (Spivak):

Romanian - they taught literature and grammar. Of the authors, I remember Ion Creangă, he wrote mostly children's literature, and also, I remember the poet, Michael Eminescu.

History - in first grade, we studied about ancient times, in second, Middle Ages, in third, modern history. *(This was also the case in Soviet schools.)*

Geography - I loved to draw maps on math grid paper, particularly with pencil, so you could erase mistakes.

Music - they taught notes, and we had a chorus. The teacher was very lenient, and we could do whatever we wanted during class.

Shop/Art - did everything with our own hands - molded, sewed

School report for Abram Kogan, my father, from 4th grade 1936-1937. It was so great to have a photo in this report.

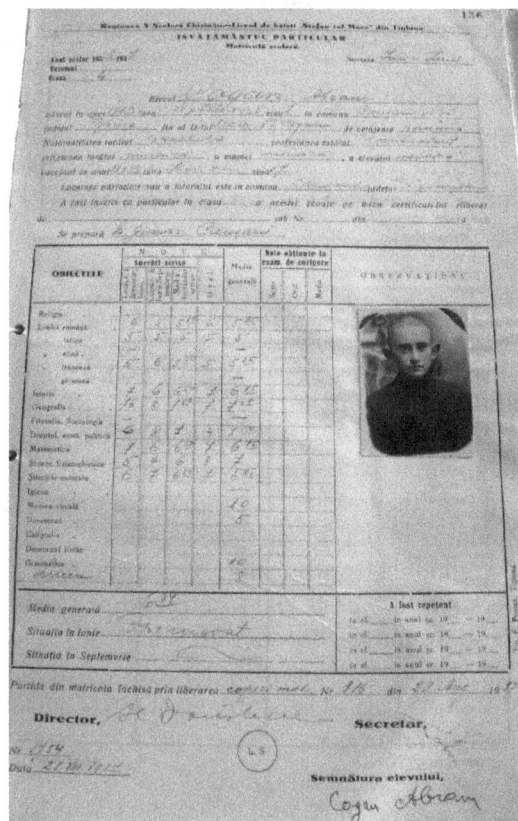

My father graduated with honors from Bendery Commercial School in 1940 before Soviet Union annexed Bessarabia and he had to go to Bucharest to receive an award from the King, but it was already the June of 1940, and the Soviets were coming, and it was dangerous to travel to Buchrest or anywhere else.

Culture and Sport

On Sunday's people went to the cinema, watching silent and sound films. Most films were in foreign languages, but always subtitled in Romanian. The Maccabi organization had quite a spacious gym with sports equipment: parallel bars, horizontal bar, rings, wall bars. In the gym youngsters were engaged in various sports activities. The older group of young men, 18-20 years old, was playing on the football (soccer) team with the same name "Maccabi". The stadium was not far, which hosted soccer matches. Every match gathered a lot of fans, mostly Jews, and children watched all the games for free.

Concerts also were in the gym. A great Yiddish singer, Sidi Tal'[83], performed in Kaushany in 1939. For the concert Jews were well dressed up. Every concert was a holiday for the people, many carrying flowers. Sidi Tal' sung in Yiddish, Romanian, French and Russian. After each song, there were

---

[83] Sidi L'vovna Tal' (born Sorele Birkental was a prominent, popular Jewish singer and actress in the Yiddish language, born in Czernowitz, Austria-Hungary (now Chernivtsi, Ukraine).

numerous standing ovations. Sidi Tal' not only sang, but also recited from various works in Yiddish and Romanian. Jews of all ages were laughing and rejoicing together. People remember performing actors and singers Tina Zlataya, Iosif Kamen' or Kamenev and a magnificent baritone James Golman, whose voice was heard on the nearby streets where a crowd of people gathered who were not able to get a ticket. There was an orchestra with 12-14 youngsters. Some Kaushaners went to Bendery to the theater to see performances of Romanian and Jewish artists.

Political Life

The political life of the town usually started during the voting campaign. Election propaganda meetings were held with enthusiasm. Many government officials, the school principal, representatives of the court, and the police participated in the elections. More Jews voted for the Liberals. But representatives of the Democrats also agitated among the Jews. Some Jews came to these meetings after a hard day's work and just relaxed or even slept during them. As early as 1937, Romania had come under control of a pro-fascist and pro-German party of National Christians; Alexandru Cuza (Cuza-Goga) came to power. Jews knew that the Germans will first imprison or kill the Jews; many in the synagogues discussed the news.

One autumn day in 1937, from the village of Zaim appeared a horse wagon with thugs in brown shirts with swastikas. At first, the Jews did not pay any attention to this until the fascist thugs started to smash windows in the Jewish shops. Police, as usual, were not around. A big noise arose and only when all the Jews came to help, could they manage to drive away the thugs. This provocation was discussed widely, and it was decided to organize a brigade of self-defense. The next day the fascists reappeared in the town, but as soon as they reached the center, the Jewish brigade appeared on horseback with whips and beat the fascists. In minutes they ran away, and such raids did not reappear. The Fascist Party in Romania in power soon was replaced in the beginning of 1938, probably after the Soviet Union declared its ultimatum to Romania. By the summer of 1940 the situation became more complicated again. There were military units and a gun stationed near the church with soldiers on constant duty. Many Jews already knew from the radio transmission that the Romanian Army and the Romanian administration would leave Bessarabia, and that soon the Russian would come. Romanians left on horseback or by car in the direction of Reni-Galati. The army, institutions and rich Romanians were evacuated to the West, though rich Jews decided to stay.

Jews were well represented in different communist and socialist groups. Some Jews from the middle class and the poor in 1936-1938 switched from the Zionist movements to "leftists". They started to read illegal literature, met "socialist" / "communist" friends. My great uncle Berl was imprisoned by Romania for his communist actions. His sister Betya was involved in illegal activities to collect money for political prisoners. That the group held lotteries and made lists of people who gave money for such needs, and of course Betya was always in those lists and donated money. She was also a seamstress, and made underclothes and drawers for men, and bed sheets. Among her clientele was one from the police, who respected her and always had her do his sewing. One day the police found the lists of donors and scheduled a raid on these young people. So that policeman acquaintance came to aunt Betya and said, "My lady, it would be good if you didn't spend tonight at home." She of course got scared, slept at her grandparents' home in the attic. That day, several people were arrested, and aunt Betya got off with just a bit of a fright.

Excerpts from Family histories: Kogan, Spivak, and Srulevich

The first story is about a family **Kogan** and their professions from around 1910 to 1920s. Berl Kogan born c.1840, my great-great-grandfather was a steward for a landlord from the middle of 1860s.

At that time the serfdom had already been abolished[84], but the landlords needed people to manage their estates. Sometime around 1910 the landlord went bankrupt and Berl bought the whole estate. His granddaughter Roza described Berl as a very good grape grower and winemaker. After his death in 1914-16 the estate was divided among his four sons.

The oldest son Peisakh (1874-1928), my great grandfather who managed the estate, had seven sons and a daughter. His two sons, Meyer (my grandfather) and Avrum served in the Romanian army in 1920s[85], Leon (Arie) and Shimen moved in 1920s to Bucharest, Romania; daughter Khona lived in a village Leiptsig, a German colony in Bessarabia.

Peisakh Kogan with his wife Khova Tulchinskiy

1910s

Berl's second son Iosif (he was called Iosef-der-Royter) (1878-1956) lived in Kaushany.

Iosif and his wife Lyuba had son Boris and two daughters Polya and Gitl.

---

[84] Serfdom was abolished in Russia in 1861.
[85] They very likely served in the First World War.

Berl's third son – Zolman (1882-1858) moved to a large town, Bendery. He and his wife Sura had two daughters and a son Boris, who was in GULAG[86] for 9 years. One of his daughters Khaika immigrated to Palestine in 1932.

The youngest son – Moyshe (1892-1946), who fought in the First World War, did not want to work on the land. He went to Odessa to study to be an accountant, got a "government rights" license and in the 1930s worked as an accountant for 5 mills in Kaushany. Moyshe with his family used to live in the main estate building until World War II, and as his daughter Roza described that the Moldovans worked on the land and grew grapes, and other plants[87].

Moyshe with his daughter Roza in their vineyards

See below an interview with Rosa Kogan from 2010 in the section **V. Memoirs, stories from Kaushaners and their descendants.**

---

[86] GULAG – the government agency that administered the main Soviet forced labor camp systems.
[87] From the memoirs of his daughter Roza Kogan.

The second story is about my great grandfather Shloime and his wife Sheiva **Spivak**. This is what my mother Khinka and uncle Izya wrote:" My grandfather Shloime was a small-time merchant, that is to say, he had no money. In Kaushany, the bazaar was on Tuesdays, and to buy grain, farmers needed money. That money, grandfather borrowed from wealthy merchants at a percentage for one day. He bought grain at one price, and sold it at a bit of a profit, thus earning a living. In the bazaar's receiving area, there were many competitors, and each pulled these farmers to themselves - they were all bitter enemies. Thus, they lived.

Shloime and Sheiva Spivak with grandchildren Khinka and Izya.

1937-1938, Kaushany

Grandma Sheiva was a housewife: baked bread and looked after the house. They lived in their own house, where they had three rooms and a kitchen. Those are my grandparents on my father's side.

Shloime Spivak, with his close relative left in 1904 for America (or Argentina)[88] to get away from the Russian Japanese war. They decided to search the land first and if all was well, bring their families to America. Shloime came back to Kaushany after half a year; he said that he didn't want to work on the Sabbath. His relative who was with him was a tailor, worked at the factory apparently on the Sabbath as well, eventually got his own sewing factory. If Shloime had remained in America, probably his wife and children could have joined him, and my parents as well as my own fate would be very different. But he returned and the story of his tragic end during World War II is below.

During evacuation we lived in Kazakhstan next door to grandparents Shloime and Sheiva, Aunt Betty and her daughter Fania. Uncle Litman - Betty's husband - was wounded in 1942 near Moscow and spent more than half a year in a hospital. In the summer of 1943, we met him in Dzhezgazgan. He came out on a pair of crutches - on his back, an enormous backpack, and in his hands another bag, full of bread and other produce. Our joy was indescribable. The walk back from the train station was 2 kilometers. You can imagine how we all took turns carrying those bags.

I don't know and don't remember exactly how it happened, but that evening, Aunt Betty and Uncle Litman came over to us for a short while, and left grandmother and grandfather alone - and they had just cooked a large pot of porridge. When they returned, they saw that the starving grandfather and grandmother had eaten that entire pot.

Aunt Betia cried and said: "eat, now that there is something," and he answered that it was too late; he couldn't get it down anymore. In a couple of days, Shloime died, and two days after the funeral, Grandmother Sheiva died. They were a pair, from God it seemed, and died one after the other. Thus, they

---

[88] My mother told me that Shloime left for America, but when I tried to be a little more specific, she said that maybe he went to Argentina.

remained in far-away Dzhezgazgan. Grandfather was physically a very strong person, but starvation broke him. He prayed every day in evacuation and died awkwardly - not yet even that old.

The last story is about a large family of **Srulevich**, their emigration from Bessarabia, and a reunion of branches of the family that have not seen each other for a long time. It is a story about the genealogical and family success of reunion of family after 100 years apart. It all started when I registered at JewishGen.org in 2007. Such registration usually includes information about yourself, and about your relatives from towns you are trying to find. So, I added the surname Srulevich, because my great grandmother Golda's maiden name was Srulevich, and her parents were Iosif and Sheiva. Sheiva died in February of 1941 at the age of 104! Iosif and Sheiva had 12 children and lived in villages near Kaushany; Sheiva lived in Kaushany from 1938, where she was buried. Their son Yakov left for the US in 1905, and two sisters Shlema and Sophie followed him in 1906. Until the middle of 1930s the families wrote letters to each other, but the war and the Iron Curtain did not allow them to correspond after World War II. For 70 years families lived without any knowledge about each other.

In 2008, I received a message via JewishGen.org from someone claiming that he was a descendent of one of these sisters, immigrated to the USA in 1906. After careful comparison it became clear that we are related. The next week, Jeff Katz, the grandson of Shlema, arrived from New York with the case of letters and photos, and multiple stories of the life of their family. After that there was a great reunion with four generations present descendent of Shlema and Sophie and my family.

Read two articles written by Jeff Katz "Meeting after many years – Letter" and "A Photograph: The Linking of Generations" in Chapter 5. Memoirs, stories from Kaushaners and their descendants.

Rare photo from Kaushany

Kaushany flood, 1933, from family collection of Yasha Volodarskiy

50

Chapter 4. The end or decline of the Jewish Community in Kaushany

The end or decline of the Jewish community in Kaushany and many other shtetlakh in Bessarabia started in 1940. The Soviet Army occupied the land; they smashed the fragile economy, rounded up Zionists, rich Jews, and non-Jews alike and sent them to Siberia with their wives and children. Informants appeared in Bessarabia, same as it was in the Soviet Union in 1930s; people started to report on neighbors, and more arrests were made by NKVD[89]. In the next year, the Great Patriotic War started, and some Jews were conscripted to the Soviet Army, others voluntarily joined the fight, and whoever was able, run away. Romanians and Germans invaded the towns and shtetlakh of Bessarabia. Most of the remaining Jews were killed by Romanians, Germans and close neighbors. When the war ended, very few Jews returned to small towns.

June 28, 1940 – The Soviet invasion of Bessarabia

During June 28 - July 4, 1940, the Soviet Army occupied the regions of Bessarabia and Northern Bukovina, after the Romanian government agreed to evacuate its troops and administration. According to the Treaty of Non-Aggression between Germany and the Soviet Union in 1939[90] Germany acknowledged the Soviet interest in Bessarabia in a secret protocol to the Pact.

After the withdrawal of the Romanian army, for a day or two there was no government in Kaushany. Young Jewish boys and girls prepared communist slogans and red flags for meeting the Red Army. On June 28, 1940, the first column of Soviet soldiers appeared from the railway station and the road from Bendery. Infantrymen sat on trucks in forage caps and helmets with rifles and other equipment. Next cannons and cavalry columns appeared. The columns moved slowly, and the children often climbed on the vehicles and gave the soldiers cold well water and fruit. The soldiers in turn gave them coins which the children had never seen before.

A good friend of my family Aron Dvoirin on the left welcomes the Red Army *(KhK)*.

Yankel Goldshtein, right. Yankel's daughter Raisa read the original book and gave the name of her father in this photo *(Yefim K.)*.

June 29, 1940, Kaushany

Written in Russian:
06/29/1940. Meeting the Red Army.

---

[89] The People's Commissariat for Internal Affairs (NKVD), public and secret police of the Soviet Union that directly executed the rule of power of the Soviets, including political repression, during the era of Joseph Stalin.
[90] Molotov–Ribbentrop Pact was an August 23, 1939, agreement between the Soviet Union and Nazi Germany.

After a few days in the town, a 'Sovèt'[91] (council) was organized, which meant the Soviet regime. Within a few days Kaushany Jews reopened their large and small shops, and everything was sold out completely. The exchange rate was set at one ruble equally 40 lei, which was close to burglary. Often military vehicles drove by and bought out whole rolls of textiles, all colors and all fabric. They had rubles, and the products cost a penny. After that, almost all shtetl Jews lost their jobs.

Perhaps one of the first decrees of the village council was closing of all the synagogues and the prohibition of prayers[92]. You can imagine what it meant for religious Jews. Elderly people were praying at home behind closed doors, with windows and shutters closed. All trade disappeared and the lack of food strongly felt. Many were starving. When the government opened the first bakery, the bread was of such quality that no one could eat it. Almost all the Jews began to bake their own bread.

The big problem for many students was the Russian language. My mother and uncle were lucky, because their father knew the Russian language, and was able to write calligraphy and to read well. Only thanks to their parents, within two months, both learned to read and write in Russian. On September 1st, 1940, they started the school year and wrote and read in Russian much better than others. Classes were conducted by newly arrived Russian teachers. In the beginning it was very interesting because everything was new, teachers and subjects. In the new school there were different teachers of Russian language and literature, mathematics, geography, botany and zoology. At school, there were various hobby groups. Students really enjoyed it, especially sports activities, competitions in soccer, volleyball, chess and checkers.

My grandfather Leib was an accountant by profession and quickly got a job in an office under the name "Egg-Bird-Industry". The organizations began to emerge in town; little by little some Jews got jobs. Medical care was not organized at once, so some of the old and sick people died.

At first movies were shown in the military mobile movie station, and later, in the theaters. Many went to watch Russian films with interest. The bookstores, which Jews loved to visit, were opened up. The radio station began broadcasting, and the radios appeared in the homes. At the same time, streets were lit and people could walk more outside. This period was very short and for the young, it all seemed interesting.

One terrible morning of the pre-war time, the Jews heard that many Kaushaners were exiled to Siberia, including all of the "rich" and also the Zionist leaders[93]. Among the deportees were relatives, friends of my parents, the owners of the fabric shop where my grandfather worked, Kertsman and Opachevsky. After the war Kertsman told how the NKVD broke into their house, gave them four hours to get all they needed, and then sent them in closed trucks to a railway station. The wagons were already waiting. Each car was stuffed with more than 50 people. His partner from work, Opachevsky, did not make it to Siberia; he died in the wagon. The houses of these people were taken, and the furniture, horses and the rest were moved to an unknown destination.

Here is how one family was saved from eviction to Siberia. My mother's mother died in the fall of 1940 after a serious illness, and my grandfather decided to marry the widow of his shop owner, another Kogan. She had two children, and they got married shortly before the events I described above when the "rich were evicted". Since my grandfather was not rich, he saved their family from exile to distant Siberia.

---

[91] Sovèt – council (Russian), form of government in the Soviet Union villages, towns, regions, provinces, country.
[92] After the war ended, several Jewish families returned to Kaushany, one synagogue was opened until end of 1940s.
[93] Ed. Michael Berenbaum and Fred Skolnik. (2007).

"My mother's family Klyuzman were on the list to exile because they were rich, but the beginning of the war saved them from deportation", from Tsilya Dunaevskaya, daughter of Ester Maryasin (Klyuzman). She continued: "My mother Ester, her sister Perl, and parents Iosl and Ides evacuated to Kazakhstan. Perl died from typhus."

It was clear that many Jews were leaving Kaushany and settling in Bendery, or even in Kishinev. During end of 1930's, many Jews went to towns in Romania to work or study, or already lived in Jassy, Bucharest, Galatz. After the Soviets arrived most of them crossed back to the Soviet Union. They were afraid of fascist Romania. The short Soviet period (June 1940-June 1941) was in some ways like the years 1937-38 in the Soviet Union. Some people became informants of the NKVD and told authorities who were rich and whom the Soviets could not trust.

Pinya Bruter, a relative and a wealthy merchant, owned a vineyard and property, and was taken away by the NKVD with his wife Khona Kogan, the sister of my great grandfather and sent to GULAG to separate places. No one ever saw him again. Khona was found by accident by another relative, who reunited her with the rest of the family in Kazakhstan in 1941-42. According to Pinya's grandson Claude Bruter, his father wrote that Pinya was arrested by the NKVD after a report from a Jewish informant.

June 22, 1941 – the beginning of the Great Patriotic War

The winter and spring of 1941 were very disturbing. Everyone felt the approach of the war. And when on June 22, 1941, the residents were awakened by a roar of planes, all understood - the war had begun. The Soviet authorities of Kaushany lent their help to all who wanted to escape[94]. Families received carts with horses or oxen to go to the train station. From there they went in overcrowded wagons to Tiraspol, Odessa and continued into the interior of the U.S.S.R. According to my mother's recollection, the evacuation began on the July 8th[95]. Kaushaners were forbidden to go through Bendery to Tiraspol, because of fears of too many people gathering on the bridge across Dniester. My mother's family had to go to Tiraspol and pick up the daughter of my mother's stepmother. On two carts, one with horses, another with oxen, they crossed Dniester River on an empty bridge and moved to Tiraspol. Soon the front line came close to Dniester and all together they left Tiraspol on July 15th on a cargo train to Odessa. Odessa was bombed for the first time on July 21st and many families got scared and moved further east to Ukraine's depths. So did my mother's family. Several times their train was surrounded by Soviet militia and ordered them to get off the train and help collect the harvest at a farm. When the Germans advanced, they moved further to Stalino (Donetsk), Stalingrad, Krasnodar and in November of the 1941 the family arrived at Andizhan, Uzbekistan, where they lived until they moved to Kazakhstan. Many Jewish families from Bessarabia and Ukraine went to Uzbekistan, Kazakhstan, and Siberia. There was a mix of evacuees in these places: Jews from the eastern part of the Soviet Union, Soviet Germans who were forced to move out because they were Germans. People worked on farms, factories, whatever jobs they could find. In some places there was a food shortage and people starved. Shloime Spivak, the family pioneer who first went to America, but did not like it, died from hunger with his wife Sheiva in Dzhezgazgan, Kazakhstan.

Srul Khaymovich's family[96] lived in Galatz, Romania before the war and decided to move to Bessarabia after the Soviet invasion in 1940. Only one of Srul's daughters Polina (Polea) remained in Galatz with her husband. The rest of the family, settled somewhere in south Bessarabia, probably Akkerman, but in the summer of 1941 they could not evacuate, and all were caught in Odessa; more than

---

[94] Jews did not receive help in every town, or shtetl in Bessarabia.
[95] A few days later the Romanian army arrived at Kaushany.
[96] Srul Khaimovich – brother of my great grandfather Khaim Khaimovich.

35 family members were burned to death[97]! Polina lived in Galatz, Romania during the Shoah and survived.

The yellow star which Polea herself embroidered. She wore it during the years of the Shoah, and it was obtained from her afterwards.

Courtesy of Polea's son Morel, Israel

POLEA·e אלאֲצֶ יֶעֶ6ַ
אﬦֶ פֶﬡﬡֶ אﬡֲﬡﬡﬡֲ הﬡﬡ
.אֲֻﬡֲﬡ ﬦֶ אֶﬡﬡ, אֶﬡﬡ אֶﬡﬡﬡ

There are **873!** records of Jews from Kaushany in the Yad Vashem Central Database of Shoah Victims' Names. Among them are those who fought in the war, killed in their native town, in their own houses, people who evacuated to the East and some of them perished during evacuation, and those who were caught and sent to Transnistria Camps.

The fate of the Jews who remained in Kaushany from July of 1941

There was a lot of killing and death in Kaushany in July-August of 1941. By some calculation about 80-100 Jews were left in the town. Some were very old and could not leave; others could not believe that the Germans wanted to do them evil. Yad Vashem only has Pages of Testimony on 20 Jews shot and burned in the town. A number of sources[98] state that all remaining Jews were gathered by the Romanians and after removing their gold teeth and rings, poured petrol over them and burned them to death. Some of the local population assisted in the massacre. See the place where the remaining Jews in Kaushany were killed in July-September of 1941[99] at the Jewish Cemetery section above.

Following are excerpts from Pages of Testimony[100] of people killed in Kaushany, written mostly by relatives of the victims:
Shulem Blank-Garbo - "Moldovans put him in a closet, poured kerosene and burned him, 1941".
Esther-Rachel Kogan (Lobachevsky) – "Shot by a German plane flying over, June 1941".
Shmil Bruter[101] – "Grandfather was very old and blind and could not be evacuated. He was
    murdered by Romanians. They put him in a box on a street, poured kerosene and burned him.
    August - September 1941".
Leyzer Gidal – "Burned together with another Jew in his own house, July 1941".
Zeylik and Shyndl Kalitskiy – "Shot to death with the whole family on his own vineyards, July 1941".
Shaya-Zeylik Kaplun - *"Killed in Kaushany, YdV".*
Efroim Leibovich - *"Killed in Kaushany, was a forced laborer (YdV)."*
David, Rakhel and Esther Polskiy – "Killed by neighbors, 1941".

---

[97] Yad Vashem, Pages of Testimonies written by Morel, son of Polina, Srul's daughter, who survived the war.
[98] *Holocaust on the territory of U.S.S.R.* (2011). Moscow: ROSSPAN; Russian Jewish Encyclopedia. www.rujen.ru; Wikipedia, Russian.
[99] According to several elderly residents of Kaushany in 2008-2009.
[100] Yad Vashem - www.yadvashem.org
[101] Two pages of testimony. One from his grandson Lev Bruter, who survived the occupation and from 1944 was in the military fighting with Nazis.

Tsipa, Gitl and Gersh Maryasin, - "Part of Maryasin family did not evacuate and were killed in 1941".
Manya Goldner - "Was shot in Kaushany".
Iosko, Tsiviya and Khaim Sherman - Killed in Kaushany, YdV
Iosif Yatom – Rabbi, killed in Kaushany.
Ikhil Zeltser - Killed in Kaushany.

Other Kaushaners who perished in the Shoah in Moldova, Ukraine, Kazakhstan

The evacuees, who could not escape in time or were delayed in a station, were cut off by the advancing German or Romanian armies and were taken to ghettos or camps in Transnistria, and most of them perished. There are those who died from bombardments, especially in Odessa and also from hunger. Many Jews were killed in Odessa by the Romanian and German administration. Yad Vashem holds 169 Pages of Testimony for the Jews from Kaushany killed in other towns or villages.

Jews who evacuated to the East of the Soviet Union

Many Jews from Kaushany and from Bessarabia were evacuated to Central Asia republics of the Soviet Union, mostly to Uzbekistan, Kazakhstan, and Turkmenistan. With the help of the Tashkent researchers, JewishGen obtained and transcribed information about 152,000 Jews - refugees to the Central Asia areas[102]. Among them there were 87 from Kaushany. This is in no way a complete list. Probably the number of people evacuated is at least ten times higher. Above I have described briefly how families reached Uzbekistan. Many people, especially elderly and very young did not make it, and died on the way from diseases, and hunger. While travelling in awful conditions on trans, which usually transport cattle, Jews were stopped on some stations and they were forced to work on harvest, because farms did not have enough people. When Germans or Romanians advanced to these places, Jews wanted to continue their journey, and not always farms let them go.

Jews in the Soviet Army who fought against Nazis

I found seventy-nine Kaushaner Jews in the Memorial database[103] of Jews who were killed on the fronts or were missing in action during the World War II. Kaushaners fought and were killed during the defense of Sevastopol, Stalingrad, also in West Prussia, the Ukraine, and other places.

---

[102] Jewish Refugees to Tashkent: http://www.jewishgen.org/databases/Holocaust/0136_uzbek.html
[103] http://www.obd-memorial.ru/. Soviet military archives are the sources of information on the site.

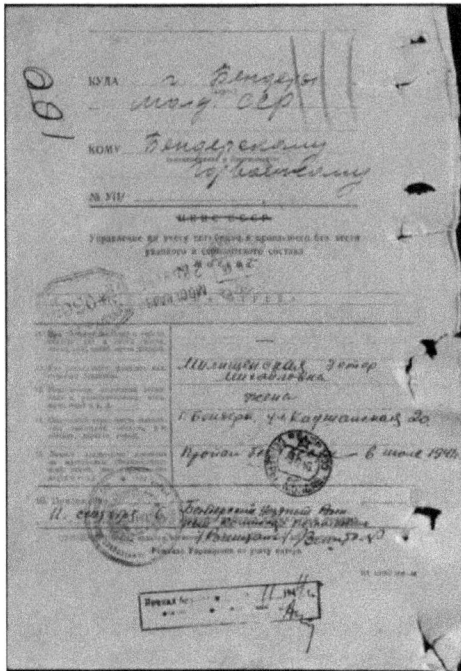

A letter to the wife of Private Isaac Abramovich missing in action in July of 1941

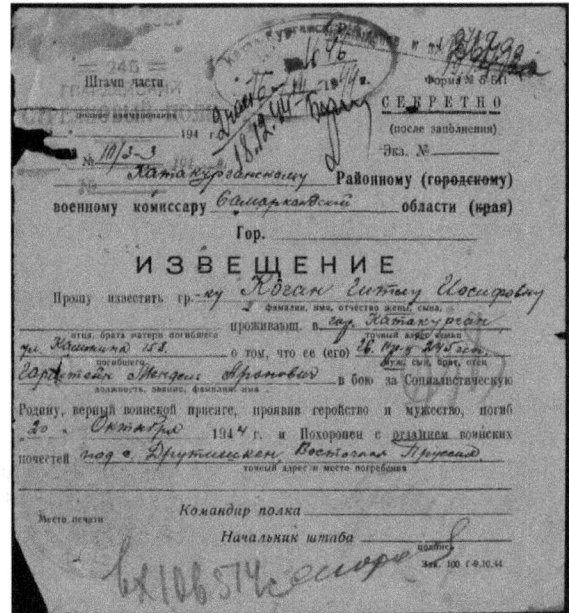

Death Announcement about Mendel Garshtein to his wife, Gitlya Kogan. He was killed in West Prussia and buried with the military honors near village of Drutishken, West Prussia.

"My father Barukh (Boris) Maryasin was enlisted in the Soviet Army, but shortly was caught and put in the camp. During the way to the camp in the train, the German soldier who accompany the wagon told all Jews to remove the yellow star, so he survived", from Borukh Maryasin's daughter Tsilya Dunaevskaya (Maryasin).

Klyzman Haim was killed or missing in action near Stalingrad in 1944. Klyuzman Bore died from starvation working on Labor front during the war.

Lev Bruter saved by a Ukrainian family

My family's good friend and distant relative Lev Bruter, born in Kaushany was saved by a Ukrainians George and Varvara Feodorovna Pelin who were honored as Righteous Among the Nations by Yad Vashem in 1996.

Below is an excerpt from the Final Report of the International Commission on the Holocaust in Romania. (2004). Bucharest, Romania (File 6853):
Pelin, George
Pelin, Varvara

George and Varvara Pelin were farmers living in the village of Malayeshty in the Tiraspol district. In March 1944, they sheltered Lev Bruter in their home. Bruter was a young Jewish native of the town of Kaushany in Moldova whom they had never met before the war.

Lev Bruter tells the story of his saviors in the village of Malayeshty in his video testimony[104]. He describes the Pelin family as very kind and compassionate. Lev was living in Odessa and later in the village of Karlovka in Transnistria under the Germans/Romanians and worked on a farm. It was 1944 and the Soviet Army advanced and the Germans and Romanians were about to retreat from Transnistria. Some of the remaining Jews as well as young Moldovans were taken away with Germans to the West. So, at this juncture, Lev decided to run from the post he was supposed to be at, and shortly ran into the house of George and Varvara Pelin. They immediately understood who he was and put him together with their son in the basement, where they hid for some time, until the Soviet Army came to the village. After liberation, Lev Bruter was enlisted into the Soviet Army, and his battalion liberated his native Kaushany, where no Jews were alive. He found some information from Moldovans and Ukrainians how his grandfather and many other Jews were killed[105].

The War ended. Where to go?

The war was over, but how to get home, and where to live? It took my mother's family from May to September to return to Moldova. In order to get money for a trip back, my grandfather, while trying to sell some goods, was arrested, bribed the arrestor, and was taken again into custody for similar operations. Finally in September they arrived in Kishinev. The family already knew what happened in Kaushany, that the Jews were killed. Many families at that time settled in larger towns, Bendery, Kishinev, and Tiraspol. A few families remained in Kazakhstan or Uzbekistan.

The problem was not only how to get an apartment in a larger town, but also how to get permission to live there. In the Soviet Union the latter was always a problem since people could not freely move from town to town. There are many stories of how people occupied empty apartments, and the militia tried to remove them by force.

My mother went to Kaushany after arriving from Kazakhstan. She found living in their house the family of Alexandra, who served in my mother's house in the late 1930s, especially helping with her sick grandmother. Not only did Alexandra not invite my mother into the house, but she also forbade my mother to look inside. I can see only one reason for that – everything inside the house belonged to my mother's family, and not Alexandra's. My mother settled first in Tiraspol, and later got married and moved to Kishinev.

The end of formal Jewish Community, 1949, 25 November, Kaushany

In 1944, when the war still raged in West Europe, several families returned to Kaushany, and found that Jewish homes were destroyed or occupied, and that part of the cemetery was desecrated. Only ruins of one of the synagogues were still standing[106]. After the war about 10-15 Jewish families settled in Kaushany. In 1949 in Kaushany the last synagogue was closed, and the Jewish community was taken out of registration because there weren't enough religious people[107]. According to the same sources, in 1991

---

[104]University of Southern California Shoah Foundation Institute, www.college.usc.edu/vhi. Video is available at Kaushany website.

[105] See section 'The fate of the Jews who remained in Kaushany from July of 1941'.

[106] Ed. Michael Berenbaum and Fred Skolnik, 2007.

[107] Ibid, p.37; also in Wikipedia, Russian.

and in 2004, six Jews lived in Kaushany, and possibly some Jews still live there now, but the Jewish Community was long before destroyed by the Holocaust.

Documents from 1949 when the Jewish Community, synagogues were closed.

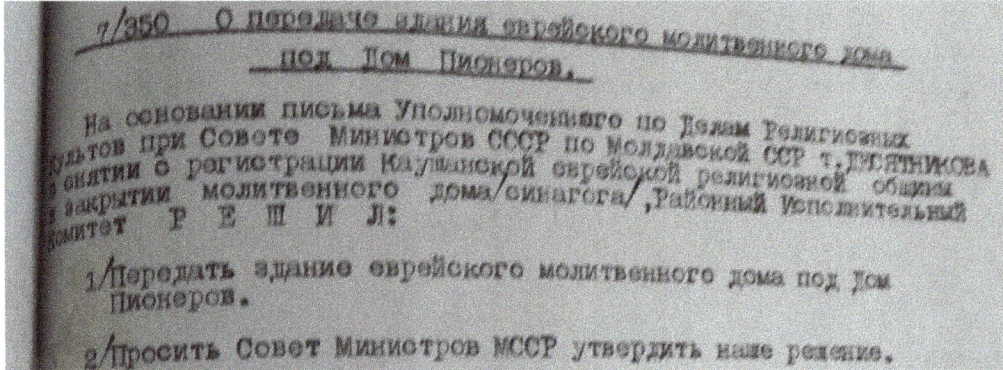

About transfer of the building of Kaushany Jewish prayer house to House of Pioneers.

Director of Religious affairs at Soviet Ministry of USSR for Moldavskaya SSR T. Desyatnikov.

Act.

1949, 25 November, Kaushany
We, who signed this Act below, created this paper:
Assistant Kaushany Rayon Sovet, others.
Based on the letter sent from November 23, 1949, #98 from Director of Religious affairs at Soviet Ministry of USSR for Moldavskaya SSR about closure of Jewish-Religious society.

This resolution was given to representatives of the religious community Korenberg N.T. (Nukhim Shliomovich), Malamud I. Kh. (Ikhil Khaskelev), and Pomos G.M. (Gedal Markovich).

Jewish representatives were familiarized with the letter, but they refused to sign this Act!

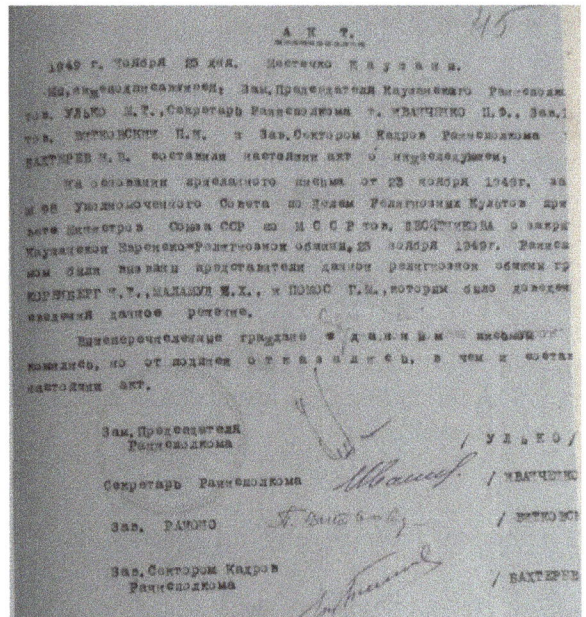

Imagine, 1949, Soviet Union, Stalin is in power, anti-cosmopolitan campaign started in 1948, large number of Jews were persecuted as Zionists or rootless cosmopolitans. Jews in Kaushany did not sign such document! They are really heroes!

Yahad – In Unum[108]

Yahad – In Unum, a leading organization investigating the mass executions of 1.5 million Jews in Eastern Europe, has started their trips to Moldova. I was in contact with Yahad – In Unum, providing them with information known to me about the killings of Jews in Kaushany.

Father Desbois[109] with his team from Yahad- In Unum was in Kaushany and close by villages. They interviewed local people who remembered the execution of Jews.

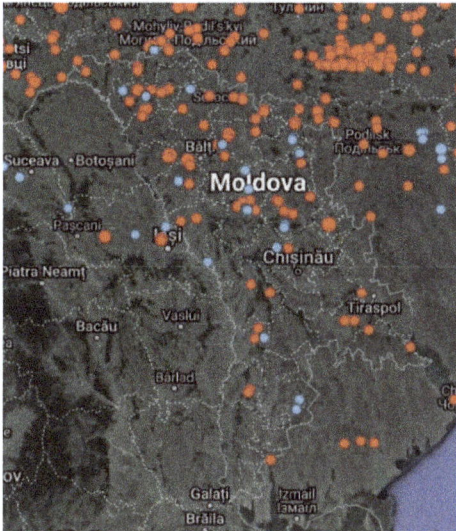

The Map of Holocaust by Bullets (Moldova).

Link to the whole map is https://www.yahadmap.org/#map/

There are so many execution sites in Moldova/Bessarabia!

You can order the following two full interviews. Go to the link below and go to "Request full video testimonies about this village". Alternatively, you can contact Oksana Miroshnyk at o.miroshnyk@yiu.ngo and she will send you the usage agreement form to complete, sign and return to her.

Here is a link to one of this excerpt of the interview: http://www.yahadinunum.orgwww.yahadmap.org/#village/c-u-eni-causeni-kaushany-koshany-kaushen-c-u-eni-moldova.836. According to the witness, about 120 Jews were killed in Kaushany execution site, near Botna river. The excerpt is only 5 minutes long with English subtitles, and the full interview is 1 hour and 43 minutes. Interview was conducted in Russian with translation into French.

_____

[108] http://www.yahadinunum.org
[109] Father Desbois is a President of Yahad – In Unum, author of a book: "The Holocaust by Bullets".

There is a second interview with a witness from Kaushany, but there is no excerpt from it, and the full interview is 39 minutes.

That interview is conducted in Romanian with translation into French.

Not the End of Jewish life in Kaushany, by Nona Shpolyanskaya (Geisman)

Thanks a lot, to Nona who presented an insight of Jewish life in Kaushany in 1950-1970s. 12 years ago, when I worked on the original research, I did not know that.

There is a header in the work for Kaushany (first edition, 2012) "The end of the Jewish Community". Perhaps it was indeed an end of a formal Jewish community. Jews remained in Kaushany, more than that many came to Kaushany to live and work from other places in Moldova. Most of them were young specialists from the 1950s-beginning of 1960s. Several Jewish families returned to Kaushany from evacuation. Of course, synagogues all were closed, no Jewish schools.[110]

I remember how families celebrated Jewish holidays. I was a child in the 1960s and helped my grandmother bake Matza for Pesach, also how I walked to our relatives and gave them shalhamunes – Mishloah Manot on Purim. Our family had Seder at my grandparents Ikhil and Ester Geisman. My grandmother always lit candles on Friday and prayed for all of us. I remember how we celebrated Bar-Mitzva for one of my cousins.

Elder generation spoke fluent Yiddish. My grandparents from father's side spoke Yiddish and Romanian, and Russian did not know well. Generation of my parents also spoke Yiddish. My father even in 1960-70s subscribed to Yiddish Journal "Sovetish Heimland" (Soviet Homeland). When anyone got married, many had a wedding Chuppah. My mother kept her Ktuba – Marriage agreement. When I got married in 1978, we also had a Chuppah, but it was already in Bendery.

I remember well, I was 12 years old, when my grandfather Ikhil (father's father) died, and he was buried by Jewish tradition. I had to go and get Takhrikhim – white graveclothes, and he was buried without a coffin. From our home to the Jewish cemetery man caried body on stretchers. The cemetery was far from home. After that minyan was gathered and people read Kadish. The mitzvah of Nihum Avelim (comforting mourners) was followed, and on a Yortsayt read Kadish.

This is all I remember. The cemetery was on the outskirts of town, on the road to neighboring Zaim village. Today is hard to talk about the size of the cemetery. Remember that it was a clear difference in monuments from before and after the war. There was a person who looked for the order at the cemetery.

The most I loved were Jewish songs at the holidays, during feast. All this took place in my lifetime in 1960-1970s in Kaushany.

---

[110] See above the document about closing Jewish community and synagogue in 1949.

Can anything else be found about Jewish life in Kaushany?

I know that this is not the end of my research and a lot more may be discovered about Jewish life in Kaushany from archives and residents of that place, Jews who used to live their long time ago and non-Jews who live in that place now.

Sergey Daniliuck, a Kaushany resident, recently found and photographed a new stone in a wooded area not far from the town. It may be a monument someone tried to put on a mass grave. There is no inscription on the stone or on a few other stones close by. I hope that future research will answer that question.

A stone was found not far from Kaushany in a wooded area.

Courtesy of Sergey Daniliuck, 2012

Chapter 5. Memoirs, stories from Kaushaners and their descendants

Jeff Katz. Meeting after many years – Letter, *June 23, 2008*

The letter you are about to read was written by Jeff Katz, grandson of Shlema Barsky (Srulevich), who in 1906 left Bessarabia with her sister Sofia. My mother, Khinka Kogan (Spivak) is a granddaughter of Golda Khaimovich (Srulevich). Shlema, Sofia and Golda are sisters. You will read about the family spread on two continents and of a miraculous gathering of Jeff and my mother in Tzur Sholom.

Yefim Kogan

Yefim:

      I have been back in New York from Israel for a sufficient amount of time to gather my thoughts and write down impressions gained after meeting your mother in Tsur Shalom.
As you can imagine, I brought to this historic visit a great deal of emotion and longing. The story of our family's loss, wandering, uncertainty and reclamation after sixty-eight years brings tears to the eyes of all who hear the story of our family's separation and our conviction in America of the family's extinction in Europe.

      In advance of our meeting, I was fearful that cultural differences and language barriers would prevent open communication and genuine emotion. When you and I met we shared a common language. We hit it off famously, volleying back and forth with questions and answers for six hours straight without catching our breath. I worried if your mother and I would be able to enjoy this seldom experienced ease of sharing our life histories.

      It became immediately evident the moment I spotted your mother waiting patiently for me in the hallway entrance of her flat that she and I would enjoy the same ease of conversation and familial connection. All my fears melted away instantly. Your mother's warmth and attention to detail was extraordinary. My Yiddish returned to me. There we were, two human beings long separated by years, distance, language and history embracing each other with great emotion and recognizing, as you and I did, several months before, the miraculous significance of the occasion.

      As you know, our family's heritage was passed down to me through my grandmother Shlema. She instinctively understood the strength of her heritage and her responsibility to transmit her tradition to the next generation. Unfortunately, in her daughter's case, she was not very successful. But Shlema had a second chance through me, her grandson. I made the existential choice of embracing this oral tradition, but after her death, I never knew if I would be able to share my knowledge and was convinced that family mysteries would remain unsolved. But you and your mother provided me with some of the answers and helped complete the transmission.

      As I looked at your mother, I was immediately struck by her physical resemblance to the Srulevich clan. There before my eyes stood a reincarnation of my grandmother Shlema. Thirty-eight years have passed since her death. At that moment, the barrier of time disappeared. There was such a strong resemblance that I shuddered. I became lightheaded and unsteady on my feet. I am not sure if my desire for your mother to resemble Shlema was greater than her actual resemblance. But it didn't matter. Her blue eyes, her nose, her wispy white hair, her voice, and mysteriously even hand gestures transported me back to the tastes and smells of childhood and to the stories and laughter that I experienced with my grandmother. Now it was your mother telling hilarious stories of Sheiva and sad stories about Golda and Feige and Gedalya and his family. Of course, we spoke about the very last letter to reach America in 1940 and about her dying mother Feige and her father Leib's certainty of war. At this time her great grandmother Sheiva was 103, having survived both her daughter and granddaughter. And here we were. I, a distant relative from America who only experienced the hardships of our people over the past one hundred years through books and film and other peoples' testimonies, speaking Yiddish to your mother, an 85-year-old woman in Israel, the last of our family to have survived the disruption of her life as brought about by Nazi barbarity and Stalinist oppression.

There we were with so many stories, so much to share and so little time to compress it all into a cruel three-hour visit. Your mother was delighted to answer my questions and to present her life story. I saw that her mind had remained sharp as she reeled off dates and facts all consistent with her memoir. But it was the anecdotes of Sheiva that immediately drew me so close to her. I captured these priceless stories of Sheiva's humor and of your mother's joy in remembering her great grandmother on video as she recalled one hundred-year-old Sheiva kibitzing with her school friends and getting the last laugh with her family doctor who while testing her senility was struck by her sharp wit and lucidity.

So, in an old housing development north of Haifa, the wanderings, separation, deprivation and reconciliation of our families came to a close sixty-eight years after the last letter before the Holocaust was written in Causani by Leib Spivak and opened in New York City by Shlema Barsky. Finally, a great circle spanning continents and oceans that began in Monzyr and Ismail in Bessarabia, then moved to Galatz, Causani and Kishinev and across the Dniester to Odessa and on to Uzbekistan, Kazakhstan, with stops in Harbin and Shanghai and New York and later in Boston, Seattle and finally returning to the Land of Israel, to Tsur Shalom. Such is the tale of Jewish history.

The world of Eastern Europe that was passed on to me by my grandmother has vanished and the stories transmitted to me had become thin and sparse over the years. But when I laid eyes on your mother and heard her voice, watched her hand gestures and listened to her sweet Yiddish stories, then the dusty past I inherited was suddenly invigorated. We both felt the significance of the moment as we laughed and cried.

How fortunate I felt to have experienced this moment. How grateful I am to the Almighty who brought me to that day and permitted me to sit with your mother and share pictures and photographs of Sheiva Srulevich with the one living relative who remembers her. Until that day in Tsur Shalom I didn't really believe that the dead share or are present in our lives. But I believe that in that small flat on Rehov Lochmei haGhettaot, on that Monday afternoon with the blinds drawn and the curtains closed to dull Israeli heat, our ancestors were present in your mother's living room. I am convinced that Shlema must now know that her instincts were correct. Tradition must be passed from generation to generation and circles, with its many wanderings and uncertainties, must be completed. That is the way, the Jewish way.

I ask you to translate this letter into Russian for your mother. (*I did it, Yefim K*)
All my best to you, Galina and your family,
Jeff

Jeff Katz. A Photograph: The Linking of Generations, *New York, December 2020*

As I age, I am left with abiding memories of childhood, of people and places that have made me the Jew I am today. This very personal memoir is a tale of how a seemingly insignificant object can have extraordinary meaning by connecting generations and nourishing the soul. Jeff.

Iosif and Sheiva Srulevich

c1910

This is a rare photo of two people born in 1830s.

My birthright came to me as a young boy in the still of the night, when our home was quiet, when all were asleep. I would awake at times and find my way to my grandmother's bedroom, into her soft bed. There was no other place that I could find comfort and no one else who stirred me so strongly with her late-night stories than my grandmother Shlema. At those moments my heritage was gifted to me in softly spoken Yiddish with stories of a vanished world in faraway Europe. Never having an interest in sports or childish games, her often repeated stories delighted me more than anything else. I was drawn to the flame of tradition that has sustained me all these many decades. I would snuggle deeper into her fleshy arms, taking in her elderly fragrances, and asked her to tell and retell me about people she had not seen for a half a century. Then she would take out old photographs that were frayed, torn and scratched. They had never been placed under glass or affixed in a family album or covered with plastic to survive the decades. For some reason they resided in a brown paper bag along with a few handwritten letters which were stored in Shlema's bottom dresser drawer. There was one particular photograph that brought more tears to her eyes than any other, the photograph of her parents, Yosef and Sheiva Srulevich.

Over the years I have stared at this photograph innumerable times seeking answers to questions that no one today can answer. These people are so familiar, yet still unknowable. An eternal link binds us, but there is so much I do not know about them. I look in vain for a familial resemblance knowing full well there is none. I recognize their facial features as characteristic of the Srulevich family, but that is where it ends. For this couple, positioned proudly, seated almost regally, know exactly who they are and their purpose in life. But as much as this photograph engenders emotion, it is equally encased in mystery.

For they are not my blood relatives; only the parents of the woman who with great love adopted the child who would twenty-five years later give birth to me.

Every Jewish family has pictures of relatives from Europe who are posing for a photographer either in a studio or in this case more naturally out of doors in front of their home in Bessarabia. The photograph was developed onto a *carte postale* and sent abroad to their children who emigrated to the West and will never again breathe the air or walk the soil of their native Bessarabia. They wanted this photograph to be a keepsake for their children, their American grandchildren and even for generations to come. As the grandchild of their daughter Shlema, I still cherish their wish. And at the same time, I mourn knowing that this eternal link, as precarious and weak as it is, will end with me. And now I fear there is no one to inherit it.

After the 1903 pogrom in Kishinev, Bessarabia, then part of the Russian Empire, several of Yosef and Sheiva's grown children realized, as did millions of Jews before and after them, that life in Europe would lead to more and more bloodshed. Even so, most remained.

As you the viewer examine the photograph, look deeply into their faces, examine their stature, their clothing, the table, the photograph propped up between their resting arms, and the crocheted tablecloth. I always hoped to see myself in their faces, but know quite well that we are not related, we only share their daughter Shlema, my grandmother, and this photograph that has endured a trans-Atlantic mailing and was saved for years to come in the bottom of Shlema's dresser drawer.

The couple is seated in either the Bessarabian, Romanian town of Galatz or Izmael. On the ship manifest that brought Shlema to New York, Izmael was written as her point of origin. Years later Sheiva moved with the family to Kaushany, in present day Moldova, a backward, landlocked and wretched place. These place names would become more familiar once I met Sheiva and Yosef's great-granddaughter Khinka and her son Yefim in 2010. But let me not get ahead of myself.

The season appears to be early spring or late fall judging from their clothing. Yosef, perhaps prematurely white, sports a traditional full beard, but without *peyot*, as was the custom of orthodox Jewish men of the region. Do I detect a twinkle in his eye, staring straight at the camera, as Sheiva is seated sternly in perfect balance with her husband. Sheiva's hair is still a dark natural color under her shawl. Bessarabian women generally didn't shave their hair and don wigs. Interestingly, in another photograph in Shlema's collection her brother Gedaliya, the oldest, is captured seated next to his wife who is wearing a wig. Sheiva in our photograph gazes ahead unsmiling, matronly, for at this point in her long life she had given birth to a dozen children with eight surviving siblings. Surely her life had been full of wonders and heart aches. Longevity is a blessing among the women in the Srulevich clan. Sheiva lived to a ripe old age of 104 without losing her sense of humor or acuity. Shlema lived to 93 and Sheiva's great granddaughter, Khinka, to 96. Shlema had the complexion of Yosef and the facial structure of Sheiva. She was pleasantly hefty all her days. In sharp contrast, my mother, Evelyn, the adopted daughter of Shlema and Aaron Barsky, was somewhat swarthy and lanky.

It was this photograph among others that my grandmother would take from her wardrobe late at night with tears in her eyes. Between sniffles she would tell me of her home, her parents, the fragrant lilacs that grew tall up to her second-floor window, her father's cattle trading business, his religious practices, her journey to America and life in the *Goldene Medina*. These vintage stories fascinated me and bound me irrevocably to Eastern-European Jewish traditions, religious orthodoxy, the Yiddish language, and to her marvelous Shabbos and Yom Tov culinary specialties. Her tales thrilled me. She spoke of family members who I knew and also those who remained in Europe and died before my time. She spoke of places I would find on a map. She gave me an appreciation of geography and a wanderlust that has been a life-long passion. I acquired her stories as my own although I was too young to realize that

65

we did not share heredity. Today they return to me as precious and ageless memories and I realize that she loved me and I loved her without question, with unparalleled affection.

Over the years in addition to photographs letters were exchanged. These would be packed with warm greetings and questions about Evelyn and Shlema's two siblings, Jacob and Sophie, and their families. Often, they were filled with Sheiva reprimanding them for failing to write more often and for financial support for their poor, ailing mother. After Shlema died I inherited a few remaining letters written in stylized Yiddish script with brown ink on lined paper often difficult to decipher. The last letter from her brother-in-law foreshadowed looming danger and then all written communication ended suddenly in a silent void in 1940.

Shlema and her sister Sophie left home in 1906 traveling by train to Czernowitz, in neighboring Bukovina, the first large city on their way to the New World. It was there that they first heard German spoken and then continued on to Polish Warsaw where they stayed with a cousin. Sophie became ill and spent the next six months in Warsaw and arrived in New York in September 1906. Shlema crossed Poland and Germany making her way to the port of Hamburg and crossed the Atlantic in steerage landing 10 days later at Ellis Island. Her brother Jacob was already in New York awaiting her arrival. Yosef, the patriarch, died in 1918-19 from the Spanish Flu pandemic that killed fifty million people worldwide. Sheiva lived on to 1941 and died at the age of 104 and was buried in a Jewish cemetery days before the Romanians came to slaughter Jews in advance of the Nazi invasion. The cemetery was demolished years later.

The central thread linking the generations in the black and white photograph is the crocheted tablecloth draped over the outdoor wooden folding table. One may ask why focus on the tablecloth, and why not on the mysterious photo propped up on the vase? The photo is regrettably indecipherable, but the tablecloth is very much recognizable and is the link that connects generations of the Srulevich family. The peripatetic crocheted pattern is found in this photograph in Bessarabia in c. 1910, again in the home of Shlema in the Bronx in 1948, and finally in Tzur-Shalom, Israel, Khinka Kogan's home in 2010. I wonder how many generations of previous Srulevich women crocheted similar patterns?

Were Sheiva or Khinka to miraculously walk into my home today I would spread before them the crocheted tablecloth Shlema labored over in preparation of her first male grandchild's *brit milah*. Shlema worked feverishly to crochet an oversized tablecloth that would cover a long table laden with homemade gefilte fish, knishes, challahs, strudels, cakes and liquor. The *brit* was held in the apartment my grandmother and my mother and father inhabited on Clinton Avenue in the heavily Jewish Tremont section of the Bronx. Shlema and my paternal grandmother cooked and baked all night to prepare a feast that all Jewish *balabustas* would have praised. And since then, for seventy-two years that tablecloth was hardly used, and today is wrapped in plastic and sits in a drawer in my closet much like the photographs in Shlema's brown paper bag that were once buried in her dresser drawer. I will never forget how Shlema's gnarled fingers could operate a crocheting needle and cotton thread with machine-like precision and make doilies and bedspreads which graced our home and were gifted to family and friends.

The extended Srulowitz (spelling this way upon arrival in the US) family now living in America consisted of Shlema's brother Jacob Schwartz (name changed in America) and her sister Sophie Silverman. Both siblings married and lived with their children in Brooklyn. Shlema and Aaron and Evelyn lived on the Lower EastSide and then in the Bronx. The families remained close. After the World War II, once the murder of six million Jews in Europe became known, Shlema reached out through the Yiddish language newspaper, the Forverts, and WEVD a Yiddish language radio station to discover if any family members were still alive after the destruction. She never received news of survivors. In 1964 when I was sixteen, I wrote to the Romanian and Soviet Embassies in Washington DC inquiring about the

Srulowitz family in the Bessarabian area. The Romanians wrote back with nothing positive to report and the Soviets ignored my letter.

Forty years later, in 2005, a saga of Jewish survival unexpectedly unfolded. Yefim Kogan, the great-great-grandson of Sheiva and Yosef, responded to a JewGen.org inquiry posted by Baruch Seff, the great grandson of Sophie Srulowitz Silverman, Shlema's sister who traveled with her to America. When Yefim and I spoke I learned of the miraculous survival of his mother Khinka, the sole member of the Srulevich family who lived in pre-War Kaushany and actually knew Sheiva in her advanced age. Khinka was still alive, and after emigrating from the Soviet Union was now living in northern Israel. At first, she was disbelieving, and then astonished to learn that a relative (me) living in the West was interested in making contact. Khinka Kogan, the great granddaughter of Sheiva and Yosef Srulevich, first survived Romanian persecution and then fled the Nazis by escaping into the Soviet Union only to survive the hardships of the war and return to the destruction that the Nazis exacted. It took until 1988 until the Soviets allowed the Jews to emigrate.

With my grandmother (1971) and my mother (2003) both deceased, I could only imagine their bewilderment and joy to discover after all these years a cousin, a grand niece was still alive, well and living in Israel. It became my mission to first visit Yefim, Khinka's son living at that time in a Boston suburb, and then to visit Khinka in Tzur-Shalom in northern Israel later that year. With each visit I presented the letters, family portraits and photos they had never seen. Khinka may have seen some of them years before the War, but all photographs had been abandoned or lost.

I have described in another essay about that momentous reunion, a story of Jewish wonder. It is worth repeating the amazement I felt when entering Khinka's flat in Tzur-Shalom and in front of my eyes were similar crocheted doilies decorating her tables and bookcases. At that moment I was united with a multi-generational tradition that I had long not experienced ever since my grandmother and mother had died. They had no idea that a remnant of the family survived the Nazi and Soviet horror and with great fortitude and courage returned to the region they knew well, and reestablished themselves after the war, only to be trapped behind an Iron Curtain until the Russians permitted the Jews to leave the Soviet Union for the West or Israel.

And in Israel, looking into Khinka's face I instantly saw before me my beloved grandmother, with her similar stature and coloring, with the same pale blue eyes, and the sweet sounds of Bessarabian Yiddish. Surely, hovering in the background were our ancestors, Sheiva and Yosef.

Each year I light a Yom Kippur yahrzeit candle in their memory and wonder what will become of this photograph and of the crocheted tablecloth made with much love seventy-two years ago for a first grandchild's *brit milah*.

Rosa Kogan. Memories, *2010*

Interview with Rosa Kogan was arranged by phone in November 2010. Rose was born in 1921 in Kaushany, and was married to Tolya Veltser (1914-1988, Kishinev). She lived in Afula, from 2011 in Jerusalem in a nursing home, died in January 2012 in Jerusalem.
Yefim Kogan

About parents and grandparents

Roza's father – Moyshe, mother – Inda. Moyshe's mother - Entel died in 1934-35, his father - Berl died in 1914-16 years. Berl was a good winemaker. Entel held a grocery store in Kaushany and Berl was the manager of the landlord. When the landlord went bankrupt Berl's family bought the whole estate. After the death of Berl estate was distributed to all four sons of Berl: Joseph Moyshe, Pesakh and Zalman.

Moshe did not want to work on the land. He went to study in Odessa and became an accountant with the state permission. After graduation, Moyshe was an accountant and served five mills in Kaushany.

Moyshe fought in the First World War, became deaf. Moyshe and the Inda were married in 1918.

Standing from the left: Boris, Roza, Menikha (daughter of Inda's sister Molka)
Sitting: Inda, Nyoma and Moyshe

~1935, Kaushany

The whole family lived on the estate until 1941. I went to Iasi in 1938 and worked there. Moldovans worked the land of the estate, and when the family was evacuated in earlier July of 1941, all was given to Moldovans, but said they would come back after the war and look.

When the news came of the death of Nyuma - I made a vow that I will never come to the old house in Kaushany.
Rosa Kogan, 2010, Afula - Tzur Shalom

Rosa kept her oath. She never came back to Kaushany. Her two brothers were killed in the war. Numa (Nachman, Nema) died August 28, 1943, and buried in a mass grave in the village of Dolginka, Izyumsky district, Cherkasy region, Ukraine. Boris (Baruch, Berl) disappeared in the early days of the war (YdV).
Yefim Kogan, March 2013

Sima Barash. About my family, *February 2023*

The Barash family is not from Kaushany, my husband Iosif Barash is from Bessarabka. I got married in 1977, and since then we have lived together in Kaushany. My maiden name is Kuchuk, my father Isaak Kuchuk is also from Bessarabka, but after marrying my mother Tatiana Geisman, in 1957 he moved to Kaushany, held leadership positions in the city, many old-timers remember him. My father worked in trade, started in a store, as they said in a department store, studied at the Polytechnic Institute in Kishinev, then received his second education in Moscow, during this time he worked in the district consumer union, then the chairman of the general store in the village Khadzhimuse, Kaushany district, and before his death (he died young at 42 in 1975) he was the chairman of the procurement office.

In 1991 we moved to Israel. Dad is buried at the Jewish cemetery in Bendery, like all my relatives and my husband's relatives.

Alexander Zeltser. Stories, *February 2023*

I remember one story that my grandma Sarah Lerner (née Archimovici) told me about her younger, beloved sister, my grandaunt Chava Archimovici (Хэйва Архимович). I clearly remember that as a little kid, I was very proud of my grandaunt, although I noticed only sadness in my grandma's voice when she was telling me this story.

Great grandfather
Psakhi (Peisakh) Arkhimovich,
father of Sarah and Chava

Grandfather
Shmil Zeltser

In 1918, after Bessarabia became part of the Kingdom of Romania, Chava joined underground movement, popular among some of the young generation Kaushany Jews, fighting for reunification of Bessarabia with the Soviet Union. Incidentally Folic Zeltser (Фолик Зельцер), younger brother of my grandfather Shmil Zeltser (Шмиль Зельцер), was one of them too. Eventually Chava was arrested by Siguranța (Romanian secret police), tried, and sentenced to Doftana prison. There she participated in a hunger strike together with other political prisoners, and as a result developed tuberculosis. Eventually she was released about a year prior to the annexation of Bessarabia by the Soviets. Because of Chava's pro Soviet activities in Romania, my grandmother's family was spared from prison, or exile to Siberia, which was the fate of most rich or even middle-class Jewish families from Kaushany. Still Soviets expropriated her brother-in-law (my grandfather Abram Lerner) business and bakery, but Chava was offered an opportunity to go to Ackerman (now Belgorod-Dnestrovsky) to study in teachers' training college and become a young Communist League leader there, which she gladly took. When Nazi Germany invaded Soviet Union and Red Army was retreating, Chava had a chance to evacuate, but decided to stay to fight Nazi occupation in underground resistance and she perished.

I talked to my 3rd cousin Senya Levit from Seattle with whom we share the same great grandfather Leib Zeltser from Kaushany. His grandfather Raful and my grandfather Shmil were brothers. As far as we know Leib owned hardware store, they sold small metal parts such as nails, screws, doorknobs, locks, door handles, horseshoes, buckets, kettles.

Raisa Rozenkrants. My Căușeni[111], *2022*

Already living here in United States, my husband and I went to Los Angeles to visit the parents of our coworker. Next day in the afternoon they decided to show us Russian "West Hollywood - Plummer's Park", where the retired "Russian Jews" played dominoes, chess and "solved" world problems. We were introduced. Having learned that I am from Căușeni, one of them began to look for common acquaintance. At the end he said *"The Căușeni Jews were the most decent people."* Although it was not quite true, it was nice and very pleasant.

So, once upon a time… No, such a beginning is good for a fairy tale. My story is a story of the beginning of my life in a former Jewish shtetl Căușeni. But for me, Căușeni is not just a "Jewish shtetl / own at the administrative center of Căușeni District, Moldova…" (Wikipedia).

My Căușeni is my father, Yaakov Goldstein, my Grandmother Beila Goldstein (dad's mother), my dearest mother Vitya / Victoria Goldstein-Letichever, my dear sister Donka Goldstein, and me, Raya / Raisa / Rukhaly (it is how my dad called me so affectionately-jokingly).

Vitya/Victoria Goldstein-Letichever

Yaakov Goldstein

1937, Kaushany or Bucharest

My Căușeni is all my beloved relatives Letichevers, Liners, and Friedmans. And I know that all of them were very decent people.

---

[111] **Căușeni** is a current name of Kaushany

I was born in the 1947 famine year in **New** Căuşeni. There were also **Old** Căuşeni with an old Windmill. For me, the word "**New**" meant a lot because in my child fantasies it was on the cusp of being a city, especially when our street with an ordinary country road, muddy in the winter and dusty in the summer, got the name - Pushkin Street.

My Căuşeni are my favorite people, that's where I played outside on the dusty street with my beloved cousin Milya. It is the town where I went to school…

My Căuşeni it's my extraordinary grandfather Berl/Berka Moyshevich Letichever, also known as "mosh Potap" for his remarkable strength in his youth. My Grandfather, madly loving his wife and children and especially grandchildren. My sister and I were not called by our last names, but "Dona, Raya lui mosh Berku, Zhidan" (Raya and Dona, the Jew-Berka's grandchildren). The word "Zhidan" among Moldovans had a totally different connotation than the Russian word "Zhid". Of course, also a label, but not mean-spirited. My Grandfather, who spoke Yiddish with the Kazakhs during the war evacuation, because they did not speak Russian also.

My grandfather, who sitting on a bench near the Club House, explained to the Moldovans that they would not find such a country where a loaf of bread costs 16 cents, and a bottle of kefir costs 13 cents. But at home, when I was sick, he sang to me the song "Dus reydaly otsakh ubergedrate (the wheel turned back).

My grandfather, who decided to walk from Căuşeni to Chisinau with a sack of flour to save my father's sisters from hunger.

My grandfather who jokingly said about his sons-in-law: "One loves guests and books, other loves newspapers, and the third one is a handyman in his own house."

Grandparents

Berl/Berka Moyshevich Letichever
Ena Abovna Letichever (Schwartz)

1952

My Căuşeni is my grandmother Ena Abovna Letichever (Schwartz). Wise and well-read she, read well in Russian and read a lot. Grandma was stern, reserved woman but very, very kind. At her young age she was left as an orphan with her younger brother Mehl / Marvin in her hands. Grandma Ena with help of my grandpa Berl raised him to 17, when he left for America to study. Only in 1968 did they find each other. Unfortunately, only through mail. Both of them named their daughters after their mother Vitya.

In 1972 my grandma Ena lived through her daughter, my mom Vitya' s death. At that time, she told me: "There is nothing worse than when parents bury their children". I was not sure if I could ever be as resilient and strong as she was. Maybe that is why the grandchildren called our grandfather with by the less formal Russian pronoun ТЫ "ty", and our grandmother with the formal ВЫ "vy".

On Jewish holidays, because there was no longer a single synagogue in Căuşeni, the entire service was held in my grandparent's house. Grandfather read and sang for the men and grandmother read for the women. My grandfather's cantor voice sent shivers down my spine.

My Căuşeni is my grandmother Beila, my father's mother, a quiet and sad grandmother who lost two children in one week, lost her husband in the evacuation, and witnessed the arrests and imprisonment of other children. She loved it when I read to her, and she told me Bible stories in Russian-Yiddish. On Saturdays, putting on a beautiful shawl, she went to visit madame Letichever, along with madame Kachkis and madame Perelman.

My dad started working at the age of 14 for a business owner as a bookkeeper. At the age of 17 he was actively involved in underground activities. After the war, he worked as a chief accountant. Both of my mother's sisters also worked as accountants: Aunt Manya and Aunt Tsilya, who I also know to be very "decent people". My dad also had a passion for books, that he shared with his children and those around him, often sharing his own books, which returned home in a terrible condition and sometimes did not return at all.

My dad tried to convince us that the cause of his youth, the struggle for happiness and justice for all, was a just cause. And at the same time, he was the one who got us the forbidden book "The Gulag Archipelago[112]." He loved the guests and talking to people. Helping people is the common feature of each of our families. When Grandfather Berl came to our house and said: "Yankl, midaf khelfn ..." (Yankel, we have to help ...)

The early death of my mother, her reburial from Căuşeni to Bendery, because the Căuşeni government decided there was no need for a Jewish cemetery in Căuşeni, it was the collapse of everything around my father. It did not contribute to his mood or health. With great difficulty we pulled him out of Căuşeni but by that time none of his friends and comrades were left there. His last couple years of life were sad.

My Mom was a teacher in a Moldovan school. At first, she taught mathematics and studied at the Teachers' Institute. My birth interrupted both - her studies and teaching math. Mom started working in elementary school. She was completely devoted to her work. By herself she sewed for 40 students in her class a folder for letters and numbers, drew visual aids. She read a lot of methodological literature, corresponded with her childhood friend Tyusha /Etel Samuilovna Natanson (1920, Căuşeni — 1998, Kiryat Nordau, Israel), who was already a professor at the Tiraspol Pedagogical Institute. Even my mama's coworker Asya Geisman wanted to send her Russian-speaking daughter to my mom's class. She also sewed clothes for our entire family - Goldstein, Letichever, Liner, and Friedman. Sometimes for her friends too. She gave Donka the start in the work of a math teacher and set me up for mathematical career as well, although I avoided teaching at school. Mom's unaccepted death at 51 was a big blow for all of us...

My Căuşeni is wonderful weekends, when guests came to us for tea, or we went to someone's house. The songs of Yasha Chulak, my father's stories about underground friends, the stories of Uncle Dima Snitsarenko about Odessa in the times of "Mishka-Japonchik"- nothing passed by children's ears. By the way, it was Uncle Dima who knocked on our window at night, after party members meeting only, to tell us about ... "the shitty congress of our Glorious Communist Party and that it turned that Stalin was not a father of all people but ...." (Galich). But on the day of Stalin's death, I could not understand why Donka was crying so bitterly and why our dad told her to stop.

---

[112] "The Gulag Archipelago" book by Aleksandr Solzhenitsyn

The years flew by. New doctors, teachers, other specialists began to come to Căuşeni to work, having received recommendations from Chisinau to contact either Letichever, or Goldstein, or Perelman if help was needed. Many of them later became family friends.

My Căuşeni are the Liner and Friedman families, which are very dear to me: Aunt Manya, Uncle Zema and their son Milya, who spent most of the summer in our house, who was a participant in all my games and pranks and unfortunately died very early (42). Aunt Manya's life was not an easy burden. When her mother, my grandmother, fell seriously ill, Manechka (12 years old) was left to cook, wash, and clean. For my mother, the main thing was to study, Tsilechka was the youngest, and Manechka became everything, and so it was all her life. After the death of my mother, she was my mother at my wedding, she raised Milya's children and helped his widow Yulia a lot, took care of Berl and Ena and from her house she saw them off on their last journey. And at the same time, she worked very hard.

My Căuşeni are Friedmans. Aunt Tsilya, Uncle Grisha and their daughter Zhenechka. Uncle Grisha is a very interesting person. He was born in the town of Chechelnik in Ukraine, and then left with his parents as volunteers in Dzhonkoy, Crimea, to develop Soviet Jewish agriculture. He started his studies as a livestock specialist. In 1939 was taken to the Finnish war. Then the whole war of 1941-1945, then the war in Japan and the "glorious" end - political camps in Siberia. It was fate that the country needed people who knew agriculture. Grisha was released. Graduated as livestock engineer and was sent to... Căuşeni. Tsilechka got reliable support and protection for all her life. He treated us, children strictly, but with love.

Donka, my dear sister is not only **My Căuşeni**, but also all her life. She was 10 years older than me. A little sad, very modest, but she was always surrounded by her friends. She did not participate in our uncomplicated games. She played in the "Timur team", very famous at those times book "Timur and his friends" by Gaidar. She read a lot. She introduced me to a little known then and very famous later Bulat Okudzhava. Quite recently she passed away, and I, sorting through her letters and photographs, again plunged into that difficult, but happy time.

In the early years of my life, our closest neighbors, across the corridor, were the Khaikin family - grandmother Ruhl, Aneta, her husband Idel and their daughter Nadia, later Mira was born. I don't remember our games with Nadia, as they left for Bendery year on, but I remember, maybe from the stories, that grandmother Ruhl shouted to Nadya to eat, otherwise she would push everything into her, like into a goose's neck.

My Căuşeni is a large field near my grandparents' house, overgrown with weeds and chamomile, where Polina and Yasha Kogan, Milya, Zhenechka and I played our simple, childhood games. Căuşeni is where a terrible explosion of a kerosene cellar took place and Rybak died. His two little girls Liza and Raya were left without a dad. Căuşeni is the old photographer Sharkansky, over whom we children, I don't know why, laughed, and then received a scolding from the adults. Căuşeni is the Perelman family with many relatives in Bendery, Chernivtsi, Tashkent and Chisinau. I was set as an example to their son Misha of how to pronounce "R". This is the Kachkis family, where Mara's and Yasha's daughter Sofa Krasnova spent her summer vacation, Căuşeni is Trager family. Căuşeni is the Shvartsman family, the first in Causeni to purchase a TV. Căuşeni is Gitlin's Samuel (Shmelka) family. Shmelka Gitlin, was the director of the Moldavian school and their children Alla (Hanna), Ira (Ita) and Peter(Peisy) were our friends.

Also, Căuşeni was the first, mostly harmless, lessons about my Jewishness. My neighbor girls, my playmates, said that there are such people, "giddy", who cannot eat candy. Having found out at home who these, "giddy" were, I really wanted to be / become Russian. Thanks to my parents, this dream did not come true, and they calmed me: "After all, even the founder of Marxism was ...". Later I realized that this was not the most painful lesson and not the most successful parental example.

Then I graduated from school and moved to Chisinau and was happy with a very beloved man, wonderful children, our pride, our grandchildren who are our happiness and pride, and…loss and loss.

My Căușeni, both New and Old, have disappeared. But there are so many memories.

My Căușeni is my childhood. Childhood has passed, **My Căușeni** has passed.

Ronni Otake. Wise / Wasserman family, *2008, 2023*

I must start with the Wise name. It was the family's name in Bessarabia, lived in Kaushany. The spelling may have changed, but the name and meaning did not. I am aware that the descendants of the oldest half-brother insist the name was Wasserman. Nobody in my records ever used that name. I have found my handwritten family history forms that I gathered around 1976-1978. They called the oldest brother Joseph, and they used the name Wise. To my mom, he was Uncle Joe. She called him that. She had never heard of Wasserman.

Joseph was the first one to come to America. His father was the same as all the Wise children. His father remarried in Bessarabia to Feige Hinda, after his first wife died. The youngest Wise son was David.

My grandmother's name was Feige Hinda Wise. She was born in 1891. Her mother was named Sureh Rivka Toben. She is our known matriarch. By the time Feige was born her father was called Abraham Wise, but he was originally Abraham Wasserman. He changed his surname from Wasserman to Wise about the time of his second marriage (to Sureh Rivka). We have scant information about Abraham. Sureh and Abraham never came to the United States, but eventually all of their children did. Feige said that her country was under Russian control at the time she was born, but there were many Romanian influences, as well.

Sureh Rivke Tobin Wise with three children

Girl on the right is Feige Hinda, next boy is David, Sureh Rivke and last one <unknown>,   Kaushany, c1907

Sureh was considered very bright. Friends and family called her "Rebbitzen", although her husband was not a Rabbi. They called her that because she was wise and learned quickly. She was frequently sought out for her advice. People used to say about my grandmother, "Her name is Wise, and she is wise".

The family owned a dairy – confectioners' shop. Some items sold there were milk, cheese, ice cream, baked goods and candies. The family had good teeth from all the calcium in the dairy products!

Sureh Rivka's father had a talent for carving wood. I own four of his carvings, see below, that have interesting designs on them. They've been handed down from daughter to daughter since the time Sureh's father, my great-great-grandfather, made them. I was told that the blocks of wood were used to press patterns in cookie dough. Perhaps they were. There is even a little bit of dough in one of the grooves. However, my research has shown me that such carved-wood blocks were more often used to imprint designs into butter. I think that is likely, considering that butter would have been sold in the dairy shop. At some point, Sureh Rivka fell down and broke her hip. It was an injury from which she never recovered. In modern times perhaps she could have been restored to health. One family member has estimated her time of death to be about 1909. She was not an old woman. No one in the family has ever seen her or Abraham's graves.

Carved-wood block

Dora Itskovich (Rybak). Farmers in Kaushany, *2023*

My husband Mekhl was 7 years when the Great Patriotic War [113] started. The whole family were farmers lived in Kaushany. They got a piece of land from someone who lived in France and paid for it.

It was one of the first days of the war. Mekhl with his brothers Moyshe and Shoil used a horse to plow the field. German plane appeared and horse got spooked and started to run which saved their lives because the bomb landed on the spot where they were just a moment before.

---

[113] Great Patriotic War – Великая Отечественная Война – 22 June 1941 – 8 May 1945 war between USSR and Germany and their allies.

Dina Vainman. Ershl Gershko Spivak 1870 – 1941, *2023*

Ershl was a Jewish refugee in Uzbekistan, Tashkent together with Priva, Elka, Dvoira, Mania, Beila and her daughter Stunya (Tunya Katz), Abrum's wife with a tiny baby Efim. During this time first Ershl passed away and after a while Dvoira also died. There was hunger and disease.

Grandma Beyla talked about the escape from Kaushany, she said that they reached relatives in Odessa and offered them to join them in the escape, but they refused, they were a wealthy family, and they said that they would get along with the Germans as they used to get along with the Romanians. After that they heard from people that this whole family was murdered by the Germans. I don't even know who they were.

All of them managed to get on the last ship that left the port of Odessa, thanks to the fact that Priva's husband that was fighting at the front, they got permission to board the ship that was full of war-wounded soldiers, after the ship left the port, began a heavy shelling of the port everyone was afraid, they turned off the lights on the ship so they wouldn't be noticed, there was a big panic, the baby Efim started crying loudly, the people on the ship were afraid they would see the ship and demanded Efim's mother to strangle the baby, they were afraid the Germans would hear the baby. She embraced him hard to her chest so he wouldn't be heard, and he was saved.

Mila Teper. Stories that I heard and recorded, *February 2024*

My mother, Ida (Ita) Garshtein, was born 12/5/1928, and her sister, Sarah (Sonya) Garshtein, born on 10/8/1931 in Kaushany. Their father, Mendl Garshtein (1908), fell in love from first sight with their mother Etl. She was beautiful but poor. Her mother was almost blind. There was no hope for a dowry. However, the family gathered some money (50 lei. Not sure if there is supposed to be more money in dowry), and the young couple eloped to Yassi to marry. Mendel wanted to marry Etl despite her financial circumstances. In Yassi they decided to spend the dowry money and have some fun, since the sum was so unsubstantial and wouldn't make much difference to their future.

Etl Garshtein (Vaysman), 1930s

Mendel was an entrepreneur. He had a small furniture store, but it was later destroyed when the Russians came. (I think I remember from my aunt that he had other businesses but didn't have much luck with them either). At the same time, Etl appeared to be not only beautiful, but also bright and hardworking. She was a skillful seamstress, did such a great job that had 5 other women working for her. Eventually the young couple had children. My mother and her sister not only looked different from each other but had different personalities. Hence, favored by different family clans. My mother was a good student, the education came easy to her, and everyone predicted that she'd become a doctor. She was a favorite of the Garshtein clan, especially of her father's sister, Freida. My aunt, however, was a favorite of the Koens family who lived in the same street. Koen's said: "we all lived in one large courtyard, and Sara was "ours".

When the war began my mother with her sister and her parents, and their grandparents (Elka and Khaikel Garshtein) evacuated. On the way they straight from the village caravan, got lost and ended up at the Астраханская область, озеро Баскунчак, not too far from Stalingrad, front lines. The situation was extremely bad for them. They starved, got sick. Mendel was sent to dig trenches, and one day he didn't come back. They exchanged whatever possessions they had for the little food that was available. My aunt Sonya said: "There were only rats and herring". The situation was dire, and adults one by one died from hunger and decease. Miraculously the girls were found and survived their horrible ordeal. Now, their fate was supposed to be decided by a commission that assigned children to the orphanages. The problem was that this commission was going to send them to different orphanages. My aunt: «We cried a lot and one woman in this commission felt sorry for us and allowed us to be together".

We were sent to a vocational school. Ida worked at the machine-tool. She had to stay on a box because she was small. She was given rations for her and me. We worked during the day and studied in the evening. We stayed at the school *(probably in the dormitory. Mila T.)*.

When the war ended, the family that survived and returned to Kishinev started looking for those that didn't come back. Especially instrumental in the search were Freida Garshtein («She moved heaven and earth»), Betya (Брана) Koen, and Betya's mother, Riva Koen. Fortunately, the girls were registered with the Red Cross in the lists of people displaced during the war, and after many letters written on their behalf, were found. When the family started filling out the required forms for their return, the plant, where Ida and Sara worked, wouldn't let them go. They were very decent girls, they worked well and studied well. Sonya was tall, very beautiful, with black hair, and Ida was a small, thin blonde. She was the secretary of the Komsomol organization. When the boss received a request for their return, he put the documents in the table and did not tell anyone.

Betya (Коен) had a friend, a war veteran, who was an invalid without a leg. He was, according to my aunt Sonya, The Hero of the Soviet Union. This could have added some weight to his plight. The relatives in Kishinev collected money and commissioned him to go to Moscow to help facilitate their return to Moldavia. The mission was successful, and Ida and Sonya reunited with the family. Upon arrival they lived with different families: Sonya with the Koens and Ida with the Garshteins. (The preferences didn't change ☺). On a serious note, when the families came back after the war, they hardly had enough resources for themselves; multiple people lived under the same roof in tiny apartments. During my childhood I've visited many places of our relatives that were in shabby small houses with yards with a lot of neighbors. Some of them lived in basements. These dwellings had a distinctive smell that I still remember very well. Nevertheless, the relatives taken in the girls, supported them like their own children, and didn't let them work at the factories or plants. Helped them to get a profession of bookkeepers. At this point their life becomes happier. My mother started working first, received a room at a dorm house and took her sister with her. They met other Jewish young people, made friends, eventually met their future husbands and post-war adult life began.

Nona Shpolyanskaya (Geisman). Grandmother and mother baked for Purim, *2021*

This is what my grandmother and mother baked for Purim in Bessarabia and Moldova: strudel, fludn and umantashen. And my grandmother also baked a large festive kolach in a real oven from a rich dough - and koylech and leykikh (sponge cake) for Purim. They baked different leykikh: *a onyk* leykikh (honey cake), *a nys* leykikh (with orchids), and *gishpritsl* leykikh (with cocoa stains). From all this they made a meshloakh manot (gift wreath) in a beautiful package, added candies and tangerines and children in costumes delivered them to relatives and friends. They exchanged and rejoiced. I also delivered when I was a child, and for this I received gifts and money. And it was called *Sholhamunys*. My mother does all this every year in Moldova and Israel and even sends it to my sister in Germany. And this year we have another lockdown for Purim. And I, and Sima (my cousin from Migdal-ha-Emik), and my sister Laura (from Germany) - we all made and exchanged *sholhamunys* via WhatsApp according to Grandma Esther Spivak's recipe.

This is how the traditions of the Kaushon shteitel of the Tighina (Bendery) district of the Bessarabian province (Moldavian SSR - Moldova) continue.

Nona Shpolyanskaya (Geisman) and her parents Usher[114] and Asya[115]. From generation to generation.

I have always been interested in my roots. I think that everything good, bright, and decent in me is due to my parents and the atmosphere that reigned in our family and our home in childhood. In 1972 we moved from my grandfather's house to our own. In our house and courtyard until 1972 lived my grandfather Ikhil with Grandmother Esther, and their daughter Stunya with her family, and son Usher with his family - my father. In the house (yard) there were three entrances to three apartments. We lived amicably and happily. Today people do not live like that anymore. But it was this atmosphere and cohesion that brought up many good qualities in me, with which I go through life, to which I try to orient my children and grandchildren.

Ikhil and Ester Geisman
with granddaughter Nona

Kaushany, 1960

---

[114] Usher Geisman (1927 – 2017)
[115] Asya Geisman (Imas) (1932 - 2023)

At the same time, we must pay tribute to the atmosphere of the small town of Kaushany, a former Jewish shtetl of Bessarabia/Moldova. I lived my childhood and youth in this town and do not regret it in any way. I am glad that I managed to ask my parents to tell me and write down what they remember from the life of this shtetl. These sketches below from dad's words (Usher) were made by mom (Asya), adding her comments.

Usher and Asya Geisman

Kaushany, 1954

Our shtetl reflected the Jewish soul as if in a mirror. All the residents had Jewish names: Esther (my mother), Dvoira, Elka, Priva, Menya, Beyla - these were the names of my mother's sisters. They were not Russified by the evacuation; they lived with these names until the end of their days. My sister's name was Stunya - May her memory be for a blessing. Her children also had Jewish names, but already translated into Russian: Shlima - Sima, Ershl - Grigory. Now they are in Israel and are not ashamed of their Jewish names.

Many Kaushaner Jews had nicknames typical of the Yiddish language. These nicknames were sometimes ironic or humorous. They largely reflected the occupation of this or that Jew. Instead of Ershl Spivak, my grandfather was called Ershl - a carpenter, and another grandfather was nicknamed Duzhik instead of Duvyd. Among our shtetl Jews there were talented people. And if a person is talented, he is talented in everything. After the war, many Jews from our shtetl found employment in Kishinev, Bendery, Chernovtsi. A small percentage returned to Kaushany.

In 2001, I visited Kaushany again. There is no Jewish community, only a few Jewish families live in the town. The majority of Kaushaners live in Israel. A few families returned to Kaushany after the war, unable to forget the places where they were born. These were our family, my father Ikhil Geisman, me – Usher Geisman, the Bargolovsky, Letichever, Lainer, Kachkis, Tsinkler, Gitlin, Malamud, Goldstein families. Samuil Gitlin was the director of the Moldavian Secondary School for many years, now he lives in the USA with his children. Many people have left for different places since the perestroika times.

Old-timers of these place will unmistakably point out where Jewish houses stood. Such living witnesses were Mokrina Varfolomey and Alexandra Dyakon. They grew up among Jews, worked for Jews and ate Jewish bread. The more time passes, the weaker the emotions. Every year it is more and more difficult to find in the appearance of the streets and neighborhoods anything related to their past Jewish life. After the war (WWII) a new Jewish - Soviet intelligentsia appeared in Kaushany: doctors Sevriver Sarra, Perelman Ester, Barg Bronya, Faerman G., teachers Sevriver Semen, Imas A.,

Krakhmalnik Anna - these were specialists sent after they graduated universities[116]. There were also Jewish specialists in other fields.

Even before the war, the Jews of Kaushany were interested in the question of the need to restore the state and political essence of the Jewish people - a nation with its own national center and language. I believe that those of us, the Kaushany shtetl Jews, who now live in Israel are fulfilling a great mission. We are here in the Promised Land and also for those Kaushany Jews who were unable to realize their ideals of L'Shana Habaa biYerushalaim[117].

Personally, I will never forget my shtetl. Even in my dreams, I walk along its streets, old and newly built.

There are no historical monuments in Kaushany that testify to the fact that Kaushany was a Jewish shtetl in the past.[118]

Aleksander Kogan. Here is what I remember.

I don't have much information about Kaushany. Here's what I know.

My great grandfather Isruel (Srul) Ochakovskiy, his wife Mamtse and children lived in Kaushany. I know four of their children: Zalman, Reuven (my grandfather), Ezra and Dintse (she was not married).[119] Families of Zalman, Reuven and Ezra lived all in Kaushany. Mendel Ochakovskiy[120], son of Ezra said that his family lived on the outskirts of Kaushany near two story mill, owned by Natanzon. Mendel remembered that his grandfather Isruel had a large white beard. Isruel was like a Rabbi, many people came to him asking questions.

Zalman, Reuven and Ezra were businessmen, they bought and sold grain. Mendel said that people came to them to buy grain even from other countries, like France.

My mother Mara ל"ז also told that when Shurka was born, before the circumcision, the children were gathered to read "Kriyat Shma" (Krishme Leinen) and she was assigned to hand out candy to the children. She also remembered that her older brother Irikhem participated in an underground circle in which they studied books on socialism/ communism. Mother was sent for a walk on the street near the house to warn if the gendarmes showed up.

I also know about the mikvahs that were in Kaushany. They are written about in the responses of Rabbi Irikhem.[121] About one mikvah he answers his son Shabse[122] that this mikvah is not kosher and the rabbi who permitted it cannot be a rabbi. Rabbi Irikhem permitted the second mikvah. He received many letters with objections. He answered them all and explained why the mikvah is kosher. The

---

[116] After graduation from Universities, Institutes in the USSR, people usually get send for a job, and for three years they could not leave that job.

[117] "Next Year in Jerusalem" ("לְשָׁנָה הַבָּאָה בִּירוּשָׁלָיִם") – last words at the seder in Passover Hagadah.

[118] I hope in a couple of years we will inaugurate a monument to Jews who lived and died in Kaushany (Yefim K.)

[119] There is one more daughter Tauba, born 8-Aug-1897

[120] Mikhail Mendel (1930, Kaushany – Sep-2022, Israel)

[121] Rabbi Irikhem was grandfather of my grandmother Leya. Irikhem (1842 – March 13 (or February 12), 1908, Dubossary).

[122] Shabsa (Shabse) (10-Sep-1856 - 1940, Kaushany)

correspondence is very interesting. More about Rabbi Irikhem and Shabse read above at section: Religious life, synagogues, rabbonim.

When the Great Patriotic War started and Jews began to evacuate, Ezra, Mendel's father went to the town's official and got a cart with a horse and they quickly moved away. My grandfather Reuven, grandmother Leyka gathered all her jewelry, and evacuated with my mother Mara 12 years old, her younger brother Shurka 4 years old. They just crossed the bridge over Dniester near Bendery and after that soon the bridge was bombed. So, Ochakovskiy families survived and went to Kazakhstan.

Grandfather Reuven and his older son Irikhem were mobilized, but soon they were released as unreliable, because they lived under Romanian rule[123]. They also joined the evacuees. In Kazakhstan family of my grandfather lived in village Samarka with the local family who gave them a place on the hay behind the stove. This was their home during the evacuation. They worked hard on farm work.

Mendel lost his parents in Kazakhstan. His mother died in the hospital, and he doesn't even know where she was buried. Mendel's father Ezra froze to death in the snow when he went to take some flatbread to his son, who had been mobilized. Mendel says that they had a hard time finding his frozen father, but there was nothing they could do. He couldn't bury his father right away because the ground was so frozen that it was impossible to dig a grave. So, they kept his body in the house for 8 days until it warmed up a bit.

When the Germans entered Kaushany, they immediately killed my great-grandmother Momtse and her daughter Dintsa, who did not evacuate. Mendel says that the Germans killed them, and my mother ז"ל said that the Romanians who entered with the Germans killed them. Momtse and Dintsa did not want to evacuate, they said: "We have good neighbors, where should we run?" Their neighbor, a blacksmith, showed the Romanians/Germans: "Jews live here."[124] They were killed in their own yard and buried there. Mendel says that when they returned to Kaushany, they reburied Momtse and Dintsa in the cemetery. There is information about them in Yad Vashem, Ida Lerer wrote this information down. It says that she is Dintsa's niece and that Israel's grandfather had 5 children. As I wrote above, I only know of 4. Ida Lerer[125] or her descendants have not yet been found.

Izya Spivak[126]. Jewish Township Kaushany, *2003-2006, Seattle, WA*

translated by David Kogan, 2021

Introduction

Being in America, several thousand kilometers away from the described locations, separated by an ocean, and most importantly - more than sixty long years of time - I will attempt to describe the life and daily routine of the township of Kaushany, in Romania, when I was born.[127] In 1940, Russia took these lands for itself, a year later, Germany-Romania occupied Bessarabia, and in 1944, the Russian army took the territory back. After the war, these lands were included in the Moldovan republic and part of the USSR. And, finally, at the start of the 90s, these lands became part of the independent Republic of Moldova.

I am Spivak Isaac Lvovich - called at home by my Jewish name Izya, would like to recall and describe the events that happened to me and my family.

---

[123] People from Bessarabia, including Jews were not conscripted to the Soviet Army until 1943.
[124] There is evidence that neighbors in Kaushany killed many Jews.
[125] Ida Lerer likely a daughter of Tauba.
[126] Izya Spivak is my uncle, brother of my mother Khinka Kogan (Spivak), Yefim Kogan
[127] Izya Spivak was born in on May 9th, 1928, in Galatz, Romania

Kaushany and Residents

The township of Kaushany was located 28 km from the town of Bendery (Tighina in Romanian) Many roads passed through it. The first went to Bendery, the second in the direction of Volontirovka, and later to Reni-Galatz, the third to Chimishliya-Kishinev, the fourth to Talmaz and Chadyr-Lunga. So, it was a four-way intersection in every direction Bessarabia-Romania. In the beginning of the 30s of the 20th century, these roads were unpaved, but in my memory, they started paving them with stones, and by 1939, you could say that through Kaushany passed the first high-speed roads, some of them even paved with asphalt, with a small sidewalk on the side and drainage for water during rainy days. The weather, and especially, the state of the roads, influenced life in the city, and us, the kids. We boys knew that in rainy weather, you can't make it to school without boots or galoshes. In general, galoshes were considered the traditional footwear of Jews in Kaushany at that time.

It's difficult to name the exact number of residents of the township. As I recalled, the Jewish population consisted of several hundred families, and if you include kids, I will guess the number of Jews came to a thousand[128]. With us also lived Moldovans, Romanians, Gypsies, and the Gagauz. I can say that in my memory, there wasn't much conflict between the different nationalities, likewise I don't recall antisemitic sentiment from the direction of the governing representatives. Those conflicts that arose at the bazaar between Jews and Moldovans during trade, could not be taken seriously. Sometimes you would hear "Hey, kike[129], you want everything for free?" - but you would take it as a term of endearment toward the Jew. I will talk in more detail about our bazaars below.

Layout

Along the roads, already mentioned above, were lots of houses and apartments. The buildings were single-story, and many were built with the intention to have apartments for adult kids. In that way, a given lot would belong to a family.

Here, for instance, is what the courtyard where I lived looked like. At the front was the house of my grandfather. It consisted of three rooms, a corridor and a kitchen. Near the house grew four beautiful trees, and next to them was a bench, on which we liked to sit with friends. On the house's windows were wooden shutters, which would be closed and locked overnight using hooks. Into the yard, there was a large gate, and a smaller one for pedestrian entry. Our house stood on a hill. We had two rooms, a corridor, and a kitchen. In addition to us, the yard also housed my father's brother - Iasha Spivak, in an apartment analogous to ours, and there also was one more apartment, which we rented out. On one side of the yard, there was a small shed, where we kept firewood and corn husks for heating the apartments in the winter. I will note that until the end of 1939, there was no electricity in Kaushany, and we used kerosene lamps for light, and primus stoves for cooking, though we also had regular stoves[130].

In every Jewish yard, there was a cellar for the storage of vegetables, fruits, and barrels with high quality Moldovan wine. My grandfather preferred the wine "Aligote". Grandfather traded in grains, so our yard also had a barn, where grains were dried prior to being shipped to buyers. We weren't rich. Well-off Jews would always have horses. When Buka Kogan rode around the township, everyone admired his beautiful gray horses, no one could look away from them.

School and Languages

At the time which I am describing, I was 10-12 years old and went to school. We had two schools, and one high school[131], though it closed at the end of 1939. Lessons in the school were taught

---

[128] Number of Jews before the war started, was more than 2,000
[129] In Bessarabia, in Russian it was жид (zhid)
[130] By that, uncle Izya meant an old iron cook wood and coal stove
[131] That was called Gymnasium

only in Romanian. We were taught handwriting, arithmetic, drawing, labor, where I remember we made little stools, we made different things with our hands. During pleasant weather, the teacher would take the class outside and would tell us about the surroundings and plants. Classes usually lasted 45 minutes, and during breaks, we would run outside and play games. Boys and girls studied in the school together.

At home, our spoken language was Yiddish. In addition to school, for a while I went to cheder-Jewish school, where we were taught Hebrew, both reading and writing, and I remember they forced us to repeat the same words over and over many times. There, we also learned about Jewish history. To my regret, I have completely forgotten how to read and write Yiddish, though I understand it, and can still speak it. My daughter does not even understand Yiddish, but my son in Israel, of course, speaks Hebrew.

Merchants

In Kaushany, there were a variety of different stores: textile, groceries, butchers, shoe stores, clothing stores, and so on. Later, I will describe the work of one textile store, where my father worked. There were also all kinds of workshops: cobblers, hatters, tailors, locksmiths, tin workers, carpenters, blacksmiths. There was also in the township a post office, a club, a sports hall, pharmacies, a hospital, a railroad station, and bakers, bars, cafeterias, and photographers. It's quite pleasant to recall all of them. We boys knew all the sellers by name. We often bought various things, and especially enjoyed candy, and we could see how pleased the sellers were to sell their goods.

We had plenty of free time, and I often went with other boys to swim in the river Botna. Late in the fall and winter, the river was almost invisible, but in the spring, after the snowmelt, it spread out, and sometimes even flooded the houses next to it. The water was very dirty, but who noticed such things? We bathed, learned to swim, tanned, and only once, very tired and dirty, returned home to eat and do our homework. Our teachers gave us homework every day, checked it thoroughly, and punished those who didn't complete it.

I will write a bit about a textile store. There were, for some reason, a lot of them. Evidently, Jews didn't buy fully made suits and dresses, but rather sewed them themselves out of fabrics which were available to any taste.

The store was called "Collaboration KOK", where KOK were the initials of the three owners: Kogan, Opachevskiy, Kerzman. The store was sizeable - there were two large doors at the entrance. Around the outside were racks with all kinds of fabrics and other related goods. You could buy fabric for a dress, a suit, a raincoat or a winter coat. They sold silk and fur, single and multi-colored fabrics in all possible shades. All the signs were in Romanian. The store employed 8-9 clerks, who were Jews, among them Avrum Blitshtein, Jacob Ochakovskiy, Milya Presman, and others. During the day of the bazaar, the store would be packed with 30-40 customers. My father - Leva Spivak, sat in an elevated position and observed the trade. A clerk would get an order, measure the material, would write out how much and of what was cut, and then father would sum up the cost and accept money. In such a manner, my father, the clerks and the owners worked all day, keeping an eye out to avoid shrinkage, i.e. theft, which occasionally happened. At the end of the workday, they would count the balance, the money would go to the bank, the remnants would be checked, and before the store closed on Fridays, the clerks would get paid, and the store would be sealed. On Saturday, all the stores of the township were closed.

Sabbath

Since I mentioned Friday, I should point out that this was a very joyous day. Jews, working as employees, would get their pay. Also, on Fridays, Jews would go to the barbers. This was a sort of ritual - each would go to their barber, naturally, would wait in line, learn the newest events, and discuss. I remember how loud it was - Jews like to talk, and often all at once. Finally, after getting a haircut and shave, everyone would return home satisfied to welcome the Sabbath.

Friday was also a difficult day in a Jewish family. My grandmother got up very early on this day to bake bread, prepare dinner, clean the house, and only after, washed herself, and waited for grandfather to come home from the synagogue. Grandfather was "Gobe" - Gabbai[132] in the biggest synagogue in Kaushany. He was deeply religious, and as many Jews of the time, had a magnificent beard. Almost all Jews went to the Synagogue on Sabbath. Even those, who did not go regularly, would definitely go on Jewish holidays. There were several synagogues, and many had their own places in a synagogue. In ours, the cantor was Syoma Kleyman. His pleasant and bright voice touched the hearts of the members, especially when he sang Kol Nidrei during Yom Kippur. Occasionally, on high holidays, the synagogue was so full, that we boys would listen to the cantor from the street. I do not remember a single instance of synagogues or cemeteries being defaced during our time living in Kaushany.

Bazaar

Sunday was the bazaar day. During this day, all women would go to buy chickens, meat, vegetables, and fruits. All Jewish workshops would await their clients, to give them finished products - suits and dresses, shoes, wooden and metal crafts, photos, and many others. During the bazaar day, people often had money and weren't against stopping by a tavern at the end of the day to have a glass of good wine.

Shmil Spivak

I want to talk a bit about my uncle Shmil Spivak - a carpenter - and how he worked on bazaar day. In those days, Moldovans, Romanians, and Gypsies would do construction work, and quite frequently would order windows, doors, fences, and floors in carpentry workshops. I would often visit uncle in his workshop and see how he took orders. Often a family would come together to place an order - a husband and wife, sometimes with their older kids. A family would come to him, and he would first ask how they were doing, how life was, etc. He would not rush the conversation, would invite them to have a seat on some stools, and take his time. Only after that would he ask what they wanted to order. Moldovans and Romanians would typically bring some sketches or plans and would discuss them with the carpenter. Having clarified the sizes, my uncle would calculate in his head how much wood he would need to build it and knowing the cost in cubic meters of that wood, would estimate the approximate cost of materials for the clients, as well as the cost of labor. All this happened with no rush, the client consulting with his wife. There would be room for barter, and after the agreement on a price, the client typically paid about 25% of the estimated price before the work started. There were times when simultaneously, my uncle's assistants would be taking orders from other clients, or there would be people paying, and uncle needed to be alerted to make sure no one swindled him, especially when dealing with Gypsies. While I am on topic, I'd like to mention that Shmil Spivak immigrated to Israel in 1972. Being elderly, he continued to do carpentry work for Arabs and Jews in his town of Akko. We met with him in Israel. He proudly showed me his Israel workshop, with all kinds of tools and benches. He worked until his final days and died at the age of 97.

Male Jews worked on Sundays without rest in workshops and stores, and women bartered at the bazaar. The bazaar was enormous. The merchants were mainly Romanians, Moldovans and Gypsies, and the buyers - Jews. Trade was very lively, with a great deal of noise in a variety of languages. It was especially interesting to see how a Jewish woman would pick a fat chicken for a celebratory soup. Along the rows of stalls walked tax collectors, who also saw to it that there were no scandals. In this same crowd, we boys would buy fruits and especially nuts for ourselves, which were necessary for games.

---

[132] Gabbai is someone who assists with the reading of the Torah.

On Sundays, it was also possible to go to a movie theater and watch silent and voiced films. Most films were in foreign languages, but always with subtitles in Romanian. All government services: court, the authorities, the post office, were closed on Sundays. In the township, there was a hospital, where all the doctors were Jews, and the rest of the personnel Moldovans and Jews. Typically, doctors would make house calls, but they also had offices to see patients. I will note that the cost of a doctor and medicine was quite high, and not every poor Jew could afford a visit.

We also had a sizeable sports hall, "Maccabee". There, I recall, we had exercise equipment - gymnastic rings, bars, and a Swedish wall. There were all kinds of sports activities there. The older group of youth 18-20 played in a soccer team under the same name "Maccabee". Nearby, there was a stadium, where the soccer matches were played. There was always a large mass of spectators, and mostly all Jews. We, kids of course watched all the matches for free.

The sports hall also hosted concerts. One, which took place in the summer of 1939, I remember well. To us in Kaushany came one of the most talented singers, Sidi Tal, the wonderful Gene Zlata, and Jacob Golman. Jews dressed up for concerts - this was a holiday for people, and many brought flowers. Sidi Tal sang in Yiddish, Romanian, French, and Russian. After each song, there were multiple ovations. Sidi Tal not only sang, but also read from several works in Yiddish and Romanian. Folks of different ages laughed and took joy in what they heard. The amazing baritone of Jacob Golman was audible in the street outside, where there was usually a crowd of people who did not make it into the concert. Later, in the 50s, I had many occasions to hear Sidi Tal in concert in Chernivtsi in the Ukraine. At the Chernivtsi cemetery, where this amazing artist is buried, she has a statue from white marble, in which she is depicted in full figure in a white dress, and on the stone below are engraved poems in Yiddish and Russian.

Weddings

I will describe how Jewish weddings went. Usually, the entire extended family would gather, from close relatives to the most distant ones. So, for example, there were 15-20 families with the last name Spivak in Kaushany, and all related. A wedding might have 100 to 200 people. Preparations for such a proceeding took two to three weeks. They would bake cakes, baklava, and many other things. Celebrations took place outside in the yards or inside houses. Guests would arrive well-dressed, and musicians would play them in. All guests would come with gifts, carefully wrapped in various colors. The actual ceremony would begin with the Rabbi when the bride and groom would enter under the huppah. The Rabbi would read prayers, and the young pair would walk around. After, the Rabbi would present the parents of the newlyweds.

Politics, fascists, and end of Romanian rule

The political life of the township began whenever we had any kind of elections. Preliminary campaign meetings were very lively. In them participated many Romanian leaders, the school director, representatives of the courts, and sometimes the police. Jews, by and large, voted for the Liberals, but the Democrats also campaigned with them. Some Jews would come to campaign meetings after difficult work, and simply rested, or even slept through them. Toward the end of 1939, the pro-fascist party "Kuza Voda" came to power in Romania. In relations to these events in the country, and, also knowing that the Germans targeted Jews first, there were active discussions on the topic in synagogues. One autumn day in 1939, from the direction of the village Zaim, came a group of horses with thugs wearing brown shirts with swastikas. At first, Jews did not pay attention to them, until the thugs began to smash the windows on Jewish stores. The police, as usual, were nowhere around. There was a lot of ruckuses, and only when all the Jews came out to help, was it possible to chase the thugs away. This provocation was discussed at length, and it was decided to organize a self-defense squad. The next day, the brown shirts showed up again in the township, but as soon as they got to the town center, our squad arrived on horses with whips and gave the fascists a good beating. They ran away in minutes and didn't attempt these kinds of outings again.

The fascist party in Romania was soon replaced, evidently after the Soviet Union declared an ultimatum to Romania. But by the summer of 1940, the situation got complicated again. Military units appeared, and a machine gun post was set up next to the church, with guards around the clock. Many Jews already knew from the radio, that the Romanian army and administration was going to leave Bessarabia, and that the Russians would arrive soon. Romanians left on horses and cars in the direction of Reni-Galatz. Included in the evacuation were institutions, the army, and wealthy Romanians.

So far, my descriptions were of the Romanian period. Next, what happened in Kaushany when the Red Army "liberated" us from the Romanian yoke.

Soviet "Liberation"

After the retreat of the Romanian army and administration, there were a day or two of no government in Kaushany. Young communist-inclined Jewish activists prepared banners and red flags to meet the Red Army. On June 28th, 1940, from the direction of the railroad station and from the road to Bendery appeared the first columns of soldiers. There were vehicles, occupied mainly by infantrymen wearing caps and helmets, with rifles and other equipment. Later came artillery and cavalry columns. The army passed slowly, and we frequently climbed onto the car step rails to give soldiers cold well water and fruits. They in return would give us some coins, of kinds we had never seen before.

After several days, a Village Council (the Village Soviet) was organized in Kaushany, which meant Soviet rule. Over the next days, our Kaushany Jews opened up their big and small stores, and everything got sold out. The conversion rate was established as 1 ruble for 40 lei, which, evidently, was sheer robbery. Army cars would drive up to stores, and buy fabric by the roll, in all colors and types. They had rubles, and our products costed kopeks. After this, our township Jews were all left without work.

One of the first proclamations of the Village Council was that all synagogues were to be closed, and that prayer was categorically outlawed. You can imagine what that meant to religious Jews. My late grandfather began to pray at home, with the doors locked and the windows shuttered. Trade rapidly ceased, and food became scarce. Many began starving. When the government opened the first bread store, the bread was of such quality that you couldn't stomach putting it in your mouth. Almost all Jews began to bake their own bread.

A big problem for us was the Russian language. Our family was lucky - my father spoke Russian fluently and could read and write well. Only thanks to him, over the course of two months, I learned how to read and write in Russian. My late mother also knew Russian, and we tried to speak Russian instead of Yiddish at home. On September 1st, 1940, when school began, I already read and wrote Russian far better than others my age. I went to 5th grade. All the lessons were taught by newly arrived Russian teachers. At first, this was very interesting. Everything was new - the teachers and the subjects. Before, I only had one teacher, and now there were different ones in Russian language and literature, mathematics, geography, botany, and zoology. The school also started a variety of clubs. Sports also began running smoothly. Classes would play one another in soccer, volleyball, chess, and checkers.

My father was an accountant, and quickly found work in an office called "Egg-poultry-prom". A few organizations sprung up, finding work for Jews. But many were still unable to find work. Medical services were not established for a while, so some elderly and sick people died.

The bazaar days remained the same, but there were twice as many tax collectors. At first, there were movies shown on military projectors, but then they started playing in movie theaters. We boys went to watch Russian films with great interest. Many bookstores also opened, which we likewise enjoyed visiting. At that time, radio transmitters began to get set up, delivering radio signals to everyone's homes. At the same time, we started getting electricity, there was much lighter outside, and we went out more. I should note that this period was quite brief, and to us kids, everything seemed very interesting. With the advent of radios in Jewish homes, current events began to be discussed in public areas, especially in government-run barbers, where there would be not just one barber working but several.

Purge of the "Wealthy"

I recall one frightening morning of that pre-war time, when Jews found out that from Kaushany were sent to Siberia all our "wealthy". Included were our acquaintances, the owners of the textile store, Kerzman and Opachevskiy. It was only after the war, having met up in Kishinev at the home of Mr. Kerzman, that he told us how the KGB broke into his house, gave him 4 hours to pack, and drove him in a closed car to the railroad station. There, a train of freight cars was waiting for them. Each car was stuffed with more than fifty people. His partner, Opachevskiy, never made it to Siberia, he died on the train. The houses of those people were seized by the government, and what was left, including furniture, carts, horses, and anything else remaining, was taken in unknown directions. Further, at that time, many of the Jews were leaving Kaushany and moved to Bendery and even Kishinev.

In our family, in the fall of 1940, my mother[133] died from a serious illness. After some time, my father began to meet with the former owner of a store, madam Honna Kogan. She had two kids, and we were two of us. They formalized the marriage shortly before the events described above, when the "wealthy" were sent away. Thus, my father saved her family from being exiled to the wilderness of Siberia. We moved to another apartment, more comfortable relative to the previous. Madam Kogan - we called her "aunt" - was very attentive to us as well as to her kids. From her first husband she had a daughter Clara and a lovely boy Lucya, handsome and very thoughtful. I was enthralled with him, and often went out with him in the yard and on the street.

Start of the War

The winter and spring of 1941 were troubled times. We could feel the war approaching. When on June 22, 1941, we were woken by the sound of planes overhead, we understood - war was here. At first, there was a period of conscription - men were immediately put into uniform and sent to the front. Those who were mobilized at the start of the war, I never met again. They all died in the first battles. Planes with fascist insignia flew low overhead and sometimes we could even see smiling pilots. Since we had no strategic value, we were neither shot at nor bombed. Usually, the planes would fly in the direction of Bendery-Tiraspol.

During the Evacuation

At the start of July, we began preparing for evacuation. The Village Council gave us papers, and the use of a cart driven by a pair of old bulls, and on July 15th we set out to Bendery. We left in the evening, planning to arrive in Bendery in the morning. We traveled along the curb, as the road was occupied by retreating soldiers of the Red Army, some in cars, others on foot - they were all retreating to Dniester. By morning, we arrived in Bendery, and quickly crossed the bridge into Tiraspol. Soon we were in Tiraspol. The city was in ruins. The Germans bombed it regularly twice a day, around noon and 4 o'clock. We sat the bombing out in a small shelter which could protect us only from shrapnel, not from a direct hit.

In Tiraspol, we stopped with distant relatives of madam Kogan. Father regularly went to the station and told us that many Jewish families were leaving using any mode of transportation. No one

---

[133] Fanya Spivak (Khaimovich) (September 15, 1896 – November 6, 1940)

spoke of an organized evacuation of Jews - and there was no such thing. After living in Tiraspol for 4 days, we collected our meager belongings, loaded them onto the cart, went to the railroad station, and by the evening of July 20th, we sat on an open wagon loaded with railroad rails and set out onward, deeper into the country. On the next day, after many stops, we arrived in Odessa.

My sister and I, along with other kids, remained on the platform, while our parents went to the evacuation center in search of food and drinking water. They returned after 4 hours and began deliberations. My dad, aunt (stepmother) and the older sisters Khinka and Clara spoke of staying in Odessa. I was categorically against it - I said I would take Khinka and continue onward. Seeing my determination, our parents agreed with me, and we continued traveling on the same platform.

Our departure from Odessa was delayed by the first bombing of the city. We traveled in the direction of the station Znamenka[134]. On the way, German planes bombed us. The train was civilian, there were no soldiers to shoot at the planes, which flew extremely low. We developed a system: if the train stopped, and there were woods nearby, we would run for cover there. If the train accelerated, we simply lay in place covering ourselves with blankets and other belongings.

We arrived in the central station of Znamenka, where there were 8-10 military trains ahead of us. We were allowed in the station last. The worst bombing happened when we were in Znamenka and thank G-d we survived it.

Describing these events, it's necessary to note that the war forced all the kids to grow up. I was 13 at the time and was in charge of acquiring food. Often, as we would approach a station, I would jump from the train while it was still at full speed, and run to the station buffet, where they occasionally sold bread, kielbasa, and other produce. My main concern was providing bread for little Lucya, who, when hungry, would cry and be beside himself, to a point where he was miserable to look upon.

On the car carrying rails, we traveled until the station Yasinovataya[135], where we were offloaded on the pretext that the train was not going further. We ended up in a communal farm 8-10 kilometers from the station. My sister and I worked in a brigade gathering cucumbers. Our hands bled, but we endured. I have to note that the owners where we were bunked did not treat us poorly. They often treated us to Ukrainian dumplings. I never heard any antisemitic comments from the Ukrainians.

Every day, we would take trips to the station and saw that more and more trains were headed in the direction of Rostov and Stalingrad. The front was approaching, and you could hear artillery fire. Once more, we gathered our few belongings and went to the station on a bull cart. By evening, in the middle of August, we got onto a train loaded with metal and began the next stage of our evacuation east.

Before the station Yelshanka, near Stalingrad, a group of police - they were about 20 - went around all the wagons of our train, and took any men who, by their estimate, could serve in the military or as conscripted workers. They took our father along with others.

Our train arrived in Stalingrad, where we all got off, and settled in the evacuation center, set up in a stadium near the station. It was after dinner, and, taking a little bread, I went to search for my father in the unknown city. After asking some policemen about the location of the conscripted, by evening, I found my father in the yard of a police station.

---

[134] Znamenka – town in Kherson oblast
[135] Town in Donetsk oblast

There were about twenty conscripted, and since they were taken without their things or food, they were upset. So, we, along with several other wives who had found their husbands, asked for the men to be released. In the end, by the end of the evening, some police captain gave everyone draft notices and told them to return at 10am the next day with clothing, a pot, cup, and food, so as to be sent to the front.

Of the twenty people receiving draft notices, two showed up the next morning, including my father. The police realized that the rest left their passports and military documents, rather than be sent to the front, and to our great joy, the officer on watch gave my father back his passport and military document, and we continued our journey. In the stadium serving as the evacuation center, there were more than ten thousand refugees. We realized that we would not leave by train soon. We hired a cart and relocated to the river port. That same evening, we applied to travel on the barge "Adzharia". We gave the sailors a significant sum, and they got us onto the barge on a plank, just over 30cm (1 foot) wide. How we did not fall in the water - G-d knows. Our aunt Kogan carried Lucya in her arms, moving with great care.

When finally, the barge departed the pier, we felt easier. All night, we traveled along the Volga. By the next morning, we arrived in Vladimirovka, where we were told to offload. The scene there was unimaginable - there were thousands of refugees gathered, and only occasional trains - with unheated cars. We didn't want to load onto such at first but seeing that our bread supplies were at an end, went onto one. To get to a place, we had to climb over three partitions.

Now began the most frightening part of the transit - across Kalmykia. The Kazakh residents on the stations wanted to trade everything for tea, but we had none. We somehow managed to trade some things for raw potatoes, carrots, anything we could eat. The train would stay at a station for 5-6 hours at a time. The weather got cold, and the worst of it was - there was no food.

Finally, we arrived at Aktyubinsk. I jumped off the train and bought 4 loaves of bread. I stuffed them into my shirt and old jacket, but still, as I made my way through the train, two were stolen from me. I yelled for my aunt to show the child, to show whom the bread was for, but to no avail. I managed to get two loaves through, and that lasted us for several days.

From Aktyubinsk, the train moved in the direction of Tashkent, where we arrived in two days. Rather than try to stay in the city, my parents decided to move to the Lenin Rayon/District of the Andizhan region. We were taken there by a work train, which was unequipped for passengers - the windows were broken, and wind blew through it. Our dear Lucya got sick, succumbed to pneumonia, and soon died at the regional hospital.

In the Andizhan Region

We got situated in a communal farm by the name of Akhunbabaeva[136], 10-12 people in a kibitka/wagon. It was cold, and there was nothing to use for heating. The chairman of the collective farm sent us to pick cotton. They gave us practically no food. Prices were incredible. By the winter of 1941st, 1kg of flour cost 100 rubles. My father would buy piece of fabric from Polish Jews at the bazaar, which asked for laughable prices, for resale. We would eat once a day.

It was cold, and we, that is, my father and I, would go with our neighbors to steal waste from the cotton harvest. One time, some Uzbeks stopped us, pulled out their knives, and threatened to undo us. Only thanks to the healthy physical strength of Garshtein[137], we were saved. We were able to turn on the Uzbeks, and they didn't bother us from then on. In general, the Uzbeks with whom we lived, were fairly hospitable - sometimes would treat us to tea and flatbread. Then, the mulberry harvest ripened, and we started cooking those.

---

[136] It is about 90 km north of Tashkent
[137] Neighbor or relative from Kaushany

At the time, we lived in incredibly tight quarters, and lice began to eat us terribly. On top of that, Khinka and I got malaria. This is a terrible sickness, which exhausts the body. First, you're cold, then you're shaking, then you're hot. In the summer, we slept on the street, and got stung by scorpions, treated by burning the skin.

By the summer of 1942, my stepsister Clara brought over her groom Syoma Libun. He was a ginger, with glasses, and played the fiddle very well. He had a hard time during the trip and got a frightening infection near his ear. My aunt took care of him util he was better, and over time, he began to play Uzbek melodies, well enough that the locals began to visit, would bring a little food, and listen to Syoma's music. Sometimes he would play classical music, but mostly he would play Uzbek motifs.

At the start of 1942, we got in touch via mail with father's father (Shloime Spivak) and his sister (Betty Roitshtein-Spivak), who lived in Kazakhstan. They sent us a request to move to Kazakhstan. In the summer of 1942, we left Uzbekistan, and moved toward Kazakhstan, to the city of Dzhezgazgan.

In Dzhezgazgan

Upon arrival in Dzhezgazgan, father found work, but he was soon taken into civil army conscription. He served in the city of Akmolinsk. Khinka and I continued to have episodes of malaria. I remember she once had a temperature of 41.2 (106 F). No one knew what to do. Then abruptly the episodes ceased - we stopped shaking - and Khinka and I started looking for work.

Khinka found work in the post office. In the fall of 42, I went to school, to the 7th grade, and in the evening, i.e. from 4 to midnight, I worked as a tuner in a military mechanical plant, to receive a bread ration card - 1kg of bread per day. At the plant, most of the workers were convicts. I learned tuning from one such convict, by the name of Alexei. He was slightly past middle age, educated, well-read, and uncomplaining. My shift was from 4pm to midnight. I would bring with me a small piece of bread and an onion. Alexei saw, but didn't ask me for anything, until one time he asked if it was possible to bring him some makhorka [a coarse type of tobacco]. I would buy a glass of makhorka at the bazaar for 25 rubles and bring him a matchbox on each shift. So, I worked as a tuner until our father returned from his civil conscription.

There were enormous lines to receive bread and other products for ration cards. Our aunt would have to get a place in line early in the morning, and she also worked as an overseer in the dormitory. By the middle of 1943, my father returned from his conscription and found work as an accountant in the local grainery. I finished my 7th year in school and went to work as an installer at the radio station. Life settled down a bit: there was more food, since father got rations of food at work.

Main Point of Interest - the Camp

A few words about Dzhezgazgan - the city where we lived. Near us was the village Kengir, with a village council, medical services, and also a nearby railroad station. The main point of interest of the village was an enormous prison camp and a military village of "vohra" - military guard. In the "vohra" club we could watch movies, and sometimes even professionally staged plays, with the convicts as actors.

Living next to the prison, we didn't know that the prisoners of the Kengir camp had staged a revolt and had been harshly suppressed by the workers of NKVD [138].

---

[138] NKVD – Народный Комиссариат Внутренних Дел - People's Commissariat of Internal Affairs

I worked at the radio station and had a pass to the camp. The leader of the camp was lieutenant colonel Kalinin, and one time he called me at the radio station. I recall, this was summer of 1944, and he asked me to set up a loudspeaker at the train station. I was surprised but did as ordered. At the station, I witnessed the arrival of a train of a hundred cars from Chechnya. In minutes, people were pushed out of the train cars, assembled in rows, and marched to the Kengir camp, where there were barracks prepared for them, formerly occupied by convicts. From the first days of arrival in Kazakhstan, the Chechens died, dozens each day. The climate is continental and harsh - the summers are very hot, and the winters very cold. German prisoners also started to arrive at the camp. The Germans worked in a copper mine not far from Dzhezgazgan.

In 1945, I was once again called to set up loudspeakers at the station. The camp was empty at the time. When I asked where everyone was, I was told that the camp was awaiting new arrivals. This time, a train of Japanese war prisoners arrived. They very quickly set up tents next to the train. There was a command to put out their things. Each Japanese prisoner had a luxurious leather bag, and inside, all kinds of things, from medical syringes to specialty meals. I got a shaving set and a wonderful knife out of it.

After

We survived despite everything. The war ended, and Jews gathered to return to their homelands. My memory of the return trip to Moldova is completely absent. I remember only that we rode in a heated passenger car. At the end of September 1945, we ended up in Kishinev, where we found temporary shelter with relatives, and then my parents moved first to Tiraspol, and then at the end of 46, to the city Izmail, in the Odessa region.

But we decided to go and see what happened to our township of Kaushany. Most homes, where Jewish families lived, were destroyed. But the destruction looked strange to us. There were no craters from bombs or artillery, only the remnants of burned-out walls. It seemed that the houses had been destroyed by the local Moldovans and Gypsies. Even the beautiful tall trees in front of our house had been cut down, likely for firewood. After the war, several dozen Jewish families returned to Kaushany, but they soon thereafter left[139], as there was no work, and Jews could not look peacefully on what had happened to our Kaushany. My mother is buried in Kaushany, and on rare occasions, I would visit her grave. But over time, the cemetery became no more. Moldovans built two-story stone houses on its place.

So, in the end, I will say there is no more Jewish township of Kaushany. There are no longer Jews living there, you can no longer hear Yiddish in the street, no Jews are arguing at the bazaar, no one sings Jewish songs. You will now no longer find Jewish settlements anywhere in Bessarabia, nor in the Ukraine, nor in Poland.

Khinka (Nina) Kogan (Spivak). History and life in letters, *1994-2017*

from Tzur-Shalom, Israel to Newton, MA, USA, 1994-2017, translated by David Kogan, 2015-2018

Before the war (before June 22, 1941)

Parents: Leva Spivak and Fania Spivak (Khaimovich)

My mom was born in the township of Tarutino, near Kaushany. My father lived in Kaushany, and there worked at a store from the age of 14, training to work the register. My mom was some distant

---

[139] Some Jews lived in Kaushany until 1990s, when they left for Israel

relative to my father; she was a very beautiful and attractive woman. They courted each other for 5 years and got married in 1920. After their wedding, they lived in Tarutino, where my brother Joseph and I were born. After that, we moved to Galatz, where dad worked in a dry goods and toys store owned by mom's cousins. I remember, whenever a new shipment of toys came in, ones with even small flaws were given to the workers. That way, I acquired a whole collection of "invalid" toys.

Kaushany

There were a lot of Jews in Kaushany. I don't know exactly how many, but probably around 5000 to 7000 *(If fact before the war there were about 2000-2500 Jews in Kaushany, Yefim)*. We had 5 synagogues. My dad and grandfather went to "Shnaidershe" - tailors'. It's not that they were tailors... it's just that it was right across the street from us. My mom knew the prayer book well and was able to translate. On holidays, she read in the synagogue among the women. There were also the New, Old, and Zionist synagogues - I don't remember what the fifth one was called. The synagogues weren't large, or particularly richly appointed, but they all had Torah scrolls, and were always clean. Of course, women sat separately from the men. Before every holiday, the attendees would donate what they could for the needs of their synagogue.

We lived in New Kaushany. Old Kaushany was behind the church which separated the town. In Old Kaushany, there were Moldovans, in New Kaushany - our people.

One more Incident from my Childhood

I had measles, like all kids. I was already recovering, but then started yelling that my stomach hurt. We had a doctor, an acquaintance of the family, and my mom called him. He looked me over, and then asked if we had cream of wheat. He said, "make some, I'll wait." Mom prepared it, and the doctor told me to eat. So, I ate, and in a few minutes, the doctor asked me, "So is your stomach still hurting?" I said, "No!" He laughed and told mom that I was just hungry. He didn't charge us for that visit.

My studies

In Galatz, I finished the 1st and 2nd grades. The school was number 9, just as yours (*Yefim: I studied in Kishinev for 8 years in school number 9, from 1960 to 1968, as did my brother Miron, cousins Dima and Miron Tismenetkiy*). On arrival to Kaushany, I went to 3rd grade. After 4th grade, I went to secondary school, which was the same for boys and girls. The subjects were the same as in Russian (Soviet) schools, plus we had two foreign languages: French and Latin, and also religion.

The director of the school was Chernenko, a very dour man - I don't remember him ever smiling - but fair. All the students were afraid of him. We were allowed to be around until 8 o'clock in the evening, and when the director came out to check on us, word of it would spread instantly, we'd hear "the director is coming" and would be gone like the wind, going home. From 2nd grade of secondary school (*1935-36*), we got a new director, Lipkan, a more sociable man, who maintained a good relationship with the students.

I had a teacher of Romanian, Lidia Zhirege; she was very beautiful, with a long braid. She liked me very much and gave me a photo of herself to remember her by, on which was written "A heartfelt symbol for my student Spivak, from Lidia Zhirege, October 30th, 1935."

That very photograph:

Lidia Zhirege, October 30th, 1935

We also had a music teacher, Mr. Moroshan. We mocked him however we could. We Jews also studied religion with a Rabbi by the name of Usim. He was intelligent, but slovenly, so we made fun of him for that. The Moldovans had a priest, but he was handsome, and all the girls made eyes at him. He was tall and well built, with a nice haircut... I forgot his name. But he didn't have many students - 80% of the students in the school were Jews.

When I was in 3rd grade, secondary school became partly private; so, half the money came from the government, the other half from my parents. It cost a lot, and studying became difficult. Government representatives came to the exams. A director by the last name of Boldir came from a boys' secondary school in Bender. My uncle Boris (dad's brother) had once studied with him, and then Boris had been arrested in 1933 for 'communism.' When Boldir learned my last name, he asked if I was Boris's relative. I fumbled and admitted that Boris was my uncle. After that, Boldir grilled me at an exam for half an hour straight, till one of the parents, who was in the committee, said, "enough tormenting her."

In the fourth grade of secondary school, the director was a fascist (about whom I already wrote), but not for long, because the school closed, and I finished fourth grade in another township - Volontirovka. After that, I didn't get a chance to study, and I was left at home till 1940, at which point we were "freed" by the soviet army. At that time, I couldn't speak Russian at all, but I understood it some. The other students were the same. So all the students were shifted back two grades, so instead of 9th grade, I went to 7th. I was already 17 at the time. I went to school for a year, and then the war started. After coming back from the evacuation, it wasn't time for studying, and in 1946, I got married and moved to Kishinev. Thus ended my schooling.

More about Sheiva Srulevich   (2007)

At 100, Sheiva was in full possession of her senses, and recognized people she hadn't seen in 40-50 years. One time, she came out to the gates and watched the passers-by. A man walked past, whom she had not seen in a long time. She told him "Berale, what, you don't recognize Grandma Sheiva?" He stopped in his tracks and couldn't believe that Sheiva recognized him. He lived 20 kilometers away, in Monzir, and sent her a cistern of sunflower oil afterwards.

One time, she evidently started losing it a bit and wanted to go out into the street at night. She kept saying that "zhizhile," like a sort of demon, were running around the street. My father barred the passage with a table and chairs, but she somehow managed to get the stuff out of the way. She said that it was dark on the street, and these "zhizhile" were wandering about. No amount of pleading helped, and in the end, dad woke his father, and together, they managed to tie Sheiva down, and she fell asleep. The next morning, the doctor came, and reassured them that it'd pass, and that's how it turned out. Sheiva once again recognized people and understood everything that was going on. One time she told her maid (while the maid was bathing her): "Why isn't my kerchief starched? Are you trying to save on starch?"

To get into our house, you had to get up five or six stairs without any rails. Sheiva always went up and down those stairs on her own, until one day, she fell and broke her hip. The doctor said that she wouldn't be able to walk anymore, but that she would live, because she had a very good heart.

My friends would come over, and they liked to play-tease Sheiva. They'd ask, "Grandma, how old are you?" She would answer, "However old you'd like - 60-70, or even let it be 80 or 90." Thus, Sheiva lived until February of 1941, when she died at 104 years.

Concerts in Kaushany

Many European artists came to us. I especially remember Sidi Tal', a very famous singer. After the war, she worked in the Chernovitsky Philharmonic, and before the war came to us with her troupe. There was also Tina Zlataia, Joseph Kamen' or Kamenev, I'm not exactly sure.

Jewish-Zionist organizations in Kaushany before 1940

My mom (Fania Spivak (Khaimovich) was a public figure - she was a member of the Zionist organization "Keren - Kasmes." They helped the poor; collected money for Palestine. Mom was a Zionist but didn't stop me from doing anything about it. Dad stood with the left but forbade me; was afraid I'd get caught.

In Kaushany, there were three Zionist organizations - Betar, Maccabee, and Terdania. Betar, we called "fascists," because they thought that the government (Israel) had to be taken through battle. I was a Maccabee. This was largely a sport organization. We also studied Yiddish twice a week. We had different sport sections, and an art activity. And once every two months, we had a ball. We had a bit of show, then dances, games and buffet. One times, a woman from Palestine came to us; she collected money for the country, and we had a ball in her honor. I was given two Yiddish poems to learn, but I didn't know Yiddish back then, and so they wrote the text for me in Romanian, and I memorized it and recited it with a good "Jewish" accent. The woman wanted to meet my mother and asked her how I know Yiddish so well. But mom answered that I didn't even know what I was saying. The woman was surprised and suggested that I should be taught the language.

Time passed, and around 14-15 years, the left took me, and I left the Maccabees, and started doing "leftist" things, so to speak "underground," and spent my time, as it turned out later, with nonsense.

This was another period of my youth. Dad (Buma) was never a Maccabee. With him, I became acquainted in the gymnasium.

Girlfriends.
Khinka Kogan (Spivak) far right, **Rosa Dvoirina** far left, **Basia L'vovskaya, Sara Gibrikh** and **Tsilia Letichever**
1937(38)

Another episode from my "leftist" life. I read illegal literature, but we didn't have much of it in Kaushany. So, a friend from Bendery sent me books. And so, one Sunday, a person who drove people and packages from Bendery came and gave me a package and a note. My friend decided that my dad wouldn't be home, since he usually worked on Sundays. But it so happened that on this day, dad was held up and saw that I was brought something. I quickly read the note; "If there will be trouble, take the books to whomever you see fit." I immediately started tearing up the note, and dad started shouting, ordered me to show him the books, and started going after me. He found pieces of the note and put together part - "there will be trouble"... started yelling that he'll go to the director of the gymnasium and tell him what his students were doing. I quickly took the book to another friend, and then later of course read them, but dad didn't find out. Father, of course, didn't go anywhere, and didn't tell anyone. And then the Soviet Rule came, and you didn't have to hide anymore.

Girlfriends. 30s
Khinka Kogan (left), **Basia L'vovskaya** and **Sarah Gibrikh,** both died during the war.

Holiday in Romania

This happened to me during the romanian rule. There was a big holiday - May 10th. The matter was that at the time, Romania belonged to several regions, which at different times belonged to different countries. These were Moldova, Muntenia, Oggenia, Bessarabia, Transilvania and Macedonia. And all this was called Romania - Mare (Greater Romania). Our school prepared a celebration, where different girls represented different regions of Romania. And I got the biggest role - Greater Romania. I had to learn 4-5 pages by rote, and prose, not poetry. I was even released from my lessons, and stayed home and studied, and in the evening, went to rehearsals. A teacher, Radulesku, worked with us. Once another teacher, Gobzhila, came into rehearsal, and asked "Why did you pick a kike[140] for the main role?" And Radulesku answered "First, who can speak Romanian like she does? And second, who can memorize as much?" And he continued. "I gave another girl a few words in Macedonia, and she still hasn't learned it."

The celebration was in Kaushan's theater owned by Motl Rabinovich. A teacher stood behind me, just in case I needed help with my lines. Everything went great, and I was 11 years old [it was 1934]. I remembered one more detail - the role of Moldova was given to Ozia Feldman *(later became a professor in Moscow)*. Ozia had to dress in traditional national clothes for the role. He got everything on but balked at the scarf - we barely convinced him. So that's the story.

1938

This happened in 1938. I was in 4th class of the gymnasium (8th grade). Fascism had already been in many countries in Europe and had come to us. Fascists came to power in Romania, and the director of our school became one of them. The gymnasium back then was part government, part private, so you had to pay twice as much as before. In our class, only 12 students remained - two Moldavians and the rest were Jews.

Once, one boy did something wrong, and they had him stay after for two hours. Out of solidarity, we stayed with him. When the director came by and saw us, he asked "why are you here?" We answered that we just stayed with him. So, the directory turned that act into a political one. He yelled "Ah, so you are communists! You'll be expelled." We got really scared, and changed our answers, saying that the boy

---

[140] Kike used as an insulting and contemptuous term for a **Jewish** person. In Russian – zhid.

asked us to stay because he had a headache. The director still expelled us for a week, first questioning all of us separately, like criminals. The chairman of Parents' Committee, doctor Feldman stood up for us - he's the father of Ozia Fledman, the professor from Moscow, whom you know. After that, we were taken back, but soon the school was closed due to financial troubles, and we were left overboard. Everyone went their separate ways, and some stopped studying altogether. I moved to another township - Volontirovka, near Kaushany. Right around Purim, fascism was overthrown - the Soviet Union put forth an ultimatum that if Romania didn't get rid of the fascist party, the Soviet Union would move into Bessarabia.

Thus, it continued until June 29, 1940, at which point we were "freed." That's the sort of uneasy youth we had, and it was great.

June 28, 1940, Kaushany. (2010)

At that time, far from everyone had radios. Near our house, Sarah Gibrikh, my friend, had a radio, and so did our neighbors across - Klyuzmans. There was a guy there, Haim, a year older than I, and sometimes we chatted on a bench near my grandfather.

And so, on June 28th, I was down with another flu - the lymph nodes in my throat were inflamed, and I often had a fever. In the evening, this Haim runs out and yells "Hin-ka! To-mo-row russ-ians are com-ing!" I jumped up, quickly got dressed and ran to the gymnasium. There was already a gathering of youth there, and we were making signs. Suddenly, we heard a rumblin. We thought that our "comrades" were coming. But it turns out to be just the local landowner, who ran off with his family on a tractor.

And the Red Army, we met the next day at the stone bridge. The soldiers stopped, came out to us. We met them throwing flowers in the air, celebrating. Then on the second day, back to the routine. We opened the stores, and our "comrade friends" swarmed them like locusts. For them, it was dirt cheap. The exchange rate was set at 1 ruble = 40 lei, so all the stores were cleaned out in two days.

When I realized that I don't have summer shoes, and that there was nothing left to buy in Kaushany, I went to Bendery and bought at least some sports shoes.

There were intervals without groceries, too, but gradually life returned to normal. Izia and I studied, father - Leva worked at a poultry exchange, mother - Fania was sick, and great-grandmother Sheiva lay in bed and waited to be fed.

Two acquaintances from Kaushany   *2011*
I knew Zonis Semen Aleksandrovich before the war, in Kaushany. He was 5-6 at the time. His father was the head accountant at a Jewish bank, and his mother of course didn't work. I don't remember her name, but she was a very interesting woman. After the war, I never heard anything from them, until you (*Yefim K.*) mentioned your physics teacher Zonis Semen Alexandrovich.

School #34, Class 10B, 1970

The Class-Teacher – Semyon Alexsandrovich Zonis, third from the left, Yefim Kogan behind Zonis on the right, then further to the right Misha Kleyner, Boris Braudo, Vitya Mak, Iosif Kuperman, Sasha Kogan (my second cousin), Yura Daylis, Viktor Sapozhnikov, and others

Milya (Sharkanskiy-Rosenberg) I also know in Kaushany. He was the adopted son of photographer Sharkanskiy. He taught him the profession of photography. At our gymnasium, Milya only studied one year, but he was in our group. After the war, he was already married to Shura, and I heard that his last name was Rosenberg. How and why that happened, he never told us. Overall, we met rarely, but when we did, we were always very happy. Later, I was the matchmaker of Iosif *(Khinka's nephew)* and Inna (Milya's daughter), and we met as "махэтунем". That's all I remember.

"Boys":
    Hazin Malamyd, Petia Blishtein, Nona Galigorski, **Milya Sharkanskiy (Rosenberg)**, Aaron Lipkanski, Josl Kliuzman.

1939-1940
Kaushany

About the Kopanski Family in Kaushany   *2009*

In the Kopanski family there were four brothers: Abram, Khaim, Joseph and Moyshe. Abram had two sons: Yana (der grober (from Yiddish - fat) since he was large). He was older than I by a couple of years. After the war, he married Aunt Ester's cousin - Zinia Vinnitzkaya. Moyshe's second son was a pretty boy about uncle Izia's age. During the war, he was taken by the Germans, but a Russian woman saved him. I don't know what happened to him after that. Khaim had three daughters: Nona, Liza and Dvoira. Nona married Mogorimova from Old Kaushan. Liza also got married to someone from Benders. Dvoira had a different fate. In primary school, she was raped by the director of the Dumitresky school (along with another girl, Riva Klyuzman). A few years before the war, she married Moyshe Goldamer, who died during the war. She returned from the evacuation with her sister Liza, and they lived together in Chernovtsy. Dvoira started to live with the husband of her sister. That husband told Liza - "If you want, we can all live together, but if not, I'll leave you and marry Dvoira." It was true, Dvoira was more beautiful than his wife Liza. So, they lived all together, and everyone in Kaushans in Chernovtsas knew about it. What happened to them later, I don't know.

Joseph had one son Yana (der diner (*from Yiddish - thin*)). Let me step back a bit. I had a girlfriend, Zhenia Erlih. Her family was very wealthy. When the gymnasium was closed down, Zhenia studied in Galatzes in a french gymnasium, Notre Dame. When we visited on holiday, we met with Jiana *(der diner)*. In 1940, when the Soviets came, she gave up Notre Dame and studied in one class with me. Then, May 15th, 1941, came, and Zhenia (Shena, as we called her), was sent away - her father in one direction, and Zhenia, her brother and mother - in another. Somehow, Jiana learned where the latter were, and went there. There, he signed a marriage license with Zhenia, changed her passport, gave the brother his last name, and in one day, got them out of there. They all lived in Kemerov after the war. Jiana finished an institute, and she also finished something. They had two daughters. The brother lived in Kishinev, married, and had kids. Zhenia ofter came to Kishinev, and visited me for a full day, and we still didn't get enough time to catch up. Her daughters married and lived in Moscow. When Jiana died, they all went there (to Kemerov). After that, I don't know what happened to them. I'm in Israel, and them - only God knows.

Moyshe (Michael) had one son Yana (Jacob), he got called Yana the small, and later, as you know, he became an important person.

Moyshe and Jyana (Jacob) Kopanski
1950 years.

Jacob Michal Kopanski (23-Mar-1930, Kaushany – 18-Jul-2006, Kishinev) is a moldovan, soviet, jewish historian, doctor of historical studies (1978) and a professor. He is the author of 13 monographs about the modern history of Moldova and judaica.

Kaushaners - Borukh Mariyasin, Esther Klyuzman and Zeltsers   *June 7, 2015*

Got an assignment from Fima yesterday and immediately went to work. Today, I looked through the book with Kaushany residents' last names[141]. It mentions Borukh Mariyasin and Esther Klyuzman, and it so happens that I remember them.

Borukh Mariyasin owned the first car in Kaushany and used it to make a living. I wrote to you that I once used his services. I gave him Izia's address [*Yefim: apparently in Benders*], and Borukh brought him over at night, because mom had an episode and badly wanted to see him.

I know little of his family - only that he married Esther Klyuzman. Esther lived across from us, and was about 5 years older than I. She had three brothers: Motl, Haim, and one more whose name I don't remember. Haim was a year older than I. He often came over to our place. He was a stutterer. I remember that on June 27th, there was an order that the Russians would come on the 28th *1940. (I wrote about it above).* They were rich: the three Klyuzman brothers owned a mill. I don't know if they got sent away or not in 1940. It was said that they treated their workers well. Later, Esther married Borukh Mariyasin.

---

[141] From the original version of the book: https://www.jewishgen.org/Bessarabia/files/FinalPaper.pdf

During the war and after - in Kishinev - I don't know what happened to them. Also, the father of Esther Klyuzman was the brother of Feiga, the wife of uncle Yankel, the brother of Grandma Sheiva.

One more story. Motl, Esther's brother, was engaged to Lena Dubosarskaya, a very beautiful woman, but when the Soviets came in 1940, she refused him (*likely because he was from a rich family*). After the war, Motl married the cousin of Mania Klyuzman. They had a son, and seemed to live reasonably well, but he soon committed suicide, and no one learned why. That's all I remember about Borukh Mariyasin and Esther Klyuzman.

I only remember a small bit about the Zeltsers. They had a metalworks shop. The father had three kids: Falek, Elman, and a daughter whose name I don't remember. I know that Falek spent time in Daftana [a prison in Romania] for leftist activities, and the daughter came to Israel for the wedding of Paul Kogan [*Yefim: our relative through my father's side*]. I had a photo from the wedding. That's all about the Zeltsers.

Two Extreme Events

I'm home alone, naturally sad and bored. It never used to occur to me - or rather - I never used to dwell on what happened many years ago. But they're showing news about flooding in the Far East on TV, and it reminded me of two events that happened in Kaushany during the "liberation".

The Soviets arrived on June 29th, 1940, and at the start of July it started to rain, quickly turning into a downpour. We lived on grandfather's property, on a little bit of a hill, but the street was already covered with a torrent of water. The bridge in the center of town overflowed, and the flood headed toward Zaim, i.e. toward us. Our bedroom windows went all the way to the floor, and there was a large gap there, so water came into the house. Mom was already sick at the time, and dad was at work. Izia, Grandma Sheiva, our help Alexandra and I had no idea what to do. We tried plugging the hole with rags, but it didn't help. We called grandfather and he took a shovel and started redirecting the water. He slaved for a long time before he finally managed to get it flowing away. By then there were 20 cm of water in the house, and Alexandra and I started bailing it by hand. Of course, it's far from what I saw on TV, but for us, it was a serious incident. I ended up getting a cold, and it took a long time for me to clear the resulting bladder infection.

The second event was November 10th, 1940. As you know, mom died in November, and we were all in rough shape, so we went to sleep early. Abruptly, in the middle of the night, dad wakes us yelling "Earthquake!". We - that is - dad, Izia and I - ran outside, but grandma [ed: great-grandmother Sheiva] stayed behind. On the roof of our house was a brick chimney, and we saw that it started to fall, making

huge racket. I thought the whole house was collapsing! I started yelling - "grandma, grandma!" When we saw that the house remained standing, I started crying, ran inside, found Grandma Sheiva and started kissing her.

[Yefim K: mom wrote this at 90 years old and remembered the exact date of the earthquake! I looked it up online, and found that on the night of November 10th, 1940, was the Vrancea[142] earthquake, the largest in that area in the 20th century. June 22, 2013]

During the war (June 22, 1941 – May 9, 1945)

Evacuation

On July 8th 1941[143], evacuation began in Kaushany. Every family was given a cart with horses or oxen. Kaushanians were forbidden to go through Bendery to Tiraspol', because of fears of too many people gathering on the bridge across Dnestr. Everyone was told to go to Jaloveni, and from there, on pontoon bridges across Dnestr River.

My stepmother had a daughter Clara - you probably remember her. So, Clara worked in Kishinev, and by then had left for Tiraspol, so aunt said - we are only going to Tiraspol'. So, on two carts - we, and aunt's sister-in-law went through Bendery to Tiraspol'. We were on horses, and the second cart was on oxen. The road was filled with servicemen and evacuees, and on approach to Bendery, we stopped to wait for the second cart. In the morning, we came up to the bridge, and there was no one there. We calmly crossed Dnestr and came into Parkan. By 9 o'clock, we were in Tiraspol', with aunt's sister-in-law. There lived her brother, whom she had not seen for 22 years. They greeted us very well. After dinner, we went to look for Clara, but we had no address. We knew that in the evening, people went around on the main street, even in such times, and we met her there and brought her back with us.

We spent five days in Tiraspol', and when the Germans (and Romanians) advanced close to the city, we went to the train station. This was July 15th, and the last passenger train from Kishinev arrived at the train station. Of course, we didn't get in: everything was overfilled, and we had a lot of baggage. In the evening came a cargo train, and we loaded ourselves into a train car with some sort of vats, and by morning arrived in Odessa. In Odessa, we stopped in the port, which is to say, transferred to another cargo train and sat there for 5 days. But they fed us very well: 3 times a day for free and gave us passes so we could go to the city, which we did in turns. On July 21st, Odessa was bombed for the first time. We naturally got very scared, and that same evening, our train left, and we moved into Ukraine's depths.

Thus, we arrived in the city of Stalino (later called Donetzk), where the police surrounded us and ordered us off the train, so that we would help gather the harvest. Thus, we ended up in an agricultural commune, 35 kilometers from the railroad. A woman farmer took us in, and we started working in the fields. There was plenty of food. There we spent over a month, and again the Germans approached, and we had to move on.

The chairman of the commune said that he had no carts for us. My father then told him "You can keep us here, so that the Germans kill us, but our people will find out, and you'll be sorry." The chairman got scared, and gave us a cart with oxen, and all night we traveled to Stalino, and in the morning, again ended up in a cargo train car, which brought us to Krastnodarsky lands, Eja station. There, the same story repeated itself - the police took us off the train and brought us to a commune, but this time only two kilometers from the train station. There we worked until around September-October, I don't remember

---

[142] Vrancea is a county in Romania with main town of Focșani.

[143] Moldova Jews were "lucky", they had more than 2 weeks to get out. That is because Romanian soldiers were not good soldiers, and it took them long time to occupy Moldova. They were in Kishiniev only on July 16th, 1941.

exactly, and then moved on, got as far as Stalingrad. There was an already established evacuation-center, with thousands of people.

We were soon given passes to a barge to cross the Volga. With great difficulty, we got on the barge, and in the morning, were already on the other side, in the city of Vladimir. There came a whole echelon with closed train cars. People were divided 50 people to a car. As soon as it arrived, we had to grab a car, which we did, but ours had evidently been used to transport fish, because there was 20 cm of water in it. We wanted to go to another, but they were all full.

We were forced to scoop the water out, and it was already November, and cold. I froze my feet; during the day, they got numb, and I didn't feel much pain, and at night, we covered up and got warm, but my feet hurt in the warmth, and I cried like a baby. In those train cars, we arrived in Andijan. There, everyone was split up among agricultural communes. I forgot to mention that my stepmother had a boy, Liuska, five years old. He was very pretty, but immediately got the measles, then pneumonia, and died in a hospital eight kilometers away. This was a heavy blow to us.

In the start of 1942, we found out the address of my grandfather (Shloime Spivak) and aunt Betia. They lived in Dzhezgazgan, sent us a summons, and we sold all we had that was worth anything, and went to them. In Dzhezgazgan, we lived until September 1945, but that's another "sippur" (story).

At first, dad (Leva Spivak) went with us on evacuation, but when we arrived in Dzhezgazgan, he was recruited into the Labor army. He was not very far from us - near Karaganda. There, he had an operation for a hernia and was left home for 3 months. With us, he got a job in a grain warehouse as the head accountant, and with the help of his director-Kazakh, he did not go back to the army. The Kazakh later said that army recruiters also "wanted to eat." After that, we didn't go hungry, and dad worked there until we left for home.

We lived in Dzhezgazgan in the north of Karaganda region. I worked at the postal office on the telegraph - twenty-four hours at work, then two days at home. There were camps around Dzhezgazgan, where different people were held - from bandits to artists and "traitors" of the motherland. Those who behaved themselves had passes and could go around. We knew several carpenters and installation men who came to us to work. The post office had two entrances - a central one into the main area, and one on the side, into the telegraph area. The telegraph entrance led into a small hallway, then to us. The door had a little hook for a lock; the first door was locked with a broom. One time on my shift, late at night, I heard knocking on the door. I didn't think much, undid the hook, and see there's a man on the street, pulling the door, and I'm pulling it back toward myself. He's pulling and I'm pulling! The others that worked with me said "Nina, have you gone mad? Open up; it's Molchanov from the mine." I let him in, of course, and he laid into me. "How could I have opened the door? What would have happened, if he had been one of 'them - bandits?'" He was our repairman, came to fix the broken line. That's how it was, when someone forgot themselves for a moment.

I worked at the post office, and Clara (daughter of my stepmother) worked at the radio station. I needed shoes - I had nothing to wear. I gathered up money - 1500 rubles, and we went on a trip to Karaganda. I had to mark myself off in the Ministry of Communication, as did Clara.

So, Sunday morning, we arrive at the flea market, where you can find anything. There are locals, evacuees dealing there, and of course thieves. We noticed that some youth are watching us. Clara and I are speaking Romanian, so that no one will understand. Clara says to me: "Hold on to your money." The youth keep on after us. So, we decided to go first to the Ministry, in the new city. We have to take a train, and the youth follows, even helps us climb into the wagon. We decided to switch wagons, the youth came after. We decided not to try to run anymore but sit and wait and see what'll happen. We sit down on a bench, the youth across from us. Clara says: "If this was at night, I'd have gone mad!" The youth start laughing, and we realize that he understands Romanian... he was just lonely, was looking for people from back home. He spent the day with us, showed us the city. Later, we got separated, and never saw him again... don't even know what his name was.

How we met Victory Day

In 1945, Clara and I worked at the radio station. So, on the morning of the May 9th, the street was filled with people, though I knew from the evening of the 8th of May - a woman from Karaganda relayed it to us over the radio. So needed to get something ready for the celebration. We decided to make 'napoleon[144],' but had no eggs. We did have egg powder. We made the cakes, and for crème, took the powder, mixed it with milk and all the rest, and made wonderful crème. So, we had the great Napoleon, and for the first time, I drank some vodka, and we of course we were out till morning.

After the war (1945 -)

The war is over - we're going home

The war is over, but how do we get home, when there's no money? Money had to be obtained somehow. And most likely dishonestly. We might have wanted to do it honestly, but this was not possible. We were given rations for tea - 50 grams per person, but the tea was American. The tea was in packages of 1/2 kilo and didn't cost much. The warehouse overseer sold packages on the side for 250 rubles, and in Karaganda, you could get 800-1000 rubles for the same. So, my father borrowed money from his brother Yasha, bought 30 packages from the overseer, and went to Karaganda with his wife Hona.

On the second day, they went out to the bazaar: dad with 3 packages and aunt with the same; the split up, standing not too far apart. A policeman came to dad immediately and took him to the police station.

The chief questioned dad: "... where did you get so much tea?" and dad answered that we had four laborers, and in two years we collected this, and were going to buy winter boots, and so forth along those lines. He also said that he was the main accountant of "Zagotzerno" (grain procurement station), and that the chief could call the controllers and check. My aunt meanwhile went to the apartment where they were staying and hid the rest of the packages. The chief didn't know what to do with father. Father then said: "You also need tea, so take a package and let me go." The other thought about it and did just that.

After that, they sold all the tea, but not at the bazaar, but to a reseller for 800 rubles a package. Of course, the profit was still sizeable. They bought various necessities and headed home. Father also bought vodka, which sold at 500 rubles for half a liter. But the vodka was not in bottles, but in two large cans, poorly sealed. So, the vodka gave off a strong smell in the train, someone snitched, and dad was again taken into custody, a bit before Dzhezgazgan. But there was a chief who wasn't above taking a drink... thus ended that adventure. We got home with this "dirty money."

One time in life, my father undertook such an "operation," and all ended well.

---

[144] Napoleon cake

About my good friend Rosa Dvoirina (Mittleman)

Rosa arrived in Kaushani around 1937-38. Her mother married Kolman Volodarskiy from Kaushany. They lived near the New Synagogue. They had a nice house and a gazebo. Rosa and I studied in the same class at the gymnasium, and a group of us often met up at her house. There was one room where there was a couch, and carpets on the walls to the ceiling, and carpets on the floor as well. So, we'd sit down around the room and chat about different things.

My voice was heard more often than others, so her stepfather thought, we were talking about "leftist things," so he declared - "I don't want to see Khinka with her group here anymore!" The following day, Rosa came to me in tears and told me everything. I soothed her, told her we'd find another place.

During the war, I didn't know anything about what happened to her. After the war, though, Rosa studied in Odessa, finished the university, and became a French language teacher. She was dispatched to the city Reni. Later, a matchmaker introduced her to Aaron, and they married and came to live in Kishinev. That's where Vena was born.

After the war, of the girls in our cohort, only three were left: Rosa, Raia Pistol and I. Raia left (*died*) early, but Rosa and I stayed close. At all our celebrations and anniversaries, we were always together. We also often met up without particular reason.

After Aaron died, Rosa got diabetes and had heart trouble as well. Rosa and Vena went to Israel in 1991 and settled in Raaman in ulpan. We often spoke on the phone, and at the start of 1992, Vena called and said, his mother was very ill, and she was asking for me to come. I came on the second day and didn't like how Rosa looked. I told Vena that we needed to take her to the doctor immediately.

In March 1992, I went to America, and there I got a letter from Vena, that he took his mother to the hospital, and that she died there. Rosa was a very good and loyal friend. I still speak with her son Vena. To me and to my children, he's like family.

On tasty things and other food in Kaushany

I remember the small chalas baked by my grandmother Sheiva. Every Thursday, she baked bread, and always gave small chalas to the kids. They had a big Russian oven - and Sheiva could bake bread and make very tasty cookies at the same time. After that, they'd put on water for bathing in a big zinc tub. I also remember regular food: bouillon/soup, roasted beef with potatoes, cutlets, gefilte fish for Sabbath and holidays. Also, grandmother occasionally made 'mamalyga' - Moldavian food - corn porridge with butter, fried onions, cottage cheese, milk. For dessert, we had baklava and fludn, which I later also made and sent to Moscow[145] for Purim.

My grandfather and grandmother lived relatively poorly, and when there was no meat, they made "lazy roast", which is to say, would roast onion as if it were real meat, added potatoes, and used garlic for seasoning... and it was an excellent dinner.

---

[145] I studied and lived in Moscow from 1970, Yefim Kogan

My parents Buma and Khinka Kogan returned to Moldova after the war. They visited graves of mother's mother, and many other relatives at the cemetery in Kaushany, while it was still standing. They married and lived happily in Kishinev. In 1988 they emigrated to Israel. Yefim Kogan

My parents' grave at
Tsur Shalom cemetery, Israel

Will Jewish Life in Kaushany be remembered?

There is not a single

monument[146],

sign,

tablet,

or reminder

of a Jewish past for the Shtetl Kaushany.

Who will remember all who perished during the Holocaust?

Who will put stones and flowers to a monument of the Jewish residents of

Kaushany?

I will and I am sure many others too.

---

[146] I hope we will erect a monument to the Jews in Kaushany soon, Yefim K.

Appendices

Appendix A. Society "Damen Ferein" ("Serene Women")

In 2010 a young man, Serghey Daniliuk, interested in the history of his own town-Kaushany found a document at a local museum dated December 27, 1923. It was about a Jewish Women's society organization. Original document in Romanian is at
https://kehilalinks.jewishgen.org/Causeni/Kaushany_files/SocietyOriginalRomanian.pdf

Following is a translation of that document from Romanian.

Statute of a Society
Society "Damen Ferein" ("Serene Women") to help poor Jews in town of Kaushany-Noi, district of Tighina (Bendery)

(In pencil written-December 27, 1923)

The Purpose of the Society
Article 1. The aim of the Society "Damen Ferein" is to help the poor in health care, medicine, food and whichever other sustenance.

Article 2. To any poor women society will provide medical aid at home, and if necessary, the Society will hospitalize the sick in a local hospital or any other area hospital which could treat her.

Article 3. To fulfill Article 1 and 2 Society will contract with a doctor, a midwife, with one of the pharmacies to acquire the help & medicines and will permanently employ a doctor who will be available by request of the Society to visit & consult the assigned sick in order to treat her however, expenditures will be disbursed from the fund of the Society.

Construction of the Society
Article 4. The Society members can only consist of females, adult (namely, of 21 years of age) dames & damsels, excluding schoolgirls and students.

Article 5. Members of this society might be women, which will pay a monthly fee of at least 10 lei, payable a month ahead.

Article 6. With respect to members enrolled in the society, who will not pay fees as in Article 5 within six months, the general assembly will call for their exclusion from the Society.

Article 7. Member or members, who cause disorder in the Society, or act against the Society, will all be excluded from the Society, in the same manner, by general assembly vote.

Funds of the Society
Article 8. Funds of the Society consist of: a/member registration fees which will be 20 lei & above; b/of the percentage of reserve capital which remains unused, c/ from donations made by members of the Society or Private; d/ of collections which the society will organize in various weddings in Kaushany or any other town; e/ donations to the society for the orphans at a time when a person dies in the family; f/ from spectacular evening balls, benefit soirees, concerts, readings & all other similar which would be organized by the Society; g / the subscription lists that will be made by the Society.

106

Article 9. Of all amounts collected, a bookkeeping register will be kept in which the all the sums received will be entered daily.

Article 10. A similar bookkeeping register will be kept for expenses made & entered daily.

Article 11. Accounting will be kept by a bookkeeper of the Society.

Article 12. Company funds will be recorded by two of the Society's members elected each month by the Executive Committee, which they will pass onto the society's cashier also elected by the Executive Committee.

Article 13. Any revenues collected by society's recording members & Cashier will consist of the forenamed through the release of receipts.

Article 14. Any payments made by society to the poor will be made vis-à-vis receipts as well as doctor's payment following a visit of the sick.

Article 15. Aid given to the poor and be determined by the Society 's Executive Committee every time it is requested.

Society's Business management
Article 16. Business Management of the Society is divided over: a / General Assembly and b / the Executive Committee.

General Assembly

Article 17. Convening society's members in an ordinary general assembly takes place in January of every year. Extra-ordinary meetings will be convened by the Executive Committee or, as many times as it decides.

Article 18. Ordinary General Assembly will choose a/ a president of the Society to administer all affairs of the Society. The election of a president will be made annually. b / Executive Committee for a term of three years and their deputies (substitutes) for a term of a year and c / a review commission composed of at least three members for a year.

Article 19. At ordinary general meetings, the executive Committee will create an account of all operations which have effected over the course of the year & of all Society 's activities.

Article 20. The General Assembly will preside over all matters, as well as Society's activities & its operation during the year. In order for decisions to be taken by a majority of voters to resolve issues: a/ status change and wholeness and b / liquidation of the Society, a majority of at least two thirds of members present is required.

Article 21. The general assembly is legal if ___ is present

(continuation of text is missing from this point on! Translator.)
Translated from Romanian by Avi Klammer.

Appendix B. Dispute Meeting

Original in Romanian in
https://kehilalinks.jewishgen.org/Causeni/Kaushany_files/DisputeMeeting.pdf

Minutes
Today's date of August 11th, 1934

We, Diomid, I. Popa, County Board [147]Chairperson of Tighina; Ion Galațan, County Board member; Stefan Căina, the mayor of the Caușani Commune; We, the Tighina county.

Considering the fact that, through Tighina County prefecture's ordinance number 9582 of July 14, 1934, driven by the county's integral service road report number 9582 of June 5, 1934, we, the County of Tighina, have been delegated with the on-site examination, (in the Caușani Commune) of the condition of a building located in said commune, on Alba Juliei Street, at the corner of General Vernescu-the property owners of which are: **Mr. Moisei Rabinovici**, **Iacob Criuleanschi** & **Shmil Rabinovici** & whose building, as resulting from the report of the Road Service, is constructed on a site which constitutes a part of the county road.-

Considering above ordinance, we, members of the commission instituted on the basis of said ordinance (with the exclusion of Mr. Chief Magistrate, Gheorghe Goll, being absent from locality, today, on above date), having examined the condition on-site & in the presence of property owners, have ascertained the following:

1) Alba Juliei Street toward the Zaim commune is a county road & from the corner of General Vernescu Street, has the width of 15 meters-aside from the part on the right-hand-side of the building in question, where said road has only 9 meters in width-& that, through the fact that above-named proprietors, without any right, have put up a wooden booth, plastered on the exterior with clay, on said road, thereby occupying the county road-a surface area of 45 meters-namely (9 meters in length, on Alba-Iuliei-Zaim Street & 5 meters in width on General Vernescu Street). However, there is a distance of 1 meter between said booth & the [148]true corner of the road where **Mr. Rozenfeld's** property is located.-

Even from such ascertainment, it follows that the structure put up later has nothing in common with the rest of the buildings (except for road zone) & is isolated. -

On General Vernescu Street, there have been other booths installed-by the proprietor himself, however-following law-enforcement ordinance/a booth adjoining **Bruter's** house & another, opposite, of Poleae's/a [149]thing which denotes that [150]these have not been considered as proprietary-over-land which is occupied by said booths &, it is possible, too, that the land occupied by said booths, has been leased for whichever period of time.-

2) The building constructed on said site consists of three parts-a whole structure made of wood & covered with shingles. -
At present, said material is old & rotten-thus, as far as maximum material value, it amounts to Lei 3,000. -

---

[147] literally: president
[148] can verbally be also referred to as: the <u>real</u> corner
[149] what appears to be a reference to the more accurate term: 'fact'
[150] in reference to the booths

3) From a juridical point of view, proprietors have no right whatsoever over locale occupied by the booth; said locale is part of public dominion. -

Considering the public's good character with respect to (said) cause, there is no functional [151]prescription in favor of proprietors. As a result of said existing proprietors' principle & bad faith, [152]they have no right but to raise the material used for the construction of the booth without any other compensation.

With regard to the act presented by proprietors emanating from former district of 1914, this act is null & void & unopposed-as, the required forms of old law have not been met &-more importantly, no authority has provided any authorization for said cause &, in fact, (with) said road being county, the communal authority has had no justification to oppose the county road. -

4) Considering the fact that they a sidewalk is going to be laid & a road toward Zaim-[153]built, these work projects cannot be executed without tearing down the booth-as, there is not enough empty space for (the construction of) the proposed road & ditches for water drainage. -

Consequently, we are of the opinion that said booth be [154]justified by proprietor &, in case of refusal-following some simple steps for it to be torn down by the respective bodies under proprietor's control & without fulfilling other formalities-since county land which will become part of the county road, is concerned. -

For this cause, article 54 & its following & of the road law are not applicable-as, the text of this law addresses a case where the land needed for road construction is private property & only in such a case, expropriation if needed land is proceeded with.

[155]County Board Chairperson

[156](Diamant?) Popa
President

[157]Director
The proposition of the minutes at present is approved (& what) follows is making the proprietor's proposition to justify booth ('s construction) of (own) good will official, contrary to taking steps (toward) its justification & factored by proprietor's expense.[158]

Undersigned: Director

---

[151] read: remedy or help
[152] proprietors
[153] read: pave (in American English terms)
[154] read: (construction of) said booth be substantiated by proprietor
[155] said is a stamped seal of title
[156] said name & title: first name is illegible (& same with regard to name appearing scribbled underneath). same applies to indecipherable 4 following words/names (signature-like in appearance)
[157] This title & written (or signed?) name appears a little further away from above translation of manually-written commentary/remarks, to the right-hand side of hand-written President title
[158] this section is the translation of the hand-written text (dated: September 9, 1934) on this page

Appendix C. Business Directory, Kaushany 1924-1925

Occupation/Business (Romanian)	Occupation/Business (English)	Last Name	First Name
bacani	grocer	Bercovich	Shmili
bacani	grocer	Bruter	Nukhim
bacani	grocer	Chiovetski	Shmili
bacani	grocer	Dovirin	Ianchel
bacani	grocer	Fucs	Khaim
bacani	grocer	Grinberg	Itsic
bacani	grocer	Itscovich	Liuba
bacani	grocer	Kogan	Sabsha
bacani	grocer	Leibelman	Moyshe
bacani	grocer	Leibovich	Iosif
bacani	grocer	Levenzon	Chisil
bacani	grocer	Lipcanskii	Abram
bacani	grocer	Mariasin	Iosif
bacani	grocer	Matenzon	Sura
bacani	grocer	Poghoriler	Khaim
bacani	grocer	Rozenfeld	Mordko L.
bacani	grocer	Saltanovich	Leica
bacani	grocer	Shafir	Itsek
bacani	grocer	Shufman	Anna
bacani	grocer	Shvartman	Ghersh
bacani	grocer	Sobal	Ghersh
bacani	grocer	Sverdlic	Sheiva
bacani	grocer	Sverdlic	Strul
bacani	grocer	Tulchinski	Shmili
bacani	grocer	Volodorski	Moshco
bacani	grocer	Zolotova	Ilona
barbieri	hairdresser	Baranov	Iosif
barbieri	hairdresser	Moldavscaia	Neha
barbieri	hairdresser	Nukhimovich	Shlioma
birturi	innkeeper	Fucs	Ghitla
birturi	innkeeper	Mazurov	Mikhail
birturi	innkeeper	Prelutskii	Leib
birturi	innkeeper	Scharevskii	Ianchel
birturi	innkeeper	Serebreanic	Shmili
birturi	innkeeper	Zemelman	Leiba
brutari	baker	Batsian	Shmili
brutari	baker	Busel	Leizel

Occupation/Business (Romanian)	Occupation/Business (English)	Last Name	First Name
brutari	baker	Diminshtein	Beniamin
brutari	baker	Lerner	Samsha
brutari	baker	Levit	Ghersh
brutari	baker	Rashcovski	Ghidali
brutari	baker	Teper	Mendel
caciuli (ateliere)	hat maker's workshop	Chishlianski	Khaim
caciuli (ateliere)	hat maker's workshop	Polin	L
carciumari	innkeeper, tavern, saloon	Averbukh	Ianchel
carciumari	innkeeper, tavern, saloon	Averbukh	Noekh
carciumari	innkeeper, tavern, saloon	Brili	Khaim
carciumari	innkeeper, tavern, saloon	Feder	Beniamin
carciumari	innkeeper, tavern, saloon	Fridman	Zisla
carciumari	innkeeper, tavern, saloon	Garshtein	Seindlea
carciumari	innkeeper, tavern, saloon	Garshtein	Zelman
carciumari	innkeeper, tavern, saloon	Grinberg	Feigha
carciumari	innkeeper, tavern, saloon	Grinberg	Khaim
carciumari	innkeeper, tavern, saloon	Grinberg	Rukhlea
carciumari	innkeeper, tavern, saloon	Grinberg	Srul
carciumari	innkeeper, tavern, saloon	Presman	Raia
carciumari	innkeeper, tavern, saloon	Rabinovich	Ilona
carciumari	innkeeper, tavern, saloon	Shmulovich	Iosco
carciumari	innkeeper, tavern, saloon	Spector	Duvid
carciumari	innkeeper, tavern, saloon	Spivak	Shlioma
carciumari	innkeeper, tavern, saloon	Sverdlic	Bunea
carciumari	innkeeper, tavern, saloon	Vaisman	Itsec
carciumari	innkeeper, tavern, saloon	Veitman	Shlioma
carciumari	innkeeper, tavern, saloon	Volodorski	Ovshei
carciumari	innkeeper, tavern, saloon	Zemelman	Moshco
ceasornicari	watchmaker, repairs	Ghershenzon	Meyer
cismari	shoemaker, repairer / cobbler	Boianovskii	Simon
cismari	shoemaker, repairer / cobbler	Erlikhman	Duvid
cismari	shoemaker, repairer / cobbler	Erlikhman	Mekhel
cismari	shoemaker, repairer / cobbler	Erlikhman	Samsha
cismari	shoemaker, repairer / cobbler	Klinzberg	David
cismari	shoemaker, repairer / cobbler	Lisovoi	Grigore
cismari	shoemaker, repairer / cobbler	Odeskii	Ghers

Occupation/Business (Romanian)	Occupation/Business (English)	Last Name	First Name
cismari	shoemaker, repairer / cobbler	**Siciug**	Simkha
cismari	shoemaker, repairer / cobbler	**Stanislavski**	Shlioma
cismari	shoemaker, repairer / cobbler	**Troianov**	Vale
cofetarii	confectionery	**Bruter**	Shmil
cofetarii	confectionery	**Ciapchis**	Elcun
cofetarii	confectionery	**Ciulak**	Abram
cofetarii	confectionery	**Kaushanskaia**	Minta
cofetarii	confectionery	**Klinzman**	Iosif
cofetarii	confectionery	**Malamud**	Nuba
cofetarii	confectionery	**Novogrebelskii**	Chelman
cofetarii	confectionery	**Novogrebelskii**	Volco
cofetarii	confectionery	**Shincar**	Sokher
cofetarii	confectionery	**Tabacinic**	Khaim
croitori (barbatesti)	men's tailor	**Brunsher**	Meyer
croitori (barbatesti)	men's tailor	**Fucs**	Shrul
croitori (barbatesti)	men's tailor	**Kolb**	Shlioma
croitori (barbatesti)	men's tailor	**Korenberg**	Nukhim
croitori (barbatesti)	men's tailor	**Malchin**	Buium
croitori (barbatesti)	men's tailor	**Malchin**	Mosco
croitori (barbatesti)	men's tailor	**Shifman**	Moshco
croitori (barbatesti)	men's tailor	**Spector**	Abram
croitori (barbatesti)	men's tailor	**Treigher**	Abram
croitori (de dame)	women's tailor	**Opacescaia**	Rukhlea
curelari (ateliere)	leather belt maker (workshop)	**Ceapchis**	Noekh
curelari (ateliere)	leather belt maker (workshop)	**Epelman**	Aron
curelari (ateliere)	leather belt maker (workshop)	**Gherscovich**	Ghersh
curelari (ateliere)	leather belt maker (workshop)	**Sherman**	Iosco
drogherii	apothecary trivia	**Hakham**	Abram
drogherii	apothecary trivia	**Hakham**	Simon
faina (comercianti)	flour merchant	**Lipcanskii**	Shtrul
faina (comercianti)	flour merchant	**Perchis**	Shlioma
farmacii	pharmacy	**Bronfman**	Ghersh
fierarii (mag.)	blacksmith	**Feighin**	Itsic
fierarii (mag.)	blacksmith	**Liverant**	Toiva
fierarii (mag.)	blacksmith	**Rosenfeld**	Barukh
fierarii (mag.)	blacksmith	**Vinitski**	Duvid

Occupation/Business (Romanian)	Occupation/Business (English)	Last Name	First Name
fierarii (mag.)	blacksmith	**Zeltser**	Malca
furaje (depozite)	fodder (repository)	**Averbukh**	Leiba
galanterie (mag.)	haberdashery	**Cretsulescu**	Ilie
galanterie (mag.)	haberdashery	**Cunicer**	Berco
galanterie (mag.)	haberdashery	**Cunicer**	Iosif
galanterie (mag.)	haberdashery	**Mordcovich**	Leib
galanterie (mag.)	haberdashery	**Rabinovich**	Moshko
lemne (depozite)	wood (warehouse)	**Cunicer**	Ghersh
lemne (depozite)	wood (warehouse)	**Feighin**	Ianchel
lemne (depozite)	wood (warehouse)	**Presman**	Iosif
lemne (depozite)	wood (warehouse)	**Ratsiu**	Pinea
lemne (depozite)	wood (warehouse)	**Stanislavski**	Ghersh
macelari	butcher	**Schvartsman**	Motel
macelari	butcher	**Zilbershtein**	Leiba
manufactura (mag.)	fabric store	**Abramovich**	Moshco
manufactura (mag.)	fabric store	**Averbukh**	Moyshe
manufactura (mag.)	fabric store	**Blidshtein**	Moshco
manufactura (mag.)	fabric store	**Bronfman**	Itsic
manufactura (mag.)	fabric store	**Bruter**	Naftul
manufactura (mag.)	fabric store	**Cuciuc**	Moshko
manufactura (mag.)	fabric store	**Feighin**	Ianchel
manufactura (mag.)	fabric store	**Kleiman**	Melic
manufactura (mag.)	fabric store	**Kogan**	Abram
manufactura (mag.)	fabric store	**Levit**	Khaim
manufactura (mag.)	fabric store	**Moghilner**	Shlioma
manufactura (mag.)	fabric store	**Natanzon**	Nukhim
manufactura (mag.)	fabric store	**Osnis**	Iosif
manufactura (mag.)	fabric store	**Polskii**	Duvid
manufactura (mag.)	fabric store	**Svartsman**	Menashim
manufactura (mag.)	fabric store	**Zelman**	Zisman
mori (cu aburi)	steam mill	**Bacal**	Isac
mori (cu aburi)	steam mill	**Finchelshtein**	Abram
mori (cu aburi)	steam mill	**Haichin**	Khaim
mori (cu aburi)	steam mill	**Klinzman**	Reful
mori (cu aburi)	steam mill	**Soltanovich**	Khaim
mori (cu aburi)	steam mill	**Talis**	Matul
palarii (mag)	hat shop	**Bronfman**	Abram
pescarii	fishermen	**Chiovetski**	Nakhman
pielarii (mag)	leather goods, tanner	**Averbukh**	Ghersh
pielarii (mag)	leather goods, tanner	**Noekhovich**	D.

Occupation/Business (Romanian)	Occupation/Business (English)	Last Name	First Name
sticlarii (mag)	glazier, bottle maker	**Dubosarski**	Ovshei
sticlarii (mag)	glazier, bottle maker	**Koen**	Itsic
sticlarii (mag)	glazier, bottle maker	**Kogan**	Ghers
sticlarii (mag)	glazier, bottle maker	**Vaiser**	Duvid
tinichigii	tinsmith	**Lebedinski**	Izrail
tinichigii	tinsmith	**Miller**	Meyer
tinichigii	tinsmith	**Talmazski**	Rakhmil
tipografii	printing house	**Hakham**	M.
uleiuri (teascuri)	oil supplies	**Erlich**	Ana
vinuri	winemaker	**Calintchii**	Zeilie
vinuri	winemaker	**Erlich**	M.
vinuri	winemaker	**Halchin**	Malea
vinuri (depozite)	wine warehouse	**Erlich**	Moshko
vinuri (depozite)	wine warehouse	**Kalintski**	Zeilic
vinuri (depozite)	wine warehouse	**Khaichin**	Malca
vopsele (mag.)	paint store	**Vaisman**	Matus
vopsitori	painter, dyer	**Lieberman**	Abram

Appendix D. Cheder class, April 1858, Kaushany.

25 children-boys with Melamed Shimon Shesterman. The students were **aged** from 4 to 7. The families were all from Middle Class estate and paid from 2rub. 50 kop. to 5 rub.

Bessarabia Revision Lists

Searching for Any Field (contains) : CHEDER
25 matching records found.
Run on Tue, 09 Apr 2024 12:43:01 -0600

Town / Uyezd / Guberniya	Surname	Given Name	Father	Relationship	Sex / Age Last Revision / Age This Revision	Year Left / Reason	Comments	Day / Month / Year	Page / Registration # / Former Registration #	Publication Type / Archive / Fond / Microfilm / Image
	SHESTERMAN	Shimon	Abram	Melamed	M		Have a license for the Cheder from Bendery Educational commision from 14 August, 1856 #196		44 / 1	
	SVERDLIK	Moshko	Yudko	Student	M / 6		Family Middle Class, paid 4rub.50 kop.		44 / 1	
	LEYZOR	Moshko	Gershko	Student	M / 6		Family Middle Class, paid 4rub.50 kop.		44 / 1	
	BAKCHARISNKIY	Moshko	Duvid	Student	M / 4		Family Middle Class, paid 4rub.		44 / 1	
	ZONIS	Yudko	Fishel	Student	M / 6		Family Middle Class, paid 4rub.		44 / 1	
	GALIS	Perets	Ioska	Student	M / 5		Family Middle Class, paid 4rub.50 kop.		44 / 1	
	KLEYNER	Volko	Ioska	Student	M / 5		Family Middle Class, paid 4rub.50 kop.		44 / 1	
	SHVARTSMAN	Duvid	Khaim	Student	M / 6		Family Middle Class, paid 5rub.		44 / 1	
	VAYSMAN	Duvid	Khaim	Student	M / 6		Family Middle Class, paid 5rub.		44 / 1	
	VAYSMAN	Moshko	Khaim	Student	M / 4		Family Middle Class, paid 4rub.		44 / 1	

Kaushany Bendery Bessarabia	DVOYRIN	Volko	Leyb	Student	M 6		Family Middle Class, paid 5rub.		44 1	
	RABINOVICH	Mordko	Srul	Student	M 6		Family Middle Class, paid 5rub.	4 April 1858	44 1	Cheder's list NARM/2/1/6703 2382897 899
	KOGAN	Gershko	Itsko	Student	M 5		Family Middle Class, paid 4rub.50 kop.		44 1	
	MARIASIN	Itsko	Gershko	Student	M 7		Family Middle Class, paid 5rub.		44 1	
	MARIASIN	Iosko	Gershko	Student	M 5		Family Middle Class, paid 4rub.		44 1	
	APAGIN	Duvid	Simkha	Student	M 7		Family Middle Class, paid 5rub.50 kop.		44 1	
	GULOVATYY	Yankel	Zeylik	Student	M 5		Family Middle Class, paid 3rub.50 kop.		44 1	
	VOLFENZON	Yankel	Srul	Student	M 4		Family Middle Class, paid 3rub.		44 1	
	RASHKOVSKIY	Khaim	Peysakh	Student	M 4		Family Middle Class, paid 2rub.50 kop.		44 1	
	LATMAN	Mordko	Leyba	Student	M 4		Family Middle Class, paid 4rub.		44 1	
	CHIMISHLIYSKIY	Moshko	Nusim	Student	M 7		Family Middle Class, paid 5rub.		44 1	
	CHIMISHLIYSKIY	Yankel	Nusim	Student	M 4		Family Middle Class, paid 3rub.		44 1	
	GLUVSHTEYN	Abram	Shimon	Student	M 7		Family Middle Class, paid 5rub.		44 1	

	GLUVSHTEYN	Berko	Moshko	Student	M 4		Family Middle Class, paid 3rub.50 kop.		44 1	
	SHURMAN	Simka	Zanfel	Student	M 4		Family Middle Class, paid 3rub.		44 1	

Appendix E. List of Kaushaner's Jews who could vote in Bendery uezd in 1890

The list includes people who own in Kaushany Bendery uezd a property with value not less than 500 rub. and have the right to participate in town voting conferences. On the list there were also 7 non-Jews. Information from newspaper "Bessarabia Gubernia News", May 3, 1890.

##	Surname	Given Name	Sex	Middle Class /Merchant	Registered in	Property Value in rub.	Comments
1	ABRAMOVICH	Shmil	M	Middle Class	Tiraspol	900	
2	BRUTER	Daniil	M	Middle Class	Rashkov	3000	
3	BERKOVICH	Itsko	M	Middle Class	Bendery	600	
4	BRONSHTEYN	Itsko	M	Middle Class	Bendery	900	
5	GARSHTEYN	Volko-Khaim	M	Middle Class	Akkerman	1200	
6	GARSHTEYN	Ita	F	Middle Class	Akkerman	750	Widow
7	GRINBERG	Perlya	F	Middle Class	Bendery	600	
8	GRINBERG	Berko Froim Gerts	M	Middle Class	Bendery	1800	Possible three people from one family
9	IOYNOVICH	Zelman	M	Middle Class	Kishinev	600	
10	KAUSHANSKIY	Yankel	M	Middle Class	Kishinev	600	
11	KOGAN	Berko	M	Middle Class	Akkerman	660	
12	KUNICHER	Moshko	M	Middle Class	Bendery	600	
13	KALITSKIY	Shlioma	M	Middle Class	Bendery	2400	
14	KOMBERG	Brana	F	Middle Class	Bendery	1500	Widow
15	KOGAN	Ios	M	Middle Class	Bendery	600	
16	MARIYASIS	Srul	M	Middle Class	Bendery	660	
17	MILER	Srul	M	Middle Class	Kishinev	600	
18	NOYEKHOVICH	Yankel	M	Middle Class	Bendery	750	
19	OSNAS	Leyba	M	Middle Class	Bendery	600	
20	OPACHEVSKIY	Volko	M	Middle Class	Bendery	900	
21	PANISH	Mordko Kelm	M	Merchant	Bendery	1320	
22	ROYZEMBLAT	Moshko	M	Middle Class	Bendery	570	
23	RABINOVICH	Leyba	M	Middle Class	Bendery	1080	
24	ROYZENFELD	Sura	F	Middle Class	Kishinev	600	
25	STOLYAR	Leyba	M	Middle Class	Dubossary	900	
26	TOVBIN	Monashko	M	Middle Class	Bendery	600	
27	KHAKHAM	Rosya	F	Middle Class	Bendery	1800	
28	SHVARTSMAN	Gershko	M	Middle Class	Bendery	600	
29	ERLIKHMAN	Shlioma	M	Middle Class	Bendery	600	

Appendix F.   An article about Irikhem from Dubossary Memorial Book.

Published in Israel in 1965 in Hebrew and translated into English by JewishGen.org in 2014

הרב הגאון ר' ירוחם בן ר' שבתי הכהן זצ"ל

(רב ודיין בדובוסרי)

איש האשכולות היה ר' ירוחם. גדול בתורה וביראת שמים. חריף ובקיא. כל ימיו עסק בתורה ובהלכה וכן החזיר את נשמתו הטהורה לבורא בעת שישב והגה בגמרא. ולא רק למדן מופלג היה ר' ירוחם. כי אם גם נעים זמירות. גדול היה כוחו בנגינה ולתפילתו בציבור יצאו מוניטין בדובוסרי והסביבה. כאשר הוא ובניו היו עולים אל הדוכן לברכת כהנים. נשמעה ברכתם כשל להקה מוסיקלית וקהל המתפללים היו מאזינים לברכתם תפילתם בהנאה מרובה. ולא בכדי. שכן בניו של ר' ירוחם נתנו כולם בקול ערב ובכשרון מוסיקלי ושימשו בחזנות בקהילות גדולות — אחד בקישינוב, ואחד

באודיסה. וש'נ"מה הצעיר בארצות-הברית. שלושתם אינם כבר בחיים.

נער הייתי וזקנתי ועד היום זכורים לי ניגוניו של סבא בברכת כהנים ובהלל.

הרב ר' ירוחם חיבר ספר בשם „כהן צדק" — הגהות על הש"ס. לתרץ את הקושיות על הגאון ר' עקיבא אייגר ז"ל. כן חיבר שא'ות ותשובות „התשבי". שהוא כפר גדול על ארבעת חלקי הש"ע. ספר זה נועד לבירור הלכה ברורה ולהלצה מסבך המבוכות שבאחרונים. שזה בונה וזה סותר. ואכן „התשבי" מתרץ הקושיות. ברר הכל על נכון בטוב טעם ודעת. על ספר זה קיבל סבא הסכמות מגאונים רבים וזקנים רבות עסק בהכנתו להוצאה לאור. בנעורי עוד הספקתי לראות את הספר עב הכרס בכתב ידו של סבא. ממון רב היה דרוש להוצאתו ולצערנו לא זכה לראותו מודפס בחייו. ייזכר לטובה דודי. ר' שלמה הכהן ז"ל. אשר נתן ידו להוציא את הספר בארצות-הברית.

כפי שידוע לי נבחבו ע"י ר' ירוחם עוד ספרים שאינם מוכרים לי. אך בידי נמצא החיבור שלו „בריש גלי" — פירוש על ההגדה של פסח. ספר קטן זה מצטיין בבאור יפה. בפשט נפלא. ויש בו גם ליקוטים אחרים של מדרשי פליאה על פסוקים ואגדות חז"ל. בכ'ף ההגדה מצוי דרוש לשבת תשובה במוסר השכל. סבא קרא לספר זה „בריש גלי" על שם התעוררות הגאולה האחרונה. ואת הפסוק „ובני ישראל יוצאים ביד רמה" מתרגם אונקלוס „בריש גלי". באותיות אלה ברומזות בר"ת שמו של המחבר ירוחם בן ר' שבתי.

לפי שמסרו לאמי ז"ל. בתו של ר' ירוחם. היה זה ב'עשרה לאדר תרס"ח. בעת שסבא ישב והגה בגמרא ובבית היתה רק בתו רחל'ה. פתאום שמעה נקישה מנפילת כובע הקטיפה שלו הקשה על הרצפה. היא נכנסה לחדר לראות סיבת הנקישה

ומצאה את ר' ירוחם כפוף על הגמרא ללא רוח חיים. הוא מת בנשיקה בעסקו בתורה ובעבודה.

אשתו. הסבתא אדילה. משושלת הבעש"ט וכבעלה מצאצאי הש"ך. היתה אשה צדקנית ועזר כנגדו כל ימי חייה. יהי אף זכרה ברוך.

נכדם. שבתי קרדינסקי

118

Yerucham, son of Rabbi Shabtai Hacohen, z'tz"l

by his grandson, Shabtai Kardonsky

Translated by Eti Horovitz

Reb Yerucham was an erudite person, great in the Torah, in his devotion to God, exquisite and proficient. He studied the Torah and the Jewish laws all his life, and even passed away while studying the Talmud. He was not only a great scholar, but also had a pleasant voice for singing. He was very talented in music and the reputation of his public prayers was spread throughout Dubossary and the surrounding areas. Whenever he and his sons came up to the podium for the Benediction of the Cohens, their prayers sounded like a musical group and the praying public enjoyed listening to it very much. There was a reason for that: the sons of Reb Yerucham were all gifted with pleasant voices and musical talent. They all served as cantors in big communities – one in Kishinev, one in Odessa, and the young Shlomo in the USA. The three of them are no longer alive.

I was a boy, and I grew old, but until today I remember the chanting of grandfather in the Benediction of the Cohens and in Halel.

The Rabbi Reb Yerucham wrote a book named "Cohen Zedek" – interpretations about the six books of the Mishna, to settle the questions of the Gaon Reb Akiva Eiger of blessed memory. He also wrote Questions & Answers "Hatishbi", which is a big book about the four parts of the "Shulhan Aruch". This book elucidates the laws and clarifies the abstruseness when one is corresponding, and the other is contradicting. And indeed, "Hatishbi" answered the questions, clarified everything in good taste and wisdom. For this book, grandfather received approvals from many Rabbis, and he worked many years preparing for it to be published. In my youth I had seen the thick book in my grandfather's handwriting. It took a great deal of money to publish it, and unfortunately, he didn't get to see it printed in his lifetime. My uncle, Reb Shlomo Hacohen of blessed memory, will be well remembered for contributing to the publishing of the book in the USA.

As well, Reb Yerucham wrote other books that are not familiar to me. But I do possess his essay "Be Reish Galei" – an interpretation for the Hagadah of Passover. This small book excels in its beautiful explanations and magnificent simplicity. It also has collections of other interpretations about Torah verses and stories of Hazal (our Sages of Blessed Memory). At the end of the Hagadah there is a discourse for Shabbat, an answer with a moral. Grandfather named the book "Be Reish Galei" after the latest redemption awakening movement, and the verse "and the children of Israel are leaving fearlessness" is translated by Uncalos As "Be Reish Galei". These letters imply the initials of the writer, Yerucham's son of Rabbi Shabtai.

According to what they told my mother, of blessed memory, Fige, daughter of Reb Yerucham, it was the 10th of Adar 1908, while grandfather was studying the Talmud. His daughter Rachel suddenly heard the sound of his velvet hat falling to the floor. She went into the room to see what this noise was and she found Reb Yerucham bent over the Talmud, not breathing. He died painlessly while studying the Torah.

His wife, grandma Adila, offspring of the Baal Shem Tov, and like her husband, the offspring of the "Shach", was a righteous woman and his right hand her entire life. May her memory be blessed as well.

Appendix G. List of Jews from Kaushany serving in the Great Patriotic War

(1941-45), from Memorial of fallen on site **http://www.obd-memorial.ru**

57 Jews found in that website from Kaushany, from that **34** were Missing in Action, **6** were killed, **one** died from wounds, **6** Jews survived and were demobilized after war ended, we do not have information about **11** people.

Full Name	Date of Birth	DoD or Date missing	Rank	
Abramovich Isaak Abramovich	1907	Jul-1941	Private	MIA
Abramovich Shoil Moshkovich	1911	May-1942	Soldier	MIA
Averbukh Shulim Yankelevich	1894	Dec-1942	Soldier	MIA
Batsiyan Moyshe Shmelevich	1925		Private	
Briker Moyshe Shmulevich	1901		Private	
Brunsher Khamel Yakovlevich	1922	1942	Soldier	MIA
Bruter Danil Petrovich	01-Aug-1915		Lieutenant	
Brutter Lev Naumovich	16-Jul-1923		Medical lieutenant	demobil.
Chapkis Shmil Naumovich		Aug-1944	Private	MIA
Feder Mikhail Benyaminovich	19-Mar-1914	Oct-1944	Private	MIA
Finkelshteyn Froim Abramovich	1901		Private	
Frayman David Meerovich	1903	Dec-1941	Soldier	MIA
Garshtein Izrail Mikhaylovich	1898		Private	
Garshtein Mendel Aronovich	1908	Feb-1945	Private	MIA
Gaysinskiy Boris Iosifovich	1918	Oct-1944	Private	MIA
Gluzberg Markus Davydovich	02-Sep-1923		Lieutenant	demobil.
Guber Moisey Khaimovich	1910	1941	Private	MIA
Ilesh Isay Iosifovich	1919	17-Jan-1945	Soldier	killed
Khakham Yakov Shaevich	1905	02-Jul-1943	Private	killed
Khamelis Meer Yankelevich	1903	Nov-1944	Soldier	MIA
Khaikin Raful Gersh	1895	Apr-1945	Private	MIA
Klyuzman Khaim Iosifovich	1921	Dec-1944	Soldier	MIA
Klyuzman Abram Ikhilevich	1920	Oct-1944	Private	MIA
Klyuzman Beysa-Rifim Khunovich	1922	Dec-1943	Soldier	MIA
Klyuzman Iosif Kh.	1923	Dec-1944	Soldier	MIA
Kopanskiy Mikhail Abramovich	17-Sep-1924		Junior lieutenant of technical service	demobil.
Korenberg Noikh Nukhimovich	1914	Dec-1944	Private	MIA

Name	Year	Date	Rank	Fate
Krinberg Veniamin Yakovlevich	1920		Private	
Levinzon Leontiy Kisilovich	1916	Nov-1944	Soldier	MIA
Levit Moisey Abramovich	1914	Nov-1944	Private	MIA
Linskiy Idrul Iosifovich	1919	27-Sep-1943	Guardsman private	killed
Linskiy Moisey Iosifovich	1923		Private	demobil.
Lipkanskiy Ilya (Yekhiel) Izrailovich	27-Jan-1903		Lieutenant engineer	
Liverant Shika Taevich	13-Jun-1914		Junior lieutenant	
Mechtovich Mordko Meerovich	1915	Jun-1944		MIA
Moldavskiy Todoris Moiseevich	1913	Feb-1943	Captain	died from wounds
Natenzon Iosif Davydovich	1907	Jul-1944	Private	MIA
Nukhimovich Meylikh Ikhilevich	1905	Sep-1941	Soldier	MIA
Odesskiy Mordko Srulevich	1907	23-Jun-1941	Private	MIA
Opachevskiy Borukh Elikovich	05-Mar-1927		Senior Lieutenant Engineer	demobil.
Osnas Shulim Iosifovich	01-Mar-1909		Major of the Medical Service	demobil.
Polskiy Matus Davidovich	1906	Jul-1944	Soldier	MIA
Presman Eolman Ikhilevich	1913	1941	Private	MIA
Presman Toyve Ikhilevich	1919	1941	Private	MIA
Rabinovich Simkha Shmilevich	1908	Nov-1944	Sergeant	MIA
Raskin David Mikhaylovich	1912		Private	
Reznikov Moyshe Froymovich	1913	Jul-1941	Soldier	MIA
Serebryanik Mikhail Samuilovich	1910	23-Apr-1944	Private	
Shafer Mendel Tsukovich	1916	Dec-1944	Soldier	MIA
Shafir Fishel Itskovich	1912	Nov-1944	Private	MIA
Shmulevich Samuil Iosifovich	1903	Oct-1944	Soldier	MIA
Spivak Abram Gershkovich	1909	Jun-1944	Private	MIA
Tovbin Ishko Berkovich	1921	06-Jan-1944	Soldier	killed
Zaborov Shmil David-Khimovich	1905	Nov-1944	Private	MIA
Zaslavskiy Mikhail Davydovich	1922	Juk-1943	Private	MIA
Zisman Pinya Zelmanovich	1908	08-Jul-1944	Senior Sergeant	killed
Zismanovich Volf Moiseevich	1911		Private	killed

Appendix H. Excerpt from Land document of Kaushany

Original
document in
Romanian

Read translation
on the next page

Village administration of Novye-Kaushany, district Tighina

Inventory
of all Jewish immovable property located on the plots of these community

	Surname and Name	Property	Value in lei
1	Klyuzman Charna	1 house made of stone with 5 rooms, 2 corridors, covered with tin, 1 kitchen in the yard, 1 cellar. Yard 80 square meters	150,000
2	Lumer Itsik	1 house from the earth covered with shingles, 3 rooms and corridor, 1 kitchen and storage room, covered with tiles.	20,000
3	Levit Mendel Duvid	1 house from the earth covered, 3 rooms, 2 kitchens and storage room, covered. Yard 40 square meters	20,000
4	Nukhimovich Khaika	1 house from the earth, 8 rooms, storage room, covered. Yard 35 square meters	30,000
5	Genis Strul	Place for the house and yard 80 square meters.	2,000
6	Guber Khaim	Place for the house and yard 80 square meters.	2,000
7	Kripleaski Yanku	Place for the house and yard 400 square meters.	6,000
8	Kluzman Iosif	1 storage room from the earth, covered with tin, place for yard 2,000 square meters	8,000
9	Opachesky Srul	Place for the yard and house, yard 800 square meters	8,000
10	Spivak Ester	Place for the yard 500 square meters, 1 old house with 3 rooms, an entrance hall covered with shingles, a storage room and a stable in the yard	4,000
11	Levit Mendel	1 house with 5 rooms, 1 corridor, 1 kitchen, 1 storage room covered with tin. Yard 300 square meters	18,000
12	Gelman Nukhim	Place for the house, yard 500 square meters	3,000
13	Gukius Aron	1 house with 4 rooms, 2 corridors and a kitchen. Two stables covered with shingles and one with tiles, the yard is not fenced with a stone wall 400 square meters, 2- ?, 1 storage room, covered with shingles, yard 800 square meters.	35,000

Appendix I. List of Jewish families who lived in Kaushany
from the 19th century to 1990s

The list provides surnames and names of people with their professions, businesses who lived in Kaushany from 19th century. For many families we have dates of birth and death. It also tells what happened to the family during the war. If parents lived in Kaushany, but children did not, they usually be included in the list, but not their children.

You find for many families their estate/class. Every Jew in the Russian Empire (before 1917) supposed to be in one of three estates. Most of the families were in the Middle Class (Мещане) estate, a few families were Merchants (Купцы) and Farmers (Земледельцы). Originally many families in Kaushany in 19th century were farmers, but in 1864, most of them were re-listed as Middle Class. For each estate families are supposed to register, and in many cases, you see that families living in Kaushany were registered in Bendery, Kishinev, Soroki, or other places.

Several families were citizens or subjects of other countries: Turkey, Moldova Principality, Romania. A few young people from wealthy families were sent to study in France, and Belgium. There are families who emigrated to Israel (at that time Palestine).

Below is information about Jews from Kaushany that I found from different sources.

WWI   **10 Jews** from Kaushany fought in WWI and were wounded, killed or were missing.

1930s   **14 Jews** were communists during Romania period, went to prisons.

One Jew in Kaushany was killed in 1930 in an antisemitic incident.

GULAG **12 Jews** from Kaushany were deported to GULAG and most of them died there.

One Jew was Zionist and was killed.

One Jew from Kaushany went to fight for Spain International brigades in Spanish Civil War (1936-1939).

WWII   **88 Jews** from Kaushany fought in WWII, got killed, or were missing, see the whole list at Appendix F.

One Jew was in Auschwitz concentration camp and survived!

Another Jew was in Buchenwald concentration camp and survived!

100 Jews who remained in Kaushany after Germans and Romanians invaded Bessarabia. All of them were killed, mostly by locals! Information about **20 Jews** killed in Kaushany below.

More when 2,000 Kaushaners evacuated to the East, and **230 died** from bombardment, starvation, exhaustion.

1970-80s **One Jew,** son of Kaushaner participated in hijacking a plane by Jewish students in Leningrad, USSR, to go to Israel in 1970s. He was jailed and after serving time emigrated to Israel.

One Jew who moved to Israel was wounded at the Arab terrorist attack in 1980s.

124

2023 **A granddaughter of a Jew** from Kaushany was killed on October 7, 2023. She was at the Nova Musical festival.

2024 **Rabbi Tzvi Kogan killed** in November in Dubai was a grandson of a Jew from Kaushany.

Where this information is coming from, sources.

There are several important sites on the internet where you can find information about ancestors. Also, there are many Kaushaners who wrote memoirs, who helped in collecting the following information about our families.

1. JewishGen.org – the main database for Jewish families *(JG)*.

Romania database include Bessarabia database too

The JewishGen Romania Database

2,992 total matches found

You can see different records for Jews from Kaushany.

(only records that refer to "Romania or Moldova")

Town (phonetically like) : KAUSHANY in Bessarabia Run on Fri, 05 Apr 2024 09:59:17 -0600	
Description	**Press the Button to view the matches**
JewishGen Family Tree of the Jewish People →	List 4 records
JewishGen ROMANIA	
1901 Klyachkin Business Directory →	List 21 records
JewishGen BESSARABIA / TRANSNISTRIA	
Bessarabia Birth Records →	List 665 records
Bessarabia Business Directory 1924 →	List 166 records
Bessarabia Death Records →	List 32 records
Bessarabia Duma Voters List →	List 300 records
Bessarabia Marriage and Divorce Records →	List 10 records
Bessarabia Revision Lists →	List 1,751 records
Jews Involved In Public Life In Bessarabia →	List 3 records
Russian Jewish Fallen Soldiers of WWI - Bessarabia →	List 7 records
Vsya Rossiya Business Directory for Bessarabia →	List 21 records
JewishGen RUSSIA	
Jewish Religious Personnel in the Russian Empire, 1853-1854 →	List 3 records
Vsia Rossiia 1895 Business Directory →	List 3 records
JewishGen JewishGen Holocaust Database	
Jews Killed in Dubossary, Moldova / Transnistria →	List 1 record
JewishGen JewishGen Online Worldwide Burial Registry	
JewishGen Online Worldwide Burial Registry - Bessarabia →	List 5 records

Birth records

Marriage records Revision lists

Burial records for people who were from Kaushany

125

2. Romanian Business directory for 1924-25 *(B24)*. Original pages of the directory are available in Romanian at the Library of Congress:http://lcweb2.loc.gov/ - FIND LINK! .

3. Memorial of fallen in the Great Patriotic War (1941-45), original site: http://www.obd-memorial.ru *(Mem)*.

4. Victims Of Political Terror in the USSR, https://base.memo.ru *(VT)*.

5. Jews refugees to Middle Asia in 1941 (Tashkent, other towns in Uzbekistan, Kazakhstan in 1941 *(J-R)*.

6. Video Testimonies of HOLOCAUST SURVIVORS, University of Southern California Shoah Foundation Institute *(Video)* *https://vha.usc.edu/home* :
   Basia Spiegel (Leibovich),
   Olga Wainberg (Berdichevskiy, Leibovich),
   Marcus Leibowitz,
   Marim Lewin,
   Lev Bruter,
   Ravail Tabachnik,
   please find all videos on Kaushany KehilaLinks website:
   https://kehilalinks.jewishgen.org/Causeni/Kaushany.htm

7. Yad Vashem *(YdV)*.

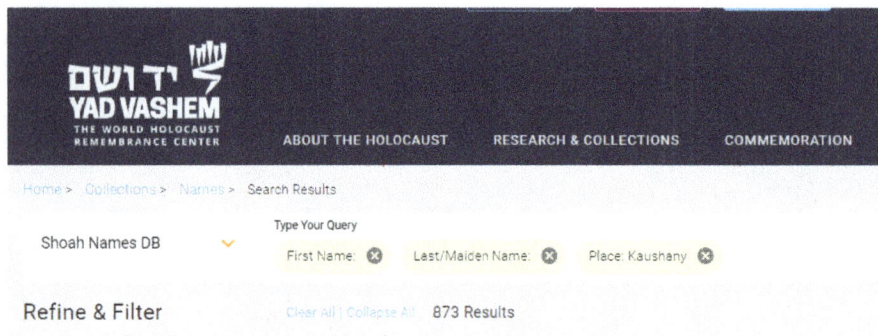

Among **873** people in that collection, you can find Jews who fought in the war in different regions: Stalingrad, Sevastopol and more. Also, there people who were evacuated to the East of the USSR, many of them died from bombardment, starvation, etc.

8. Memoirs of a Kaushany resident **Khinka Kogan (Spivak)** *(KhK)*.

9. Memoirs from **Nona Shpolyanskaya-Geisman** and her mother **Asya Geisman (Imas)** *(G)*.

10. Memoirs from **Raya Rozenkrants (Goldshtein)** *(RR)*.

11. Memoirs from **Tsilya Dunaevskaya** *(TsD)*.

How to use the following Family list?

All families in the list are in alphabetical order by surnames.

There might be many families with the same surname, in this list they divided by a space line. Find comments about a person or a family written by Kaushany residence.

In some families we do not know a person's name, "__?" is written instead.

Please see an example of two families with surname **Kuperman** with comments below.

Kuperman.
      Abram (1-Jan-1897, Kaushany -), Merchant of 3rd gild, father – **Pinkhas,**
        wife **Dora** (Bendery – 1941, died under bombardment near Stalingrad),
          daughter **Sara** (1923, Kaushany -), "it was my classmate in Kaushany gymnasium in
                1930s " *(KhK),*
           husband **Moisei Kogut** (1920, Bendery – 1942, fought in the war and was MIA),
              see **Kogut** family,
          son **Aron** (2-Feb-1925, Kaushany – 7-Sep-1999, Tel Aviv, Israel), graduated from
              Kishinev University, worked as Engineer,
           wife **Khona Lev** (Kishinev -),
          son __? (1930s, Kaushany – died young).

      Leib (1899 -),
        daughter **Rakhel** (1919, Kaushany – 1941, Transnistria), not married, died on the way
          to Transnistria camp.

Here are two families with head of households **Abram** and **Leib**.
Abram's estate was Merchant of 3rd gild. Also known his father's name – **Pinkhas**.
Dora, **Abram**'s wife was born in Bendery, there is no year of birth, and she died under
      bombardment near Stalingrad. They had three children.
Sara, their daughter born in Kaushany in 1923, and there is a comment from **Khinka**
      Kogan who wrote that **Sara** was her classmate.
Moisei married **Sara**, and his surname was **Kogut**. **Sara** would also be **Kogut** after marriage.
Aron son of **Abram** and **Dora** has a full date of birth, and full date of death, he was an Engineer.
Aron married **Khona**, her maiden name was **Lev**.
The third son of **Abram** and **Dora** is without name, we do not know his name, but know that he was born
      in 1930s in Kaushany and that he died young.

Leib is written after a space line in a tree, likely **Leib** and **Abram** are not related or their
      relationship was not found.
Rakhel, **Leib**'s daughter was born in Kaushany and died on a way to Transnistria death camp.

There are **tabs** and **spaces** used to show brothers/sisters from same parents, like **Sara, Aron** and __?
above.

Spelling of Surnames and Names. Surnames and Names might be spelled many ways.
Example Rachel, Rakhel, Rukhel, Rochel or Feiga, Feyga, Feige. I tried to use spelling close to
how it was written in Russian, or how people pronounced it. Not sure if I always succeeded.

Jewish Families with people born in Kaushany or lived in Kaushany in 19-20 centuries.

Abramov.

> **Isaak** (14-Oct-1910, Kaushany -). Lived in Balashov, Russia, and in 1938 was arrested by NKVD for espionage. In 1940 got 5 years in prison *(VT)*.

Abramovich.

> **Shmul,** Merchant of 2nd Gild, father – **Shloime,**
>> wife **Beila,** manufacturer, Merchant of 3rd Gild. Father – **Shimon,**
>>> son **Daniil** (3-Jun-1866, Kaushany -),
>>> son **Moshko (Moyshe-Ios)** owned a fabric shop *(B24)*, was in Middle Class registered in Tiraspol,
>>>> wife **Frima,**
>>>>> son **Shoil** served in the Soviet Army, was MIA since 1941 *(Mem),*
>>>>>> wife **Ester Milishchenskaya,** father – **Michail,**
>>>>> daughter **Dvoira** (26-Mar-1897, Kaushany -),
>>>>> son **Samuil** (5-Jun-1899, Kaushany -).

> **Isaac** fought in the war, was MIA since 1942 *(Mem),*
>> wife **Reyzya,** father – **Abram.**

Arhimovici (Arhimovich).

> **Psakhi (Peisakh, Pinkhas)** (– died during evacuation in Krasnaya Gorka, Bashkiria), had a very distinctive white beard. He owned a tavern,
>> wife **Dvoira,**
>>> daughter **Sara** (1898 – 1978, Kishinev),
>>>> husband **Abram Lerner** (1896, Kaushany – 1941-42), owned a bakery, had a large hall in the yard, which was rented to an organization "Makkabi", see **Lerner** family,
>>> son **Gerts,** before the war moved to Galatz,
>>> son **Aba** (7-Sep-1901, Kaushany – 4-Aug-1990, Belgium), left Kaushany, when he was 20 to France or Belgium to get education. During the war he was in Belgium Resistance movement and in 1944 was captured as a Jew, not as partisan. Deported to Buchenwald, after 8 months he was liberated by Americans in 1945. After the war got Belgium citizenship, worked in a bank,
>>> daughter **Hava (Kheyva),** participated in communist movement in Romania, jailed by sigurantsa – Romania secret police. Before the war, she was a young communist and was sent to Akkerman to study. When Nazi invaded, she volunteered to stay to organize underground resistance, was captured and executed.

Arnold.

> **__?** "I remember a doctor with this surname. He was also an owner of many houses and shops on the main street" *(KhK)*.

Averbukh.

> **Yankel,**
>> son **Moshe** (1889 -), "I remember **Moyshe,** a great joker" *(KhK)*, owned a fabric shop *(B24)*,

wife **Estra** (1884 -), father – **Iosif,**
    son **Gersh** (1917, Kaushany -),
    son **Iosif** (1926, Kaushany -),
  son **Shulim** (1898, Kaushany - 1942), trader, **Shulim** fought in the war, was MIA
                since 1942 *(Mem, YdV),*
    wife **Golda Opachevskiy**, father – **Ruvin,**
    son **Mikhail.**

Leiba, sold fodder *(B24).*

Gersh had a shoe store and was a tanner *(B24).* "He was a father-in-law of my friend
        Sema Sirkis. Died in Israel" *(KhK).*

Noah and **Anchel** owned a tavern-saloon *(B24).*

Shmuel (Shmil),
  son **Srul,** was in Middle Class, registered in Kishinev,
    wife **Inda (Hinda)** ,
    daughter **Elka** (4-Jan-1915, Kaushany -),
  son **Yosef,**
    wife **Maryas,**
      daughter **Khaya** (26-Nov-1915, Kaushany -), from twin,
      daughter **Liba** (26-Nov-1915, Kaushany -), from twin.

Shloime,
  wife **Riva (Rivka),**
    son **Zalman** (1904, Dubossary –1941-42, murdered, died in Shoah *(YdV).* Lived in
      Kaushany before the war.

Feliks, lives now in Haifa, but claims that he was born in Kaushany. (*G and*
    Rozetta Kupershlak, who was from Kaushany).

Bakal.
    Isaak owned a water mill *(B24).*

    Sukher (Yisokhor), was in Middle Class, registred in Akkerman,
      wife **Rukhlya (Rakhel),**
        daughter **Sura-Malka** (23-Apr-1876, Kaushany -),
        daughter **Elka** (9-Sep-1878, Kaushany -).

Baranov.
    Iosif was a barber *(B24).*

Barash.
    Iosif (Bessarabka, Moldova).
      wife **Sima Kuchuk** (1958, Kaushany), married in 1977, lived in Kaushany,
        daughter **Inna** (1978, Kaushany),
          husband **Ziv Rakhamimov**, children **Ben, Tal, Noy** and **Bar,**
        daughter **Elya-Elvira** (1982, Kaushany),
          husband **Artel Dadon**, daughters **Lii and Lipaz**, sons **Liam and Lipan,**
        son **Eduard** (1988, Kaushany),

wife **Karin**, married in September of 2014, children **Ori, Oshri and Toar.**

Barber.
>**Mendel,**
>>wife **Ida,**
>>>daughter **Roza** (1905, Kaushany -), bookkeeper,
>>>son **Nakhman (Nashka)** (1909 or 1911 – 1942, Sevastopol),
>>>>daughter **Sonya**, seamstress,
>>>>>"I remember **Nakhman Mendelevich**. Family had a small pharmacy store. He was also a nurse and people called him to do a massage, injections, etc. **Nakhman** fought and died during defense of Sevastopol *(Mem)*. Mother - **I.C.**, daughter **Sonya** was a seamstress. She sewed many cloths for me and my mother" *(KhK).*

Barenboym.
>**Semen,**
>>wife **Anya Koen** (Kaushany -), one of five **Koen** sisters. In 2018 lived in Rishon LeTsiyon,
>>daughter **Galya,**
>>son **Alik.**

Barg.
>**Efim** (- 1990s, Kishinev), was an accountant in the regional finance department.
>>Father – **Bogdan,**
>>wife **Bronya** (-2020, Germany), doctor infectionist in Kaushany Regional Hospital.
>>>Father - **David.** Family came to Kaushany in the beginning of 1960s,
>>son **Arkadiy (Alik)** (1955 -), engineer, businessmen, lives in Moldova,
>>daughter **Olga Oleynik** (1958 -), lives in Germany with family,

*Barg family moved to Kishinev in the beginning of 1970s. **Bronya** moved to her daughter to Germany. "Family was close friends of my parents, and I studied with **Arkadiy** in the same class (G).*

Bargolovskiy.
>**__?**,
>>wife **Ester Spivak.** (25-Apr-1901- 1989, Israel), was married, and soon divorced. Lived in Kaushany whole life (except during the war). She did not have children, was a housewife. She did not speak well Russian. Mostly spoke Yiddish. She lived with her younger sister – **Soybel Spivak** (see **Spivak**).

Batsian.
>**Shmil.** "owned a bakery; I remember they baked nice bagels *(KhK)*. Owned an inn *(B24)*,
>>son **Iosif.** "He was a great singer, a khazan in a synagogue" *(KhK).*

>**Moyshe** (1925 -), served in the Soviet Army during the war *(Mem).*

Beitenbroyt (Beytenbrant).
>**Zis,** private in WWI, missing from December 1914.

>**Moyshe (Moshe),** was in Middle Class, reg. in Trostyanets, father – **Gershko (Tzvi),**
>>wife **Makhlya,**
>>>son **Israel** (1892, Kaushany – 1942, bombardment near Stalingrad), craftsman,
>>>>wife **Brana**, cooper,

son **Tsvi (Gersh)** (1924, Kaushany - 1942, bombardment near Stalingrad) *(YdV)*,
son **Avrum (Abram)** (1895, Kaushany – 1945, MIA), trader,
  wife **Sima Averbukh,**
    daughter **Idl** (1928, Kaushany – 1945, MIA), shoemaker,
    son **Mikhael,** survived the war,
son **Pinya** (1910, Kaushany – 1944, served in Soviet army and killed), baker, not married *(YdV),*
daughter **Ester Leya** (1904, Kaushany – 1941, during evacuation),
  husband **Leyzer Spektor**. Relocated to Kishinev before the war. Died during evacuation *(YdV).*

Benderskiy.
Sima (1909), her father - **David** *(YdV)*. Lived in Kaushany before the war.

Berinskiy.
Samuel cloth cutter,
  son **Lev** (1939, Kaushany -), poet, translator, lives in Israel. See more at
    https://biographs.org/lev-berinsky ,
  son **Sergey** (1946, Kaushany – 1998, Moscow) – Russian, Moldavian composer.
    See more at https://www.last.fm/music/Sergey+Berinsky/+wiki.

Berkovich.
Shmil owned a grocery store *(B24)*.

Bershadskiy.
Brakha (1879 – 1941, Odessa, murdered in Shoa), widow, parents **Moyshe** and **Shifra,**
  husband **Ekhezkil (Dov) Chulak** (died before the war), see **Chulak** family.

Bersudskiy.
Leib (Laibesh). "I remember **Leib**, was a partner in a mill and the family was rich.
                They lived on a "Bud gos" - Bath Street *(KhK),*
  son **Khaim,**
  son **Moyshe (Moisey)** (1917 -), served in the military and was MIA,
  son **Shuya (Shulim)** conscripted to work in a coal mine in 1940 and was killed by a
                wagon,
  daughter **Rosa,**
    daughter **Sonya,**
  daughter **Golda,** "got married for a good men **Abram Trakhtenberg.** She died in 60s"
    (KhK),
    husband **Abram Trakhtenberg,** see **Trakhtenberg** family.

Blank.
Itsik,
  son **Aron** (- 1941, killed in Kaushany, murdered together with wife and two children,
    son and daughter).

Yankel,
  wife **Sosi,**
    daughter **Sura-Feiga** (24-Sep-1878, Kaushany -),
    son **Isaf** (1902, Kaushany -).

Iosif,
> wife **Tsilya**. Arrived to Kaushany from Talmaz. After Kaushany lived in Bendery,
> daughter **Sarra,**
> son **Yakov.**

Blank-Garbo.
> **Sholom (Shulem, Shlema)** (1865, Kaushany – 1941, killed in Kaushany), melamed-
> teacher, killed by locals in school,
> wife **Paya** (1869, Kaushany – 1941, died in evacuation) *(YdV),*
> daughter **Tzilya** (1907 -),
> son **Israel** (1908, Kaushany – 1942, Kazakhstan), salesperson, single. Was in Labor
> army where died.

Blitshtein (Blidshtein).
> **Peisakh,**
> wife **Dvoira,**
> daughter **Rukhlya (Rakhel)** (3-Dec-1878, Kaushany -),
> son **Moyshe** (8-Jan-1887, Kaushany – murdered near Odessa), owned a fabric store
> *(B24),* "later in 30s the store did not exist and he worked in a same place as my
> father **Lyova. Moyshe** traveled to markets with fabric to Monzyr, Volontirovka.
> Everyone in the family was killed in Odessa *(KhK),*
> wife **Ena Bruter** (1895, Kaushany – 1941, murdered near Odessa), parents **Shmuel**
> and **Khaika,** sister of **Naum Bruter,**
> daughter **Ada (Udel, Odel)** (1925, Kaushany - murdered near Odessa), studied in
> gymnasium before the war,
> daughter **Ita** (1920, Kaushany – murdered near Odessa),
> daughter **Blyuma** (1928, Kaushany – murdered near Odessa),
> son **Abram** (1895, Kaushany – 1973, Kishinev), Merchant,
> wife **Etel Abramovich** (1900, Kaushany – 1965, Kaushany), parents **Sheyl** and
> **Sura,**
> daughter **Bella (Belka)** (15-Sep-1922, Kaushany -), teacher. **Belka** "studied in
> the class with your father" *(KhK),*
> husband **Boris Dvoirin,** see **Dvoirin** family.
> son **Peisa (Petya),** "my very good friend, surved in the army, the only one
> survived from the whole family. Peisa returned from the war limping" *(KhK).*

> **Borukh,** *(likely this family related to one above)*
> wife **Liza,**
> son **Peisakh** (1909, Kaushany – 1941, murdered in Shoa) *(YdV).*

Bolyasnyy.
> **__? ,**
> wife **__?** (- Kaushany), teacher,
> daughter **Nonna** (1954 -),
> daughter **__? ,**
> *Father with daughters emigrated to Israel. Lived in Beer-Sheva. I studied with **Nonna** in*
> *Musical school (G).*

Boyanovskiy.
> **Semen (Simon)** shoemaker, cobbler *(B24).*

Braverman.

>> **Vladimir (Volf)** (1911, Bendery – Caucasus, MIA), bookkeeper, father – **Iosif,**
>>> wife **Raisa (Rashel) Buksdorf** (1911, Kaushany - Jan-1977, Kagul), parents **Abram**
>>>> and **Feiga,**
>>>>> daughter **Fanya Bondar** (28-Oct-1935, Kaushany -).

Briker.

>> **Moyshe** (1901, Kaushany -), fought in the war, was private *(Mem)*. Father – **Shmul.**

Bril.

>> **Khaim** owned a tavern, inn. *(B24).*

Brodskiy (Brotskiy).

>> **Itskhak,**
>>> wife **Polya,**
>>>> daughter **Sara** (1921, Kaushany – 1942, Damanevka, Odessa), lived in Kaushany
>>>>> before the war, "was under Germans together with my good friend **Sara Gibrikh.** I was
>>>>> told that **Sara B.** was alive after the war but got typhys and died from it" *(KhK).* By
>>>>> *(YdV)* died in Shoah in 1942 at the Domanevka camp, Ukraine,

>> **Ziska (Ziske)** (1890, Baymakliya – 1941, Nikolaev), father - **Abram ,**
>>> wife **Enta** (1897, Bendery - 1941, Nikolaev) lived in Kaushany before the war
>>>> son **Meyer** (1915, Kaushany - 1941, Nikolaev) ,
>>>>> wife **Fanya (Feiga) Lyubarov** (12-Feb-1909, Bendery - 1941, Nikolaev), parents
>>>>>> **Lavi** and **Gitel,**
>>>>> son **Leivi** (1940, Kaushany – 1941, Nikolaev),
>>>> daughter **Sara** (1920, Kaushany died in Nikolaev in Shoah *(YdV),*
>>>>> **Ziska, Enta, Meyer, Fanya, Leyvi, Sara** died in Nikolaev in Shoah *(YdV).*

>> **Shloime** (– 1920),
>>> wife **Ekhevit Nakhovitsa** (1839-1939 or 40, she was 101 when died in Kaushany),
>>>> had 6 children,
>>> daughter **Sprintsa** (1879-1963) (Video),
>>>> husband **Iosif Leibovich.** (~1870, Kaushany – 1961, Bronx, NY). Emigrated to
>>>>> USA before the war. Had 3 sons and 2 daughters, see at **Iosif Leybovich**
>>>>> family,
>>> daughter **Roza,**
>>>> husband **Shloime Kogan,** children **Malia, Riva, Ana, Ita** and **Froike,**
>>> son **Itsil** died in Shoa,
>>>> wife **Neta Gaisinskiy,**
>>>>> son **Meyer,**
>>>>> daughter **Sarah.** **Itsil** and **Sarah** died in Shoah *(Video),*
>>> son **Ziska,**
>>>> wife **Rivka Kumerfeld,** children **Eser, Izya** lived in Paris, **Manya** and **Ita.**

>> **Shloime's** 4 siblings: **Itsik, Gedalia, Elek, Nehemiah.**

>> *Not sure if following families are related to above*

David,
>> wife **Rivka Klaymen** .

Ioske,
  wife **Adelin.**

Itskhak
  wife **Fanya.**

Ita,
  husband **Ruven Ochakovskiy,**
    daughter **Manya.**

Bronfman.
  Shloime,
    wife **Khaya-Sura,**
      son **Pinkhas** (11-May-1878, Kaushany -), *(YdV),*
      son **Abram** hat master *(B24)*, was *in* Middle Class, registered in Kishinev,
        wife **Genya-Brana**   ,
          son **Moisey** (18-Feb-1897, Kaushany -),
          daughter **Rivka** (2-Feb-1899, Kaushany -),
          daughter **Leya (Liya)** (3-Jul-1903, Kaushany - died in Shoah *(YdV)*,
            husband **Goldman**, lived in Tatarbunary before the war,
          son **Fishel** (1903, Kaushany -),
          daughter **Ida** (1910, Kaushany -), *(YdV)*, **Fishel** and Ida were together during
            evacuation.

Not clear how Itsik and Gersh are related to the family above.
Itsik owned a fabric store *(B24)*.

Gersh pharmacist *(B24)*.

Bronshteyn.
  Itsko, Middle Class, reg. in Bendery, was on 1890 Bendery Voter's list.

Brunser (Bronsher, Brunsher).
  Nekhemya-Gersh, father – **Iosko**, lived in Kaushany,
    wife **Pesya,**
      son **Meyer** – men's taylor *(B24)*, Middle Class, registered in Kishinev,
        wife **Genya**, father – **Srul,**
      daughter **Liya** (6-Jul-1897, Kaushany -),
      son **Itskhok** (19-Sep-1903, Kaushany -).

  Yakov – Leib (- died near Odessa), lived in Kaushany before the war,
    wife **Ester, 5** children,
      daughter **Yakhad** (1919, Kaushany or Petrovka – 1941, murdered in Shoa near
            Odessa), lived in Kaushany before the war,
      son **Kheml** (1915, Kaushany or Petrovka – 1941, was in the military, died in East
            Prussia).

Bruter.
        Five brothers born from 1872 to 1895.
  Daniel -David (1856, -), was in Middle Class, registered in Rashkov,
    wife **Yenta (Yentali)**

134

son **Shmil (Shmuel)** (4-Aug-1872, Mogilev-Podolskiy – 1941, killed in Kaushany)
owned confectionary store. Killed by locals in Kaushany,
  wife **Khaya,**
    daughter **Ena (Enta)** (1901 – 1941, Odessa), *(YdV),*
    husband **Moyshe Blitshteyn** (see **Blitshteyn** family),
    daughter **Feiga** (6-Mar-1903, Kaushany – Sep-1941,Transnistria, murdered),
    husband **Moyshe Katsap**, died in Transnistria in 1941*(YdV),*
    son **Naum** (1898, Kaushany – 1942, camp Karlovka, Transnistria,died in Shoah)
owned a grocery store, merchant *(YdV),*
      wife **Riva Abramovich** (Chimishliya – 30-Apr-1945, Odessa),
        daughter **Etl (Etya)** (1921, Kaushany - 1987),
        daughter **Udl (Ada) Getsenshtein** (1925, Kaushany -),
        son **Lyova** (July 16, 1923, Kaushany -). "**Lyova** is my very good friend. He
lives in Israel" (*KhK, Video),* was under occupation, in 1944 was in the
military, fought in the war, demobilized as lieutenant of medical
services.
        wife **Tatiana**
    son **Motl (Mordekhay)** (24-Jan-1903, Kaushany - 1975) owned a grocery store.
He sold sugar, bread and sunflower seeds,
    son **Ilya,**
    daughter **Rakhel** (20-Jun-1910, Kaushany – 25-Sep-1941, murdered in Shoa),
seemstress,
    husband **Shimon Yanovich** (1941, Orgeev -),
    daughter **Sara** (Kaushany - 1987, Kishinev),
  wife **Khana** (second wife of **Daniel-David**),
  son **Natan (Nuta)** (21-Aug-1874 – 1941), owned a fabric store,
    wife **Maliya (Manya) Spekterman** (15-Mar-1889, Pavlovka – 1941) Both died
in Shoah *(YdV).* Before the war they lived in Kaushany, had 6 sons,
    son **Israel (Srulik)** (15-Sep-1922, Kaushany – 1941, Odessa), "my very good
friend, died in Odessa in 1941 *(KhK, YdV), he* was a student, single" *(KhK),*
    son **David** (1-Nov-1909, Kaushany – 16-Nov-1977, Nice, France), emigrated
to France before the war,
      wife **Matilda**, children **Adin** (Montreal) and **Jan** (Nice),
    son **Abraham (Abram)** (21-Apr-1911, Kaushany – 1941, murdered) *(YdV),*
      wife **Chernya (Yelena)** (1911 -), father -**Yuliy**, daughter **Sima,**
    son **Monya (Moyshe)** (23-May-1914, Kaushany – 1999),
      wife **Manya,**
        sons **Arkadiy** and **Anatoliy** "who was involved in an underground left
activities in 1930s together with my uncle **Boris Spivak**"(*KhK),*
    son **Mendel** (27-Oct-1915, Kaushany – 1941, Transnistria), worked as a
cashier, died in Transnistria in 1941 *(YdV),*
      daughter **Shoshana (Sima),**
    son **Mikhel (Mikhail)** (24-Apr-1917, Kaushany – 1991, Kishinev),
    son **Isaak**
  son **Pinkhus (Pinya, Pinkhus-Zelig, Petya)** (25-Nov-1876, Kaushany - 1941)
merchant**,** owned a fabric store, winery, houses. Died in GULAG,
    wife **Khona (Khana-Leya) Kogan** (11-Oct-1880, Kaushany -), was deported
to Siberia for Anti-Soviet Activities *(JG).* 3 sons and 2 daughters,
    son **Ovshey (Shuka)** (2-Jan-1904, Kaushany - Australia), doctor,
      wife **Roza Gershkovich**, lived in Soroki, divorced, son **Sasha** (1930?),
      wife (second) **Sofiya** from Poland. Twins **Anya** and **Richard** 1946,

daughter **Sura (Sara)** (10-Mar-1905, Kaushany – 2000, Kiriat-Gat, Israel),
husband **Aleksander Vaynshteyn** (- 1988, Kotovsk, Moldova), doctor,
son **Boris** (13-May-1909, Kaushany – 23-Aug-1989, Compiegne, France),
went to study to Strassburg, France in 1930,
wife **Valentina Temel** (14-Nov-1914, Paris – 14-May-2005, Compoegne),
son **Claude** (4-Jul-1937, Paris), daughter **Anna** (1947,Rodez, Fr.),
son **Daniel (David)** (19-Jul-1914, Kaushany - Kirijat-Yam, Israel), fought in
the war, demobilized as lieutenant.
wife **Musya**, son **Petya,**
daughter **Enna** (3-Aug-1916, Kaushany -),
husband **Zelik Kogan** (Kalarash - 1942 killed on the front of the war). After
husband **Leonid (Iona) Shamis**, doctor. Lived in Barder, Moldova, went to
Israel, where died in 2009,
son **Naftulya (Tule)** (14-Oct-1884 -), according to *B24* owned a fabric store,
wife **Sarra** (5-Jun-1885 -),
daughter **Klara** (28-Apr-1913 -), studied for a doctor in Belgium,
daughter **Dobrish (Dolya)** (9-Apr-1915, Kaushany - 2006), from twins,
husband **Lev Garshtein** (see family **Garshtein),**
daughter **Ester (Fira)** (9-Apr-1915, Kaushany -), from twins, married for
Moldovan and worked in the shoe factory died in Stalin GULAG,
son **Daniel (David)** (12-Aug-1918 - Kishinev) "Was tall, handsome guy,
named **Dudele,**
daughter **Enna (Genya)**, died young from tuberculosis,
daughter "**Golda (Koka)** (1-Feb-1922, Kaushany -), studied with me in the
same class in gymnasium. Lived after the war in Kishinev" *(KhK),*
son **Nukhim** owned a grocery store *(B24),*
wife **Rivka,** daughter **Etel.**

Buksdorf.
    Abram
     wife **Feiga,**
      daughter Raisa (Rashel) (1911, Kaushany - Jan-1977, Kagul),
       husband **Vladimir (Volf) Braverman** (1911, Bendery – Caucasus, MIA), see **Braverman**
       family.

Bushel.
    Leyzel owned a bakery *(B24).*

Chapkis.
    Noikh, father **Gershko,**
     wife **Etlya,**
      son **Avigdor** (6-May-1899, Kaushany -),
      daughter **Freida** (9-Aug-1903, Kaushany -), *(JG).*

    Shmil, fought in the war and was MIA since 1944 *(Mem),* father - **Naum**

    Elkun, confectionery *(B24).*

Chernyavskiy.
    _?__ was a journalist of local newspaper,
     wife **Evgenia Yakovleva,** father – **Yakov,** was Math teacher in Russian school and my

classroom teacher *(G)*,
daughter **Nelli Chernyavskaya (Yakovleva)** (1951, Kaushany -),
son **Michail Yakovlev** (1953, Kaushany -). Live now in Natania, Israel.

Chiovechi.
Nakhman – fishermen.

Shmil owned a grocery store *(B24)*.

Chobrutskiy.
Aron, father – **Itsko,**
wife **Ita,**
daughter **Khaya** (28-Jul-1915, Kaushany -).

Usher (15-Oct-1929 – 22-Jan-1972, Bendery), father **Nusim,**
wife **Sonya Kuchuk (- ,**Migdal-ha-Emek, Israel). Came to Kaushany from Romanovka
(Bessarabka) in the beginning of 1950s. **Usher** worked in trade. **Sonya** was a housewife,
son **Milik** (1951, Kaushany -),
daughter **Ella** from twin (1955, Kaushany -),
daughter **Fira** from twin (1955, Kaushany -).
*Family moved to Bendery, **Sonya** with children emigrated to Israel. **Milik** with sisters*
*live in Migdal-ha-Emek, **Sonya** died and buried there (G).*

Naum
wife **Sarra.** Arrived to Kaushany from Romanovka (Bessarabka). *They lived in*
*Kaushany for short time. **Naum** worked in procurement office. Moved to*
Bendery and emigrated to Israel (G).

Boris (1928), father – **Grigoriy.** Lived in Kaushany from 1945 with his mother – widow.
Mother died of older years in Kaushany. Before the war lived in Lambrovka, not
far of Kaushany,
wife **Fanya** (- Kaushany), who was an accountant,
son – **Grisha** (1961).
***Boris** with children emigrated to Israel, lived in Ashdod (G).*

Chulak (Chiolac).
Abram owned a confectionary *(B24)*.

Ehezkil-Dov (died before the war),
wife widow - **Brakha Bershadskiy** (1879 – 1941, Odessa, murdered in Shoa),), father
Moshe, mother - **Shifra,**
son **Moyshe (Moshe)** (14-Sep-1902, Kaushany -),
daughter **Enya (Henia)** (1906, Kaushany – 1941, murdered in Odessa),
son **Asher**, lived in Israel.

Aron (1894, Kaushany – 1944, died in Shoa), parents **Iosif** and **Feiga, Aron** owned a
milk farm. Lived before the war in Galatz, Romania, both died in Shoah in 1944
(YdV),
wife **Feiga Itskovich** (1896, Kaushany – 1944, murdered in Shoa). Parents **Nakhum**
and **Fania.**

Shloime. Worked in trade, selling fabric. Worked together with **Isak Kuchuk** *(G)*.

Darakhov (Dorakhov).

> **Naum,** after the war lived in Kaushany and was mathematics teacher in Moldovan School. Father – **David,**
>> daughter **Anna** (Kaushany -), graduated from Kishinev University, after marriage lived in Uzbekistan,
>> son __? died young *(G).*

Diminshteyn (Dimenshteyn).

> **Benyamin** owned a bakery *(B24).*

> **Meir,** was in Middle Class, registered in Kishinev, father – **Leib,**
> wife **Tsipa,**
>> son **Leib** (3-Aug-1899, Kaushany -).

Dubosarskiy (Dubossarskiy).

> **Ovshey-Ber (Yekhoshua-Dov),** was a glassier *(B24),* china-shop owner, was Middle Class, reg. in Tiraspol, father – **Yankel,**
> wife **Dvosya,** father – **Lusor,**
>> daughter **Basya** (11-Dec-1897, Kaushany -),
>> son **Moyshe** (1889, Kaushany –25-Mar-1953, Bendery), was in Middle Class, registered in Tiraspol. He inherited his father's china-shop,
>>> wife **Pesse-Ida (Idos) Rabinovich** (Romanovka - Ivano-Frankovsk), during the war was in Eastern Kazakhstan with their daughters who worked in the tin mines there, after the war returned to Bendery. After **Moyshe**'s death, **Pesse-Ida** moved to her daughter **Rukhl** to Ivano-Frankovsk,
>>> son **Semen (Shimon)** (5-Jun-1914, Romanovka – 2-Apr-1989, Bendery), lived in Kaushany, during WWII with his wife and daughter were evacuated to Frunzenskiy district, Stalingrad region. On front since 1942 or 1944. He was a private artillery battery driver, awarded a Medal of Bravery. After the war lived in Bendery,
>>>> wife **Anna (Khana) Rozenfeld** (1916, Romanovka -), parents **Reveka** and **Boris**, **Semen** and **Anna** married on 29-Jul-1939,
>>>> daughter **Tatiana** (1941, Kaushany – died during evacuation),
>>>> son **Boris** (3-Feb-1947, Bendery – 1-Nov-2017, Kishinev), Composer, violinist, professor, Maestru în arte of Moldova (born after WWII in Bendery, but the only famous person in the family),
>>> daughter **Leah (Lana)** (26-Aug-1918, Kaushany – 23-May-2005, Beer-Sheva), after the war lived in Bendery, emigrated to Israel in 1991,
>>> daughter **Rukhl (Raya)** (17-Jul-1923–26-Feb-2008), after the war married, and lived in Ivano-Frankovsk, and emigrated to Israel in 1988,
>> son **Yankel** (Kaushany - was private of 135 Kerch-Enikal regiment, perished (abandoned on the battlefield) at Seret river August 1, 1916 (WWI),
>> daughter **Miriam** (6-Apr-1900, Kaushany – 23-Dec-1983, Bendery), after the war lived in Bendery,
>>> husband **Samuil Soyfer** (do not know where he is from and whether he lived in Kaushany),
>>> daughter **Fira Soyfer** (1927, Kaushany – 28-Dec-1950, Bendery),
>> son **Lusor (Eliezer)** (12-Aug-1902, Kaushany -), *(JG),*
>> daughter **Liba (Ljuba),** after the war lived in Kishinev.

"**Moyshe** owned a china-shop, had two daughters **Lana** and **Raya**. **Raya** was my friend, married and lived in Ivano-Frankovsk, after that in Beer-Sheva, where she got sick and died in a nursing home. I often spoke with her on the phone" *(KhK)*. *Information from JG records, and Julia Maksimova.*

Dvoirin.

"I remember five sons, but do not remember the names of the parents. The youngest son **Aronchik**, the husband of my dear friend **Roza**, also sons **Tsoka, Moyshe, Iosif,** and one more, who moved to France. Their father was a merchant, and the family was not rich, but not poor too" *(KhK)*.

Matvey (Mark). Merchant. Lived in Kaushany before the war,
    son **Moisey** (6-Jan-1906, Kaushany – 17-Jun-1977, Bendery**),**
    son **Aron (Aronchik)** (14-Jul-1914, Kaushany – 28-Jan-1981, Kishinev),
    son **Tsalik (Tsoka),**
    son **Iosif,**
        wife **Golda,**
            son **Boris** (1-Apr-1921 -),
                wife **Bella (Belka) Blitshtein** (15-Sep-1922, Kaushany -), teacher. **Belka**
                    "studied in the class with your father" *(KhK)*,
    son __?, emigrated to France before the war. *Information from JG and YdV.*

Leibl,
    wife **Beila,**
        daughter **Risl** (1878, Kaushany – 1941, Bolgrad, Bessarabia-murdered),
            husband **Khaim Ochakovskiy**. See **Ochakovskiy** family.

Yankel (1863 -), owned a grocery store and apothecary trivia store on the main street in
                Kaushany *(B24),* father – **Iosif,**
    wife **Maria** (1868 -), lived before the war in Kaushany. Father – **Nukhim.**

Eizner.
    Girsh (Gershi),
        wife **Perel,**
            daughter **Rakhel,**
            daughter **Sonya** (1898, Chmishliya - 1941),
                husband **Sheivakh Lipkanskiy**. All lived before the war in Kaushany,
                    daughter **Tsilya** (1926, Kaushany-old - 1941),
                        Sonya and **Tsilya** died in Shoah *(YdV)*.

Elkis.
    __?, Moved to Kaushany at the end of 1950s. Was a great operating doctor
                Otolaryngologist,
    wife **Uliyana** doctor laboratory assistant. Had two daughters, do not remember
            their names. Moved to Kishinev, and later to Israel *(G)*.

Epelbaum.
    Khaya (Kaushany – 1941, died in Shoa in bombardment *(YdV),*
        husband **Iosif Slepoy** (14-Jan-1899 – 1-Jun-1974, Romanovka),
            see **Slepoy** family.

Epelman (Epilman).
    Aron owned a belt-lather shop *(B24)*.
    Yefim,
      wife **Khova,**
        son **Vladimir** (1913, Kaushany – 1944, killed on the front of the war),
          wife **Adelya.** *(YdV),*
        son __?,
          daughter **Sonya** (1934),
            husband **Toyve (Tolya) Opachevskiy.** See **Opachevsky** family *(G),*
          daughter **Tsilya Balyasnaya** (1938). Emigrated to Israel with her son *(G).*

    Vladimir (1902), father - **Ikhil** *(J-R).*

    Adela (1906), father - **Solomon** *(J-R).*

Erlikh.
    Anna owned an oil press business.

    Smul,
      son **Moshko** (1886 -), was a wine maker*(B24)*, and owned a bank – Jewish-Bessarabia,
        wife **Khaya-Leya** (1894 -), father – **Ayzik.**

    David, was a private and wounded in WWI in September of 1914. Father – **Iosif,**
      wife **Feiga,**
        son **Zelman** (1886, Kaushany – 1942, killed in Shoah, *YdV*), two children. Family
          relocated before the war to Tiraspol.

Erlikhman.
    Shlioma,
      wife **Sheina,**
        son **Duvid,** show maker *(B24),*
        son **Yosef (Yoska)** (15-Jul-1866, Kaushany -).

    Mekhel, shoemakers *(B24)*. It is possible that **Mekhel**'s father is **Shlioma.**

    Shamsa, shoemakers *(B24).*
    It is possible that Mekhel's and Shamsa's father is Shlioma.

Faerman (Faverman).
    Yankel,
      wife **Sose,**
        son **Shloma-Zelman,**
          wife **Perlya (Perel),**
            son **Moshka/Moshe** (- 29-Jun-1884, Kaushany),
            daughter **Ginda (Hindi)** (- 16-Jul-1884, Kaushany), both died from Diphtheritis,
            daughter **Pesya** (22-Mar-1887, Kaushany -),
            daughter **Khana** (31-Jan-1903, Kaushany -),
        daughter **Tovba** (6-Oct-1878, Kaushany -).

    Yakov (1900, Kaushany – 1942, killed in military service), was a baker,
      wife **Ester** (1900, Kaushany – 1943, murdered in Shoa).

G__, doctor, gynecologist. Lived in Kaushany after the war,
son **Yuriy** (1951, Kaushany), lived in Moscow *(G)*.

Borukh (- 1941, served in Soviet Army and killed) owned and run a restaurant,
wife **Feiga Fridman** (28-May-1888, Kaushany – 1941-42, died from bombardment
near Stalingrad), lived before the war in Bendery,
daughter **Zinaida.**

Feder.

Benyamin, was in Middle Class, registered in Kletsk, Minsk gubernia, innkeeper, tavern,
father – **Borukh,**
wife **Enta** (1882 -), father – **Mark (Mordko),**
son **Mikhel (Mikhael)** (19-Mar-1914, Kaushany – 1944, fought in the war, and was
MIA,
daughter **Beno** (1918 -),
son **Mendel** (1925, Kaushany -),
daughter **Indo (Inda)** (1926, Kaushany -),
daughter **Sheiva,**
daughter **Sheindl.**
"I remember how my grandfather sent me to buy a half a liter of wine for dinner. They had three
*daugthers: **Sheiva**, **Sheindl** and **Inda** and son **Mikhel**" (KhK).*

Fefer.

Simkha (1882, Kaushany - 1942, murdered in Shoa), blacksmith, parents **Iosl** and **Doba,**
wife **Khaika** (1885, Tiraspol - 1942, murdered in Shoa), parents **Sonya** and **Yoyna,**
family lived before the war in Kaushany. **Khaika** remained in Kaushany and she was
shot during column movement of Jews probably to Transnistria *(YdV)*,
son **Yoyna,** had two daughters, one – **Sonya.**
The family had a blacksmith shop in Zaim.

Feldman.

Sarra (1923 -), accountant, father - **Georgiy** *(YdV)*.

__?, doctor. "I know his son **Ozya** – my good friend at school." *(KhK)*.

Feigin.

Yankel, owned a fabric store and a lumber store *(B24)*,
son **Monya.**
"I remember well **Yankel**. I did not know them well, but with one of their sons –
Monya, in my age met recently in Kirijat-Motskin, Israel *(in 1990s, KhK)*.

Itsik, father – **Srul (Isroel)** was a blacksmith *(B24)*,
wife **Ester-Gitlya,**
son **Mendel** (5-Jan-1866, Kaushany -),
son **Usher** (1870, Kaushany – Aug-1941, killed in camp, Transnistria), served in the
synagogue,
wife **Enta- Leya** and four children. Before the war they lived in Tolmaz,
daughter **Ester** (3-Jan-1902, Kaushany -),
son **Zislya** (9-Aug-1876, Kaushany -),
daughter **Beilya** (9-Oct-1878, Kaushany -),

son **Favel** (19-Oct-1902, Kaushany -).

Fikhman.

     Samuil – chief Veterinary doctor of Kaushany region,

       wife **Sofa** (1939 -), nurse. Before the war she lived in Tiraspol,

         son **Senya**, graduated Kishinev Agriculture Institute,

         daugher **Diana**.

*Family emigrated to USA in the beginning of 1990s. **Samuil** died several years ago. **Sofa** lives in Los-Angeles (G).*

Finkel.

     Molka (1880, Kaushany – 1941, Tiraspol, killed in Shoa) *(YdV)*,

       husband **Mendel Pokhis**, lived before the war in Tiraspol,

Finkelshtein.

     Abram owned a water mill *(B24)*, father – **Semen**,

       wife **Rakhel,**

         son **Froim** (1901, Kaushany -), fought in the war, was private,

          wife **Anna**

         son **Simon (Shiman)** (1907, Kaushany -), lived before the war in Kaushany. Merchant, served in Soviet Army and was killed on the front,

          wife **Khaya-Leya (Khova) Lvov** (1909 -), parents – **Bendik** and **Yakhed,**

           son **Meyer** (1936 – 1942, killed in Shoah *(YdV)*,

         son **Aron** (1907 -),

          wife **Sura** (1909 -), father – **Moisey,**

           son **Sema** (1929 -),

           son **Markus** (1937 -).

     Khaim Nakhman (1888, Kaushany – 1942, murdered in Shoa), parents **Iekhil** and **Bila** *(YdV)*.

Fishman.

     Leyzer ben Shimon, was private in WWI and MIA since November 1914.

Flisfish.

     Yankel (Yankel-Shamshen), owned an Apothecary trivia store *(KhK)*, was a mohel,

       wife **Libe,**

         son **Berka-Zeev** (14-Feb-1876, Kaushany -),

          son **Benya (Beniamin),**

         daughter **Freida** (17-Sep-1878, Kaushany -),

         son **Srul (Yisroel)** (20-Nov-1887, Kaushany -).

     Zus (1895 -), father **Itsik,**

       wife **Ita** (1907 -),

         son **Shos** (1932 -), *(J-R)*.

Frank (Frenk).

     Shmul,

       wife **Ester,**

         daughter **Pesya** (08/06/1897, Kaushany -),

         son **Ber** (06/13/1899, Kaushany -),

daughter **Reyzlya (Reiyzi)** (12/19/1902, Kaushany -).

Zisya, father – **Itsko,**
  wife **Gitlya,**
    daughter **Basya** (16-Nov-1866, Kaushany -).

Yitzkhak,
  wife **Elka Garshtein** (1889, Kaushany – 1941, Odessa, killed in Shoa), parents
        Yitzkhak and **Molka,**
    daughter **Malka (Molka)** (Kaushany – Israel)

__?, "We had a doctor **Frank,** but I thought that he lived not far in another place –
        Monzyr. Other people with that surname I did not know" *(KhK).*

Frayman.
    David (1909 – 1941, fought in the War and was MIA since 1941), father – **Meir,**
    wife **Khaika** *(Mem).*

Fridman.
    Shulim, was a Merchant of Third Gild, grocer, his father – **Usher.**
      wife **Zisl (Zislya)** owned a tavern *(B24),*
        daughter **Feiga** (28-May-1888, Kaushany – 1941-42, died from bombardment
          near Stalingrad), lived before the war in Bendery,
          husband **Borukh Fayerman** (- 1941, served in Soviet Army and killed) owned and
            run a restaurant. See **Fayerman** family,
        son **Shloime** (25-Feb-1899, Kaushany -),
        daughter **Khaya** (24-Mar-1902, Kaushany -).

    Yakov,
      wife **Miriyam,**
        son **Kolman** (1885, Kaushany – 1941, died in Shoah *YdV),*
          wife **Ita Nukhimovich,**
            son **Yakov.**

    Gutman,
      son **Beniamin** (1906), tailor *(J-R).*

Fuks.
    Aron, father – **Zanvel,**
      wife **Khaya,**
        son **Yankel** (1-Feb-1866, Kaushany -),
        son **Tanya** (24-Mar-1876, Kaushany -),
        daughter **Malka** (24-May-1878, Kaushany -),
        son **Meir-Ber,**
          wife **Malka,**
            son **Khaim** (9-Dec-1887, Kaushany -), owned a grocery store,
            son **Borukh** (24-Apr-1899, Kaushany -), owned a confectionary store,
            daughter **Perlya** (8-Dec-1903, Kaushany -),
            daughter **Leya** (1886, Kaushany – died in Shoa) *(YdV),*
              husband **Abram Gofman,** they lived before the war in Bendery,
              daughter **Sabina Bunfeld.**

Gitlya owned an inn, tavern *(B24)*.

Srul was a man's tailor.

Furman.

> **Mikhail,** prior the war family lived in Kaushany, during the war were in Romanovka,
>> wife **Khana** (1895, Kaushany – murdered in Shoa, *YdV*), her parents **Abraham** and
>>> **Gita,**
>> daughter **Elena.**

Gaysinskiy.

> **Iosif,**
>> wife **Sura,** father – **Itsko,**
>>> son **Boris** (1918, Kaushany – fought in the war, private and was MIA, *Mem*).

Galperin.

> **Gersh (Hersh)** (Shargorod -),
>> wife **Brukha,**
>>> son **Leib** (1912 – 1941-42, murdered). Lived before and during the war in Kaushany. He was hung for partisan activity during the war *(YdV)*.

> **Sasha (Sander),**
>> wife **Vera Gitlina,** worked in commerce, had 2 daughters and a son. Emigrated to Israel, lived in Kirijat Gata.

Garshtein (Gorshtein, Gershtein).

> **Nukhim,** was in Middle Class, registered in Akkerman,
>> wife **Gitlya (Tovbe-Gitlya),**
>>> daughter **Ita-Basya** (13-Nov-1876, Kaushany -),
>>> son **Zelman (Shneer-Zalman)** (12-Feb-1887, Kaushany -), hold a tavern, inn *(B24)*,
>>> wife **Ita,**
>>>> daughter **Elka** (1889, Kaushany -),
>>>> husband **Itskhak Frank,**
>>>>> daughter **Molka** (- 1941),
>>>> son **David (Dudl)** (1915, Kaushany - Israel), metalworker,
>>>> son **Khaykel** (Kaushany - 1941, Odessa, murdered in Shoa), businessman, had a grocery store,
>>>>> wife **Elka** (1874, Kaushany – 1941, Odessa, killed from bombardment),
>>>>> son **Mendel (Monya)** (1908, Kaushany-1941, died from bombardment),
>>>>>> wife **Etl Vaysman** (Kaushany - 1941, near Astrakhan, Russia), tailor,
>>>>>>> daughter **Ida (Ita)** (5-Dec-1928, Kaushany – 2016, USA),
>>>>>>> husband **David Goreshter** (1929, Galatz -),
>>>>>>> daughter **Sarah (Sonya)** (10-Aug-1931, Kaushany - 2017, USA),
>>>>> son **Osher (Usher)** (1910, Kaushany- 1941, killed in bombardment),
>>>>> daughter **Freida Hait** (c1912, Kaushany – 25-Dec-1975, Kishinev).

Elka, Etl, Molka, Khaykel, Mendel, Osher died in Shoah near Astrakhan in 1941 (YdV).

> **Moyshe (Mikhail),**
>> son **Izrail** (1898 -), fought in the war from July 1942.
>> wife **Riva** (1906 -), father – **Iosif,**
>>> daughter **Shura** (1933 -),

daughter **Maria** (1913 -).

Aron,
  wife **Sheindl,** widow, sold wine, owned a tavern *(B24)*, father – **Mendel,**
    son **Monya (Mendel)** (1908, Kaushany – fought in the war, private, MIA *(YdV, Mem)*,
      wife **Gitl Kogan** (1905, Kaushany-1968, Kishinev),
        daughter **Lena** (1941, Kaushany -),
          husband **Tolya Kogan,** see **Kogan** family,
    daughter **Roza,** lived in Kishinev,
      husband **Iosl Royzman,**
        son **Aron,** worked in a restaurant in Kirijat-Motskin, Israel and was
          wounded from a terrorist act by an Arab" *(KhK)*.

"**Rukhl** studied with me in the same class of gymnasium, immigrated to America" *(KhK)*.

Sonya married to a Russian man (KhK).

Leva (c1924, Kaushany -),
  wife **Dobrish (Dolya) Bruter** (9-Apr-1915, Kaushany - 2006) from twins,
Leyka Vaysenberg (Leva's sister).

Geisman. "The family lived close to us *(KhK)*. **Ikhil** was a husband of **Ester-Malka Spivak,** daughter of uncle **Gersh,** brother of my grandfather **Shloime. Ikhil** owned a carriage with horses before the war and traveled with goods between townlets. During the war they evacuated to the East, and after the war returned to Kaushany. **Ester** was a housewife. She kept and continued Jewish tradition in the families. She died in 1978 and was buried in Bendery Jewish cemetery, because at this time Jewish cemetery in Kaushany fell to disrepair" *(KhK, G)*.

David,
  wife **Tuba,**
    son **Ikhil** (1895, Kaushany – 30-Jun-1967, Kaushany-reburied in Bendery in 1980s),
      wife **Ester-Malka Spivak** (1896, Kaushany – February 1978, Bendery),
        son **Usher** (28-May-1927, Stepanovka village, now Shtefaneshty – 26-10-2017, Raanana,
          Israel). Lived in Kaushany before moving to Israel in October of 1991,
         wife **Asya Imas** (7-Feb-1932, Bendery - 20-Dec-2023, Raanana, Israel). After
           graduating an Institute in 1951 came to work as History teacher to school of Old
           Kaushany. In 1954 got married. Emigrated to Israel in 1991 and lived in Migdal-
           HaEmek,
          daughter **Anna (Nonna)** (1955, Bendery –). Lived in Kaushany with parents
             until 1973. Studied at Kishinev University, "House where I lived and
             grew, was owned by **Shmil Spivak,** because **Ikhil Geisman'**s house was
             destroyed during the war *(G)*.
           husband **Yakov Shpolyanskiy** (12-Oct-1955, Leovo, Moldova). Married
             in 1978. See **Shpolyanskiy** family,
          daughter **Lora** (1961, Kaushany -). Lived in Kaushany until 1975.
             Studied in Kishinev,
           husband **Efim Berkovich** (6-Aug-1956, Floreshty, Moldova),
             In 1992 family emigrated to Germany. (G),
         daughter **Stunya (Tatyana, Tunya)** (11-Jan-1937, Kaushany – 11-Dec-1998,
           Migdal-ha-Emek). Got married in 1957,
         husband **Isak Kuchuk** (27-Aug-1932 – 19-Jul-1975, Kaushany, buried in

Bendery), lived before in Romanovka (Bessarabka). "I remember we were at that wedding in Kaushany" *(KhK).* See **Kuchuk** family,
son **Moyshe,**
son **Mortykh (Mordukhai)** (1903, Kaushany – 1941, Nikolaev, died in Shoa), trader,
  wife **Golda Shikhman,**
    son **Itsik,**
      wife **Ida,**
        daughter **Tuba** (1937, Kaushany -),
        son **Abram** (1938, Kaushany -).

Leib,
  wife **Kunya,**
    daughter **Ida** (1912, Kaushany -).

Geldenberg.
    Sukher ben Abram, as private in WWI and wounded in November 1914.

Geller.
    Isroel (Israel) was a Rabbi in Kaushany before 1928,
      daughter **Rivka** (1894, Kaushany – 1942, died from typhus *(YdV),*
        husband **Eliyakhu Fishman,**
          son **Aron** served in the Soviet Army. Lived before the war in Bolgrad, Bessarabia.
        Rivka and Eliyakhu died in Shoah in 1942 (YdV),
      daughter **Tsipa (Tsipora)** (1886, Kaushany – 1942, killed in Ipatovo, *YdV*),
        husband **Natan Kishinevskiy,** see **Kishinevskiy** family.

    Israel (Srul), was in Middle Class, registered in Soroki, father – **Yehuda,**
      wife **Beyla-Liya,** father – **Geynikh,**
        son **Idel** (9-Oct-1897, Kaushany -),
        daughter **Perlya** (12-Apr-1903, Kaushany -).

Gershenzon.
    Meyer "was a watchmaker. Also, he owned a haberdashery on a main street."*(KhK, B24).*

Gershkovich.
    Gersh (1871, Bayramcha – Nov-1941) owned a belt shop *(B24),* father - **Yankel-Yosef,**
      wife **Leya** (1874 – Nov-1941), lived before the war in Kaushany,
        son **Shika** (1908 – Nov-1941), saddler,
        son **Daniel** (1911, Kaushany – died in Shoa),
          wife **Frida,**
        daughter **Sosna** (2-Jan-1914, Kaushany – Nov-1941, Odessa, killed),
          husband _? **Zaychik** and had two children twins (1939),
        son **Zyoma,** survived, was in the Soviet Army, and after the war stationed in Galatz,
             Romania, where met a relative **Polina Khaimovich,**
        son **Shmil** (1918 -).
    Gersh and Leya, Shika, Daniil and Sosna died in Shoah in Odessa in 1941 (YdV).

Gibrikh.
    Ershl (Gersh), from Tiraspol, but family lived in Kaushany,
      wife **Khova Novogrebelskaya.** Had his own business – Chicken and Eggs production
        together with the father of **Basya Lvovskiy,**

daughter **Sara** (2-May-1924 – 1941, Odessa, killed in Shoa), was my very good
friend, studied together in gymnasium *(KhK)*,
son **Don,**
daughter **Dina** (1921 - died in Shoah, Odessa),
daughter **Lyuba** (1923 - died in Shoah, Odessa),
son **Abram,**
son **Erhele** (crippled).

Gidal.

Leyzer (Kaushany – Jul-1941, killed in Kaushany by locals *(YdV))*.

Gitlin.

Khaim-Leib, Middle Class, registered in Soroki, father – **Itsko,**
wife **Perl Blitshtein,**
son **Itsik** (1902(8?), Kaushany – 1942, murdered in Shoa),
son **Peyts (Peisakh)** (1897, Kaushany – 1942, murdered), grain-grower,
wife **Etl Kuchuk** (1906, Kaushany), parents **Khona** and **Ikhil,**
daughter **Ita** (1937, Kaushany – 1941, murdered in Odessa),
daughter **Khona** (1935, Kaushany – 1941, murdered in Odessa),
daughter **Khaya-Feiga** (1910, Kaushany – 1941, murdered in Shoa),
husband **Shaya Levit**. Lived before the war in Bendery,
*Itsik, Peyts, Etl, Ita and **Khaya-Feiga** died in the Shoah in Odessa 1942 (YdV).*
son **Gersh** (12-Jan-1915, Каушаны -),
wife **Sima Sverdlik** (1918, Kaushany – 1941, died in Shoa). Lived in
Lambrovka before the war. *(YdV)*, parents **Abram** and **Tzipa,**
daughter **Shmelka.**

Leib,
son **Samuil,** lived in Kaushany after the war. Many years **Samuil** was director of
Moldovan School in Kaushany. After retirement moved to Kishinev *(G),*
wife **Busya,**
daughter **Anna,**
son **Peter,**
daughter **Zlata** (**Zinaida**) "…my kindergarden teacher in Kaushany *(G)"*,
daughter **Vera,**
husband **Sasha (Sander) Galperin**, both worked in commerce in Kaushany. Had 2
daughter and a son,
son **Milya Galperin, medical** assistant. Emigrated to Israel and lived in
Kirijat-Gat *(G).*

Glinzberg.

David - a shoemaker *(B24).*

Gluzberg.

Duvid (David), father – **Moshko-Khaim,**
wife **Basya (Batya),**
son **Markus** (2-Sep-1923, Kaushany -), "**Markus** is my good friend, lives now in
Israel" *(KhK),* was on military service from 1-Apr-1942, demobilized as
lieutenant *(Mem),*
son **Khaim,**
daughter **Rita,**

son **Avram (Avraham)** (23-Sep-1915, Kaushany -),
son **Khaim,**
daughter **Lea,**
daughter **Charna.**

Gold.

Michail (Milya) (1927 - Baltimore), father-**Semen**, Engineer,
  wife **Daria** (1937, Bendery -), father-**Akim**, Russian language and literature teacher in
    Russian school,
    son **Akim (Kim)** (1955, Kaushany -), graduated from Kishinev Agricultural institute,
      mechanical department. Got married and moved to Moscow in 1977,
    son **Sasha** (1966, Kaushany -).
      Parents emigrated to USA in the beginning of 1990s and lived in Baltimore. (G).

Goldfarb.

"**Benya** was a Shoichet- ritual slaughter. He died from typhus in Aktyubinsk,
      Kazakhstan during evacuation,
  wife **Malka Varshavskiy**, sister of aunt **Inda**, wife of **Meir Kogan**, see **Kogan** family.
      Her nickname was "di shoiketke". **Malka** was a head of a Jewish woman
      organization. She had two sons and a daughter.
    son __?, The younger son was involved in communist activity, and was in jail in
      1936-37, where he got tuberculosis,
    daughter **Menikha,** took care of him and she also got sick and died right after soviets
      came in 1940. She was the first buried in a "new way", in a coffin and with the
      red flag on top,
    son __? The older son went to Bucharest or Yassy, and later died during the war in a
      partisan brigade" *(KhK).*

Iosif,
  wife **Khana,**
    son **Uda-Leib (Yuda Leib)** (19-Dec-1876, Kaushany -),
      wife **Khaya,**
        son **Shulim (Shalom)** (19-May-1902, Kaushany -),
    son **Nasanel** (1888, Kaushany – killed in Shoa), trader, *(YdV),*
      wife **Dvoira Viner,**
        daughter **Pnina Finkelshtein**. Lived before the war in Romanovka.

Goldgamer. "I remember two brothers **Moyshe** (1918) and **Shloime**" *(KhK).*

Srul (Israel) (1894, Kaushany -), parents **Srul** and **Zisla,**
  wife **Sura Kofman** (1892, Kaushany – 1962, Kishinev), parents **Moyshe** and **Kunya,**
    son **Moyshe** (1918, Kaushany – 1941), was a mechanic, fought in the war and was killed
      in military service, 1941,
      wife **Dora Kopanskiy** *(KhK),*
    son **Shloime,**
    son **Khuka** (4-May-1926, Kaushany – 1956, Kaushany),
    son **Khaim** (1-Jun-1931, Kaushany -).

Goldshtein.

Shmil (Samuel, Shmul) (1874 - 1943, Pestravka, Kuybyshev obl., USSR). Lived in
      Kaushany before the war, father – **Shaya,**

wife **Beila Zonis** (1887, Romanovka –1968, Kaushany), father – **Yakov,**

son **Yakov (Yankel)** (1909, Kaushany – 1988, Kishinev). Bookkeeper. During Romanian rule, between the wars he was jailed for revolutionary activity in infamous jail "Doftana". After the war, he worked as senior accountant in Kaushany "zagotkontora". In 1985 moved to Kishinev,

wife **Molka Kharnash** (1913 -), seamstress, father **Moisey,** also engaged in underground activities,

daughter **Dona (Donka, Domka) Landsberg** (1937, born in jail - 2021), graduated from Tiraspol Institute as a Math teacher, moved to Kishinev,

husband **Lippa Landsberg** (1929, Nisporeny – 2000), taught theory of music in conservatory,

daughter **Alina-Khaya** emigrated to Israel. Lives in Petah-Tikva,

daughter **Svetlana** (1944,) lives in Israel with children, grandchildren and great grandchildren,

wife (second) **Viktoria (Vitya) Letichever** (1920, Kaushany – 10-Aug-1972, buried in Kaushany, and re-buried in Bendery) after the war was teacher in Kaushany Moldovan Elementary school *(G, RR),*

daughter – **Raya (Raisa, Rukhaly)** (1947, Kaushany) – studied in Russian school in Kaushany, graduated from Kishinev University as Math and Informatics,

husband **Yefim Rozenkrants** (1945), from Kishinev,

two children **Victor** and **Bella,** now live in San-Diego, USA *(G, RR),*

daughter **Sonya** (1911, Kaushany-1990, Kishinev), before the war **Sonya** engaged in underground activities, was beaten by Romanians-gendarmes, after the war moved to Kishinev. Her husband was killed on front of the war, they did not have children,

daughter **Ester-Fira** (1915, Kaushany-2000, Israel), after the war moved to Kishinev and emigrated to Israel,

husband **Zelik Zeltser**, they divorced, no children.

Goligorskiy.

Peisakh (c. 1880, Bayramcha – 1941, killed from bombardment near Odessa), father - **Iosif,**

wife **Etl Soltanovich** (1885 - 1941, killed from bombardment near Odessa), *(YdV),* father – **Yankel,**

son **Naum (Nona),** lives in Israel. **Nona** "studied with me in gymnasium. His father worked as a mechanic on a mill in Old Kaushany" *(KhK).*

Granik.

Moshko,

son **Bentsion,**

daughter **Miriam** (1888, Kaushany – 1941, murdered in Akkerman), *(YdV),* husband **Elieser**, lived in Akkerman,

son **Aharon (Aharon-Meir),** was in Middle Class, registered in Ochakov,

wife **Feiga (Rakhel?),**

daughter **Rakhel-Leya** (1890, Kaushany – 1941, died in Shoa, *(YdV),* husband **Meyer,**

son **Tsvi.** Lived in Akkerman before the war,

son **Gersh** (14-Sep-1915, Kaushany -).

Grimberg.
    Israel (1892 -), father – **Semen,**
      wife **Anna** (1900 -), father – **Emanuel,** family lived in Kaushany,
        daughter **Nyusya** (1925 -),
        daughter **Mariya** (1928 -).

    Gedania (1921) fought in the war and was MIA since 1941 (Mem).

Grinberg, Grunberg, Greenberg.
    Hertz (20-Jun-1914, Kaushany -), during the war was in Galatz, Romania *(JG)*.

    Itsik owned a grocery store *(B24)*.

    Srul and **Feiga** owned a taver-saloon *(B24)*.

    Khaim, subject of Romania,
      wife **Ester,**
        son **Shulim** (11-Apr-1897, Kaushany -), owned a taver-saloon *(B24)*.

    Mark,
      daughter **Rukhlya Leya** (- killed in Shoa), owned a taver-saloon *(B24)*.

    Abram (Avrohom-Ben), citizen of Turkey,
      wife **Livshe,**
        son **Yekhiel** (19-Aug-1878, Kaushany -),
      wife **Malka-Khaya,**
        son **Shimon-Gersh** (11-Jul-1887, Kaushany -).

    Pinkus (1904, Kaushany -), was arrested in 1943, got 10 years in GULAG. Father – **Naftul** *(VT)*.

Grinshpun.
    Moisey,
      daughter **Rakhil** (1877, Kaushany -), Lived before the war in Kaushany.

    Khaim, was in Middle Class, registered in Kishinev,
      wife **Khava-Reiza,**
        son **Danil-Mordko** (29-Aug-1876, Kaushany -).

Groysman.
    __? ,
      wife **Vera Fedotovna** was a labor teacher in Russian school,
        son **Valeriy** (1952),
        daughter **Natasha** (~1954) *(G)*.

Guber.
    Khaim, father – **Abram,**
      son **Moisey** (1910, Kaushany – fought in the war, private, was MIA from 1941).

Guz.
    Shmuel,
      wife **Miriyam,**

son **Moyshe** (1914, Odessa – 1942, killed), tailor. They lived before the
war in Kaushany. **Moyshe** served in the Soviet Army and died in 1942 *(YdV)*,
daughter **Ester.**

Guzinskiy.
Pnina (1900, Lublin, Poland – 1943, Kaushany, died in Shoa) *(YdV)*,
husband **Menashe.**

Idls.
Surka had a store selling threads and needles at the main street in Kaushany in 1930s.

Iliesh.
Isay (1919, Kaushany - fought in the war and killed 17-Jan-1945 in Poland, *Mem*),
father – **Iosif,**
wife **Olga.**

Itskovich.
Aron (Aharon), was Citizen of Moldova Principality, from Leove, father -**Yitskhok,**
wife **Khana (Sara?),**
son **Elkhuna** (27-Oct-1866, Kaushany -),
son **Nokhem (Nukhem)** (1870 – 1943, Kharkov, murdered), carpenter, citizen of
Romania,
wife **Khenya (Genya) Latman** (1870, Kaushany – 1943, Kharkiv, murdered),
lived before the war in Kaushany, both died in Shoah in 1943 *(YdV)* ,
daughter **Ester Beker,**
daughter **Feiga** (1896, Kaushany – 1944, murdered),
husband **Aharon Cholak,**
son **Yakov** (12-Sep-1902, Kaushany -),
son **Mordkha** (2-Nov-1899, Kaushany -).

Leib, Citizen of Moldova principality, from town of Yassy,
wife **Maryasya,**
son **Gersh (Gershon)** (13-Feb-1866, Kaushany -).

Shlema, father – **Shoil,**
wife **Liba.** In 1941 evacuated to the East, after the war lived in Bendery,
son **Rafuel** (20-Jun-1902, Kaushany -), was in Middle Class registered in Kishinev,
wife **Ides (Yehudit) Kiovetskaya** (21-Feb-1902, Kaushany -),
son **Moyshe** (1929, Kaushany -),
son **Shoil (Shula)** (1932, Kaushany -),
son **Mekhel (Mika)** (1934, Kaushany -),
wife **Dora Rybak,**
son **Yakov** (6-Oct-1903, Kaushany -).
Information provided by Dora Rybak and Yad Vashem

Kachkis. "Yes, remember them, do not know what they did" *(KhK).*
Noah, according to *B24* owned a belt/leather shop.

Eleun owned a confectionary shop.

Shlema,

wife **Roza (Tzirlya-Brukha** maybe second wife) (1874), father – **Shika,**
    son **Shmarya** (1-Nov-1876, Kaushany -),
    son **Samshen** (4-May-1878, Kaushany -),
    son **Isaak (Itsik)** (27-Dec-1887, Kaushany -),
      wife **Khana** (1900 -), father – **Meir,** lived in Kaushany before the war,
        daughter **Kheyna** (1917 -), was a teacher *(J-R),*
        son **Beniamin (Binel)** (1918, Kaushany -), teacher,
          wife **Fanya,**
        daughter **Mara** (1922 -), secretary,
          husband **Yasha Soltanovich**, from Bendery. Fought in Spain International brigades. His nickname was **Krasnov**. In the beginning of 1930s **Yasha Soltanovich** and **Yasha Goldshtein** went to Palestine to build happy life. **Yasha Goldsh**tein returned to Kaushany, but **Yasha Soltanovich** went to Spain.
    son **Itich** (1888 -).

    __?, an elderly man was French language teacher in school in Kaushany, and after that worked in publication. His wife was housewife,
    daughter **Rosa** (1950/1951), graduated Kaushany Russian school. Moved from Kaushany at the end of 1960s.

Kalitskiy (Kalisskiy, Kalishski, Kaliski, Kalskiy).
    Shlioma,
      son **Zeyli (Zeylik)** (c.1880, Kaushany – 1941, killed in Kaushany), was a winemaker *(B24)*, own land,
      wife **Sheindl**. All were killed on their winery in July 1941 *(YdV)*,
      wife **Malka** (second wife after **Sheindl** died),
        daughter **Shlima** (22-Dec-1899, Kaushany -),
        son **Finkel** 6-Oct-1903, Kaushany -),
      son **Srul-Gersh (Israel),**
        wife **Bunya,**
        daughter **Liya (Leya)** (15-Mar-1902, Kaushany -),
        son **Shloimo** (1903, Kaushany – 1943, killed Odessa),
          wife **Roza Stanislavskiy** (1905, Kaushany – 1943, killed in Odessa),
            daughter **Enta** (1940 – 1943, killed in Odessa), **Roza, Shlomo** died in Shoah in Odessa in 1943 *(YdV)*.

    __?
    wife **Khana Letichever** (- Kaushany, buried in Kaushany), father **Moisey**
    son **Volodya (Velvl)** with his wife lived in Kiev,
    daughter **Mada** with family emigrated to Israel from Sambor.

Kaplun.
    Shaya-Zeylik (1920, Talmaz, near Bendery – Aug-1941, killed in Kaushany), during the war lived in Kaushany, where was killed *(YdV)*, father – **Abram.**

Kashelevskiy.
    Ikhail (1886), father - **Motel** *(J-R).*

Kaushanskiy.
    Elya (Eliyahu),

wife **Brukha,**
  daughter **Tsivya** (28-Sep-1876, Kaushany -),
  daughter **Khaya** (290-Dec-1878, Kaushany -),
  son **Azriel,**
    wife **Rakhel (Rukhlya),**
      son **Moyshe (Moyshe-Israel)** (14-Sep-1914, Kaushany -),
      son **Pinkhus (Pinku, Puyu)** (1921, Kaushany – fought in the war and was MIA),
          before the war was a bookkeeper.
*"**Pinku** studied in the same class with your father, all named him **Puyu**. His family lived in a*
village not far from Kaushany." (KhK), he fought in the war and was killed on the front (YdV).

Kertsman.
  Sholom (Shulim),
    wife **Etl,**
      son **Gersh (Tsvi)** (1921, Kaushany – 1941, killed on the front near Odessa in 1941 *(YdV)*.

Mekhel.
  Yankel (**Mikhel**'s brother) – owner of a store – KOK: **Kertsman, Ochakovskiy,**
      Kogan, where worked my dad, **Leib Spivak.**
    wife **Gitl,**
      daughter **Sheiva** (1920, Kaushany – died following evacuation) "studied with me in
          gymnasium, we went together to a resort in Bukovina – Vatra-Dorney. **Sheiva**
          earlier married but died young. She was a very nice, but frail girl" *(KhK).*

Kesler.
  Moisey (Moshe) (1906, Kiliya - 1942), carpenter, fought in the war and was MIA since
      1942 *(YdV)*,
  daughter **Roza**, family lived before the war in Kaushany.

Khaikin (Haikin).
  Meir (- 1941-43,died in evacuation),
    wife **Rukhl Saltanovich** (- 1962, Czernovitsy),
      son **Shmil** (11-Jan-1912, Kaushany – 14-Feb-1997, Israel),
        wife **Polya (Perlya) Kogan** (20-Oct-1908, Kaushany – 30-Oct-1983, Bendery),
          daughter **Lyuba** (1948, Bendery),
            husband **Tolya Kogan**, father - **Eynekh** (see **Kogan**'s family),
      son **Yakov** (- died in Sevastopol),
      daughter **Khaika** (Kaushany -),
        husband **Smil Norel** (Bendery -),
          son **Miron (Meir)** (1943, Kazakhstan - killed in 1966, Bendery),
          son **Monya** (1948, Bendery –), lives in Bendery,
      daughter **Edl (Ida)** (- died in Tallin),
        husband **Gidaliya Saltanovch** (Kaushany - died in Tallin),
          son **Miron.**

  Gershko (c1870 -),
    son **Shmil** (1898, Kaushany -), evacuated to the East during the war. Evacuated to the
        East of the USSR,
    daughter **Feiga** (1898, Kaushany -).

  Shoel,

wife **Gitlya,**
  son **Moyshe-Iosl** (31-Jan-1876, Kaushany -),
    wife **Zelda,**
      daughter **Leya** (1900, Kaushany – murdered in Shoa),
        husband **David** (1900, Kaushany – murdered in Shoa, *YdV*). Parents **Nekhemia**
           and **Freida,**
  son **Meer-Leib** (7-Feb-1878, Kaushany -), evacuated to the East in 1941,
    wife **Rukhlya** (1882, Kaushany -),
      son **Idel,**
        wife **Anneta,**
          daughters **Nadya** and **Mira,**
      daughter **Frima,**
  son **Gersh** ,
    wife **Khaya-Sura,** father - **Isaak**
      son **Raful** (1895, Kaushany -), fought in the war, private, was MIA
      daughter **Liba** (15-Sep-1897, Kaushany -),
      son **Eliahu (Elya)** (1-Jan-1902, Kaushany -),
      daughter **Reyzya** (2-Jan-1903, Kaushany -).

Malya was a wine maker.

Khaim owned a steam mill *(B24).*

Abram,
 wife __?,
  son **Reful** (1816, Kaushany -),
    wife **Reizya,**
      son **Zanvel Zvi** (1834, Kaushany -),
        wife **Gitl** ,
          daughter **Rukhl** (1857, Kaushany – 6-Nov-1924, Buenos Aires),
           husband **Vaisman,**
           husband (second) **Lev Mogilner,** see **Lev Mogilner** family,
          son **Abram** (11-Feb-1866, Kaushany -),
          son **Israel David,**
          son **Mordko,**
           wife **Malka,**
             daughter **Tsipa** (3-Mar-1897, Kaushany -),
             son **Shlomo** (1-Aug-1899, Kaushany -),
        daughter **Khaika** (1837, Kaushany -).

Abram, father – **Srul Israel,**
  son **Raful (Rafil)** (1895) fought in the war and was killed *(Mem).*

Lyuba (1900, Kaushany – 1941, killed in Shoa *YdV*), parents **Gersh** and **Sara,**
      sister of **Khava Bruter,**
  husband **Pinkus Natanzon.** Lived before the war in Strudzeny, Bendery district.

Moshe,
 wife **Zelda,**
  daughter **Lea** (1900, Kaushany – killed in Shoa, 1941, *YdV*),
  husband **David** (1900, Kaushany – killed in Shoa, 1941, *YdV*).

Gersh,
wife **Maria** (1899,), mother – **Motlya** (1876 -), **Mariya**'s father - **Lazar** (1876 -),
daughter **Roza** (1931 -),
daughter **Sara** (1932 -).

Khaimovich (Haimovich).
Khaim (Haim) (c1865 – 15-Jun-1934, Galatz, Romania), father – **Moshko,**
wife **Golda** (- 1937, Kaushany). Lived in Tarutino, Kiliya, Galatz, Kaushany,
son **Yakov** (2-Jan-1903, Monzyr (not far from Kaushany),
daughter **Fanya** (15-Sep-1896, Tarutino – 6-Nov-1940, Kaushany),
husband **Leib (Lyova) Spivak** (1898, Kaushany – 31-Mar-1964, Ismail),
see **Spivak** family.

Khakham (Hakham).
Yankel,
son **Shimon** (- 1939, Kaushany), was in Middle Class, registered in Rezina, reburied in
Kishinev Jewish Cemetery,
wife **Rivka** (- 1943, Kazakhstan during evacuation),
daughter **Liya (Leya)** (19-May-1902, Kaushany -),
son **Abram,**
"I remember that family. They had a pharmacy store (KhK, B24),
son **Shaya,** was in Middle Class, registered in Bendery,
wife **Khaya,**
daughter **Tauba** (24-Apr-1903, Kaushany -),
son **Yakov** (1905, Kaushany - fought in the war and was killed in 1943, *Mem*),
wife **Manya,** father - **Mark,**
son **Moshko, owned** a printing house, and groceries store,
wife **Rukhlya,**
son **__?** (7-Jun-1897, Kaushany -),
son **Nakhman,**
wife **Rukhlya,**
daughter **Eydya** (22-Aug-1903, Kaushany -).

Khamelis.
Meir (1903, Kaushany -), fought in the war, soldier, was MIA, father – **Ikhil.**

Kiovetskiy.
Nakhman, father - **Itsko,**
wife **Pesya,** father – **Moshko,**
daughter **Ides (Yehudit)** (21-Feb-1902, Kaushany -),
husband **Rafuel Itskovich** (20-Jun-1902, Kaushany -), see **Itskovich** family,
son **David** (16-Nov-1897, Kaushany -).

Kishinevskiy.
Natan,
wife **Tsipa Geller** (1886, Kaushany – 1942, killed in Ipatovo, Caucasus, in evacuation),
parents **Israel** and **Bella,**
daughter **Khaika** (1912 - 1942, killed in Ipatovo, Caucasus, in evacuation),
daughter **Malka** (1916 - 1942, killed in Ipatovo, Caucasus, in evacuation), seamstress,
son **Shmil** (1919 - 1942, killed in Ipatovo, Caucasus, in evacuation), had near rail

155

road station an oil depository. "**Shmil** was also a carpenter *(KhK)*.
All died in Caucases region in Shoah in 1942 (YdV).
daughter **Dvoira.**

Kislyansliy (Kishlyanskiy).
> **Yankel,**
>> wife **Tsipa,**
>>> son **Abram** (1894, Kaushany – 1942, Kazakhstan, died during evacuation),
>>>> wife **Nesya** (1894 -), father – **Iosif**. Family lived in Kaushany before the war,
>>>>> daughter **Khana** (1924 -), salesperson,
>>>>> daughter **Khaya** (1927 -),
>>>>> daughter **Tsilya** (1930 -),
>>>>> son **Shmuel,**
>>> son **Khaim** was a hat master, his son worked with **Lyova Spivak** *(KhK),*
>>>> wife **Sura,**
>>>>> son **Moyshe** (18-Jul-1914, Kaushany -).

Kizhner.
> **Pavel (Favel),**
>> wife **Golda** – housewife. He worked as a supplier of agricultural products,
>>> son **Vova,** was a musician,
>>> son **Grisha,**
>>> daugher – **Klara.**
> *At the end of 1960s family moved to Bendery and at the beginning of 1990s emigrated to Israel.*

Kleyman (Cleiman).
> **Melik** owned a fabric store *(B24).*

> **Syoma** "was a cantor in a synagogue" *(Izya Spivak).*

> **Khaim Avram,**
>> son **Wolf** (1872, Kaushany -),
>>> wife **Tsilea** (1882, Kaushany -), parents **Naftule** and **Reizl,**
>>>> daughter **Ana** (1906, Bendery -).

Klyuzman.
> **Zelman,**
>> son **Khuna,** was in Middle Class, registered in Obodovka, Podolia gub.,
>>> wife **Khaya Rivka,** father - **Reful,** had 3 sons and 3 daughters,
>>>> daughter **Feiga Levit,** was called 'mima Feiga',
>>>>> husband **Yankel Levit.** See more at family **Levit,**
>>>> daughter **Etl,**
>>>>> husband **Laibesh Bersudskiy.** See more at family **Bersudskiy,**
>>>> daughter **Khana** (8-Jul-1897, Kaushany -), *(JG),*
>>>> son **Iosl (Iosif, Yisrael-Yosef ben Elchanan)** (1880 - 14-Aug-1959, Kishinev),
>>>>> owned a confectionery shop *(B24),*
>>>>> wife **Ides (Ida, Yehudit)** (1885 – 1960, Kishinev) from Ukraine, had 5 children:
>>>>>> son **Motl (Mordechai ben Yisrael-Yosef)** (1911 – 1960, Kishinev),
>>>>>>> wife **Manya- Malka,** died in Carmiel, Israel, cousins.
>>>>>> son **Mikhel** (1948 – 2009, Toronto, Canada),
>>>>>> daughter **Ilana,**

daughter **Anya** live in USA,

son **Bore (Ber, Dov)** (7-Apr-1915, Kaushany - died from starvation working on labor front),

son **Khaim** (1921 – 1943, MIA near Stalingrad, *Mem*) "**Khaim** was one year older than I and lived in a house across the street (was stutter) *(KhK)*,

daughter **Ester** (1917(9?), Kaushany – 2007, Los Angeles),

husband **Barukh Mariyasin** (1910, Kaushany - 1977) Kishinev

daughter **Tsilya,**

daughter **Ira** (named in memory of **Ides**) living now in Los Angeles

daughter **Perl** (1907-1942) - died from typhus during evacuation),

son **Naum** 95 years old in Israel,

son **Efim** died in Toronto.

Iosl, Ides, Ester and Perl were evacuated to Kazakhstan (TsD).

son **Mekhl (Mikhel, Ikhil),**

wife **Charna Zemelman** (1893 – 1957, Kishinev),

daughter **Manya-Malka**, died in Carmiel, Israel,

husband **Motl** (1911 – 1960, Kishinev), cousins, see above whole family.

daughter **Riva** lives in Brooklin, NY,

son **Abram** (1920, Kaushany - 1944), worker, **Abram** fought in the war and was an MIA since 1944 *(Mem, YdV)*.

"**Abram** was related to my aunt **Feiga**. He had two sisters, **Manya** and **Riva**. **Abram** lived with us in Uzbekistan during evacuation, but then moved to Kokand, when found his family. Later we found that he died from typhus." *(KhK)*.

son **Reful** (1899 -), **Reful, Khaika and Peisya** were deported in 1940 for anti-Soviet activities *(JG)*,

wife **Khaika** (1896 - ?),

son **Peisya (Beysa)** (c1919/1922 -), fought in the war, private was MIA from 1943 *(Mem)*.

son **Iosl** (1922 – 2003, Philadelphia). "They were rich. I studied with **Iosl** at gymnasium, but after the war we did not meet. He worked on a nail factory in Kishinev" *(KhK)*.

son **Misha,**

daughter **Klara,**

daughters **Nina** (- Israel),

husband __? **Chobrutsky,**

daughter **Faina,**

daughter **Khona** probably died during deportation. The family was rich and was deported in 1941 to the East of Soviet Union.

Reful, Khaika and Peisya were deported from Moldova 13-16 June 1941, JG)

Iosl, Reful and Mekhl owned a water mill (oil mill) (B24), Motl and Bore had shares in the business (TsD).

Koen.

Itsik, Merchant owned China store, according to *B24* he was a glazier. "After the war I did not meet anyone except **Fanya**" *(KhK)*,

wife **Riva (Rivka-Leya) Kogan, Itsik** was a widower, and got a letter from Romanovka Rabbi, married 14-Feb-1914 in Kaushany,

daughter **Fanya,** from twin,

husband **Nyusya Sichuga,** had two daughters,

daughter **Roza**, from twin, a pretty girl,
  husband __? **Shtehman,**
  daughter **Bella,**
daughter **Brana (Betya),**
  husband **Isrul Tarantin,**
daughter **Tsilya,**
daughter **Anya (**In 2018 lived in Rishon LiTsion),
  husband __? **Barenboym,** two children **Galya** and **Alik.**

Kofman (Kaufman, Koifman).
  Moshko, father – **Meir,**
    wife **Sura,**
      daughter **Pesya** (7-Aug-1866, Kaushany -),
      daughter **Khana** (21-Sep-1876, Kaushany -),
      daughter **Brana** (11-Jul-1878, Kaushany -).

  Volf (1892 -), accountant, father **Itsik,**
    wife **Bunya Zeltser** (1893, Kaushany – 1943, Namangan, Uzbekistan. The whole
        family evacuated in 1941, *YdV*),
      daughter **Charna** (1916 -), seamstress,
        husband **Falik Zeltser, Falik** is **Charna's** uncle,
      daughter **Fida** (1920),
      daughter **Garnya** (1919 -), seamstress,
      son **Mortko** (1923 -), *(J-R)*,
      daughter **Molka** (1928 -),
      son **Motel,**
        son **Fima,**
        son **Senya,** live in NYC,
        daughter **Frida Friman** (YdV).

Kogan (Cogan). Many families lived in Kaushany with **Kogan** surname, some were related, for
        others relations were not established.

  Moyshe (c1820 -), was in Middle Class, registered in Akkerman,
    wife **Nekhama-Beyla,** had children **Iosif, Rivka, Leiser** and **Berl** (maybe more).

*My father, **Abram Kogan**, told me a family story that his great-great grandfather **Moyshe** when got
married took the last name of his wife **Kogan**, because he (or somebody else in the family) did not want to
go to the Tsar army for 25 years of service. (In the middle of 19 century, when the Jews started to be
recruited into the army, the Jewish Kahal often decided who will go. The family name Kogan, usually
belonged to kohanim – the priestly tribe, maybe they did not go, because of small numbers… Even
though our last name is Kogan, we are not kohanim.*

      son **Iosif-Mendel** (7-Feb-1876, Kaushany -),
      daughter **Rivka,**
        husband __?,
          son **Moyshe,**
      son **Leiser** (1-Oct-1861, Kaushany -),
        wife __?,
          son **Iosif Kogan (Iosif der Shvartser)** (October 15, 1888, Kaushany – January 18,
            1959, Faleshty). Did not have a profession. **Iosif** was natured by step-

mother **Dina,**

wife (first) **Malka Averbuch (**January 28, 1893 -), father – **Abram,**

daughter **Polya (Perl)** (September 25, 1932, Kaushany -). After the war lived in Faleshty, was a literature teacher at school. Lived in Brooklyn, Borough Park (2012),

husband **Buma Grinshpun,** Brooklyn, USA, two daughters **Mila** and **Inna,**

daughter **Golda** (May 1, 1921, Kaushany – 1986 Brooklyn, NY USA), was not married,

wife (second) **Dina** (June 2, 1865 – 1939),

son **Moyshe,** had a wife and three children **Khona, Srulik** and **Dasya.**
All were killed in a camp near Odessa.

son **Buka (Abram)** (died in 1939-1940, Kaushany), was one of the owners of KOK store,

wife **Khona Natenzon** (1902 – 1977, Izmail),

daughter **Klara Sapozhnikova** (1924, Kaushany – 1976, Izmail,

son **Lyusya,** died in 1942 in evacuation,

husband **Leib Spivak (Khona** re-married after **Buka** died. See **Spivak** family.

son **Berl (Boris)** (1850s – died before 1909), steward for a landlord,

wife (second) **Entel** (10-May-1868 – died 1934-35), had a grocery shop in Kaushany. Had 4 sons and a daughter,

son **Peisakh** (16-Dec-1874 - 1928), was a manager for the landowner estate,

wife **Khava (Hova) Tulchinskiy** (10-Sep-1878, Tiraspol – 1941, Kokchetav, died in Shoa *YdV*), lived in Kaushany before the war, they had 7 sons and a daughter, parents **Dov** and **Rivka,**

son **Meyer** (1896, Kaushany – 1941, Osinniki, Kemerovo oblast, died in coal mine *(YdV)*,

wife **Elka,** also **Kogan,** see **Shabsa Kogan** below,

son **Abram** (9-Sep-1923, Kaushany – 9-Mar-1991, Tzur-Shalom, Israel),

wife **Khinka Spivak** (4-May-1923, Kaushany – 6-Feb-2020, Tzur-Shalom, Israel), 2 sons **Miron** and **Yefim.**

daughter **Mara** (20-Jan-1928, Kaushany – 13-Dec-2006, Karmiel, buried in Haifa, Israel),

husband **Lenya Tismenetskiy** (2-Jan-1925, Bieshty, Bessarabia – 20-Nov-2020, Haifa), 2 sons **Miron** and **David (Dima),**

son **Avrum** (21-Sep-1897 – 1920s from tuberculosis) served in Romanian army together with **Meyer,**

son **Leon (Arie, Leib)** (16-May-1902, Kaushany - 1980, Bnei-Brak, Israel), lived in Kaushany, Bendery, Bucharest. Married to **Tina** in 1928, divorced, remarried to **Tsilya Fishelovich** (1907, Romania-1998, Israel),

son **Einekh** (9-Jan-1905, Kaushany – 9-Jun-1988, Bendery),

wife **Bunya** (23-Aug-1903, Bendery – 30-Dec-1984, Bendery),

son **Petya** (30-Dec-1930, Kaushany -), lived in Karaganda, after the war,

son **Tolya** (11-Jul-1938, Kaushany – 25-Dec-2011, Kirijat-Mozkin, Israel). Lived after the war in Bendery, Kiliya, Israel, was a doctor,

wife **Lyuba Khaikina** (1948, Bendery -), doctor, have two sons **Igal** and **Boris,**

son **Berl (Boris, Berku)** (9-Oct-1909, Kaushany - 1970s),

wife **Sonya,** married in 1938, divorced, remarried to **Ida.** Lived after the war in Molotov (Perm), Russia and moved to Beltsy, Moldova,

159

daughter **Khona (Khana, Ana)** (14-Nov-1911, Kaushany – 1941-42, died in
Bessarabia in Shoa, *YdV*),
husband **Iyol**, were engaged in 1936, lived in German colony Leyptsig,
Bessarabia, died in Shoah in 1941-42 *(YdV)*,
son **Gersh** (13-Apr-1914 - died in the end of 1920s or beginning of 1930s.),
son **Shimen (Simon)** (1916 – 1942, killed near Stalingrad), married,
professional photographer, lived in Kaushany, Bucharest, fought in the war,
son **Iosif (Iosif-der-Royter)** (1878 - 1956, Kishinev -), produced wine,
wife **Lyuba (Leyka) Khasileva** (1880 - died during evacuation),
daughter **Gitl** (1905, Kaushany - 1968, Kishinev),
husband **Monya Garshtein,** died in Shoah. See **Garshtein** family.
daughter **Polya (Perlya, Palageya)** (1908(12?), Kaushany-1983 Bendery),
husband **Shmil Khaikin** (1912 - 1997, Israel). See **Khaikin** family,
son **Boris (Berko)** (1910 - died in Shoah, was last time seen in Odessa,
daughter **Khona (Khana-Leya)** (1880 -),
husband **Pinkhu (Pinya, Pinkhus-Zelig) Bruter.** Three sons and two
daughters. See **Bruter** family.
son **Zolmen (Zelman)** (1882 - 1958, Bendery),
wife **Sara (Sura) Feferman** (1886 -),
daughter **Khaika** (1911-1970, Israel), immigrated to Palestine in 1932,
husband **Shimshon Gilad**, changed surname from **Goldshtein,**
daughter **Perl (Perlya)** (1912 - 2003, Bendery),
husband **Milya Feferman**, son **Sasha,**
son **Boris (Berko)** (1919 -), was in GULAG 9 years, after that lived in Soroki,
wife **Riva**, teacher,
son **Moyshe** (7-Apr-1892 - 1946 Kishinev), fought in WWI,
wife **Inda (Enta) Varshavskiy** (25-May-1894 – 22-May-1978, Kishinev),
owned a large house-estate in Kaushany,
son **Borukh (Boris, Ber)** (1919, Kaushany - 1941), accountant, fought in the
war, was MIA since 1941 *(YdV)*,
daughter **Roza** (15-Sep-1921, Kaushany - 2012, Jerusalem),
husband **Tolya Veltser** (1914-1988, Kishinev), **Roza** lived in Kishinev,
Afula, and Jerusalem,
son **Naum (Nakhman)** (1923, Kaushany – 28-Aug-1943), killed on the front in
1943 in Ukraine, Cherkassy obl, vil. Dolginka *(Mem, YdV)*.

Another large clan of **Kogans.** It is possible that the prior clan was related to this one, but no connections
yet are found.

Irikhem (1842 – March 13 (or February 12), 1908, Dubossary). He was melamed
in Tomashpol, lived in 1871 in Gancheshty, 1872 – in Kaushany, was in Beit
Din, in April 1866 was a rabbi in Ismail, was expelled. July 1866 – in Kishinev,
was one a main rabbi in town, August 1886 – Dubossary, town rabbi. Had 10
children.
wife **Adel (Gudlya).** According to the birth record of their daughter **Dvoira** and
Khaim-Volko, Irikhem was citizen of Moldova principality, later became
Romania.
son **Shabsa (Shabse)** (10-Sep-1856 - 1940, Kaushany), "father of **Elka Kogan,** my
mother-in-law. He had a grocery store *(B24)*. In 30s store sold herring and
lime – whitewash. He was also a rabbi, but not sure where" *(KhK)*.
Shabsa was in the Middle Class, registered in Dubossary.
wife **Mariam Fuks**, died in 1919, and likely **Shabsa** re-married. He had five sons

and three daughters:
son **Yankel** (23-Aug-1890, Kaushany-),
  wife **Beyla** (8-Aug-1889 -), two daughters:
    daughter **Khaika** (9-Oct-1916, Kaushany -), was married, divorced *(J-R)*,
        one son **Izya**,
    daughter **Mara (Mariam)** (3-Apr-1920, Kaushany -),
      husband **Avrum Zemelman,** see **Zemelman** family,
    son **Irikhem** (1-Jul-1918, Kaushany – 1989, Bendery), lived in Kaushany
        before and after the war and later moved to Bendery,
      wife **Manya,** lived in Kaushany after the war in 60s. Emigrated to Israel.
      daughter **Polina,**
      son **Yasha,**
son **Shmil** (24-Oct-1895, Kaushany -),
  wife **Tuba** (25-Oct-1898 -),
   son **Khaim** (1921 -),
   daughter **Mara** (1-Apr-1923), it possible that they lived not in Kaushany,
      record in the Census of 1924.
daughter **Brukhe** (4-Jan-1899, Kaushany -),
daughter **Elka** (1901, Kaushany-1969, Kishinev),
  husband **Meyer Kogan**, see above family of **Meyer Kogan,**
son **Meyer** (2-Dec-1903, Kaushany - 1966, Chernovtsy),
  wife **Betya,** daughter **Felika.** After the war **Betya** moved in Romania, but
      Meyer was not able to,
  wife (second) **Ita Khorovits**. Lived in Czernovtsy,
daughter **Leyka** (5-Mar-1892, Kaushany – 15-Oct-1967, Kishinev),
  husband **Ruvn Ochakovskiy** (4-Jan-1887, Kaushany -), see **Ochakovskiy**
      family.
son **Shimen** (3-Nov-1906 – 1946, died on front of the war in China),
  wife **Rivka,**
son **Shoil,** lived in Kaushany, died in Shoah.

Continue with children of **Irikhem** (1842 – March 13 (or February 12), 1908, Dubossary),
  daughter **Dvoira** (19-Jul-1876, Kaushany -),
  son **Khaim-Volko** (17-May-1878, Kaushany -),
  daughter **Rakhil,**
  son **Aharon,**
  daughter **Feige** (- 1924, Odessa), she was a Zionist and died because of it,
    husband **Simno ben Yekhiel ben Meir** (- June 5, 1922), was a sales person
      between towns of Kalyuzh, Lodz, Warsaw and Kishinev,
  son **Shlomo Zalman**, lived in the USA,
  son __?, cantor in Odessa,
  son __?, cantor in Kishinev, possible it was **Shabsa (Shabse)** (10-Sep-1856 - 1940,
      Kaushany),

Kogan families with whom relations were not established. Most of them were recorded at the
      Census of 1924 for Kaushany and there are records at *JG*.

    Iosif (*there are a number of Iosif Kogan above, but not clear who is this one),*
      daughter **Rivka-Leya** (1895, Kaushany -),
        husband **Itsko Koen,** widower, married Rivka on 14-Feb-1914, Kaushany. See **Koen**
          family.

Shimen,
   daughter **Perlya** (1873, Kaushany - 16-Oct-1884, Kaushany), died from diphtheritis.

Abram-Moshko,
   daughter **Rukhlya** (1813 – 24-Sep-1884, Kaushany), died from old age.

Gamshiy-Gersh (1879 -), lived in Kaushany before the war, father – **Iosif,**
   wife **Ester** (1884 -), father – **Aron,**
      son **Itsik** (1910 -),
      son **Abram (Avraham)** (26-Feb-1915, Kaushany -).

Iosif (Yosi),
   wife **Khenya,**
      son **Gersh (Hersh)** (1874, Kaushany – 1941, died during bombardment near
                  Stalingrad) *(YdV)*,
         wife **Ester,**
            daughter **Sofiya Fisher.**

Gersh owned a china store, according to *B24* was a glazier.

Gersh, family lived in Kaushany before the war,
   son **Abram** (1915 -),
   daughter **Sura** (1918 -),
      husband **Khaim Yankinzon** (1915 -), father – **Miron.**

Falik (1870 -), was in Middle Class, registered in Kishinev, father – **Khaim,**
   wife **Rukhlya-Leya** (1875 -),
      daughter **Sura** (30-Nov-1902 -),
      daughter **Dvoira** (1905 -),
      son **Iosif** (1907 -),
      son **Gersh** (1909 -),
      son **Azril** (1912 -),
      daughter **Sosya** (1914 -).

Falik (1917 -).

Einikh, was in Kaushany when war started, moved to camp Obodovka, Transnistria.

Semen,
   daughter **Polina** (1865, Kaushany – 1941, Odessa, died in Odessa Ghetto, *YdV*),
      husband **Mark Fankelzord** (1860 - 1941, died in Odessa Ghetto), lived before the
                  war in Odessa. Mechanic. Father – **Iosif,**
         son **David** (1897 – 1941, died in Odessa Ghetto),
         daughter **Sofiya** (1900 - 1941, died in Odessa Ghetto).

David (1908, Kaushany – 1941, killed on the front), owned a store, He was in the Soviet
                  Army, killed on the front during defense of Sevastopol,
   wife **Ita**. Lived before the war in Baymakliya.

Moshko (Moyshe) (1892 -),
  wife **Roza Shvartsman**(1898, Tarutino – 1941, Odessa), parents **Bentsion** and **Basya,**
    daughter **Idasya** (1936, Kaushany – 1941, Odessa),
    son **Israel** (1930, Kaushany – 1941, Odessa),
    daughter **Khana** (1923, Kaushany - 1941),
      husband __**? Kogan**, lived before the war in Kaushany.
    *Roza, Idasya, Israel and **Khana** killed in Odessa in Shoah (YdV).*
Moyshe
  wife **Basia**
    son **Bentsion** (1871, Tarutino – September 1941, Kakhovka, Ukraine), five children born in
      Tarutino, and one in Kakhovka.
    daughter **Khona** (1883, Kaushany – Aug-1942, Saratov). Died during evacuation,
      husband **Khaim Pogoriler** (1869, Kaushany – 1934, Romania/Bessarabia), see **Pogoriler**
        family.

Leyzer (1898 -), bookkeeper, father – **Ruvin.** Family lived in Kaushany before the war,
  wife **Dvoira** (1902 -), father – **Yankel,**
    daughter **Malya** (1926 -),
    son **Itsik** (1928 -).

Itsik (1879, Kaushany – 1941, died during evacuation), Merchant,
  wife **Khaya**, lived before the war in Chimishliya, merchant, died in Shoah in 1941 *(YdV)*,
Itsik's brother(?) Avrum (1872, Kaushany – 1941), lived before the war in Chimishliya,
    died in Shoah in 1941 *(YdV)*.

Meyer,
  wife **Rivka Goldshtok,**
    son **David** (1914, Kaushany – 1941, died in Shoah *(YdV)*, lived before the war in
        Lopushna,
    son **Avraam.**

Matus,
  daughter **Leya** (1899 -), lived in Kaushany before the war.

David-Zalman,
  wife **Sara,**
    daughter **Esther-Rachel** (20-Sep-1888, Stolniceni – 1941, died in Shoa),
      husband **Mordekhai (Markus) Lobachevskiy** (1887, Kiev -). Lived before the war
        in Kaushany. See **Lobachevskiy** family.

Leiba (1874 -),
  wife **Tsipa** (1878 -),
    son **Itsik** (1906 -),
    son **Shaya** (1911 -).

Rukhlya (1864 -), possible that this is **Rivka**, sister of **Berl**, see above.

Shulim (1887 -).

Aron (1900 -).

Kolb.

        Shlyoma was a men's tailor *(B24)*.

Kopanskiy.

        Yankel, father – **Mordko,**
         wife **Feiga,** father – **Mikhel,**
           son **Zus** (26-May-1897, Kaushany -),
           son **Mendel (Moshe)** (1901, Kaushany -), was a clerk in a fabric store,
             wife **Khaika (Ester?)** (1904 -), father – **Ovsha (Ovsey),**
              son **Yan (Yankel, Yakov)** (1930, Kaushany – 2006, Kishinev). **Yakov** was a
                famous historian, researcher, and professor *(Wikipedia)*. *He g*raduated from
                Moldovan State University. (My mother **Asya Geisman** knew him very well; she
                was also a historian. Lived in Kaushany before the war. Returned to Kaushany
                after the war, and soon moved to Bendery. **Yakov** from 1959 worked in
                Academy of Science Moldova SSR. He was a chair of department of history and
                culture of Jews.
             wife **Larisa** chemist, author of schoolbooks,
              son **Aleksandr** (1959) *(G)*.

      Mikhail (1924, Kaushany -), fought in the war, was Lieutenant of Technical services,
           demobilized after the war, father – **Abram.**

      Minta owned a confectionery *(B24)*.

      Dora,
        husband **Moyshe Goldgamer** (1918, Kaushany – 1941), was a mechanic, fought in the
           war and killed in military service, *(KhK)*.

Korenberg.

        Shlema (Shloime), was in Middle Class, registered in Berdichev. father **Iosef-Dov,**
         wife **Tovbe (Tobi),**
           daughter **Ita-Dvoira** (18-May-1878, Kaushany -),
           son **Zanvel** (13-Dec-1887, Kaushany -),
           son **Azriel** (23-Mar01902, Kaushany -).
           son **Nukhim (Nakhum)** was a men's tailor *(B24)*, lived in Kaushany after the war.
             son **Shlomo,**
              wife **Zina Soltanovich.** Lived in Old Kaushany,
           son **Noikh** (1914, Kaushany –), fought in the war, private, MIA since 1944.

Kotlyar.

        Khaim,
         wife **Frime** (1917, Kaushany -), father – **Shaysel,**
          son **Moisey** (1940 -).

      Khonna (c1920 - Kaushany), lived alone. Died and buried in Kaushany Jewish
             cemetery *(G., written from the words of **Rozetta Kupershlak**).*

Kotsubei.

        Aron (1870, Dubossary – 1941, died during bombardment), worked on railroad *(YdV),*
         wife **Makhlya,** they lived before the war in Kaushany,

daughter **Rebeka**   (1905, Bendery), served in the Soviet Army, MIA from 1941 *(YdV)*.

Krakhmalnik.

> **Anna, teacher** of foreign languages, father – **Iosif**, moved to her son to Germany (G).

Krinberg.

> **Yakov,**
>> wife **Anna,** father – **Beniamin,**
>>> son **Veniamin** (1920, Kaushany –), fought in the war, private.

Krinshpun.

> **Shunya** graduated Leningrad Medical Institute, lived and in Kaushany,
>> wife **Dolli** (1930 -). Both doctors. **Dolli** – ophthalmologist, graduated Kishinev
>>> Medical Institute, from Kaushany moved to Simpheropol,
>> son **Evgeniy** (1955),
>> daughter **Irina.**
>
> *In the beginning of 1990s emigrated to Israel. Last years of her life, **Dolli** lived in hostel in Ramat-a-Sharon. She was a friend of my mother from youth when they together worked in Kaushany (G).*

Kriulyanskiy.

> **Zeylik,** family lived on the main street *(1934, court document).*

Kuchuk (Cuciuc),

> **Moyshe** owned a fabric store *(B24).*

> **Shmerel-Leib,**
>> wife **Ygidasya (Yehudeisse),**
>>> son **Aron** (25-Oct-1878, Kaushany -),
>>> son **Ikhil** (1920 -),
>>> daughter **Liya-Dvoira** (26-Apr-1887, Kaushany -),
>>> daughter **Zlota** (1883, Kaushany – 8-Jul-1884, Kaushany), died from seizures,
>>> daughter **Pesya** (May-1884, Kaushany – 19-Sep-1884, Kaushany)), died from
>>>> seizures.

> **Ikhil,**
>> wife **Khona,**
>>> daughter **Etel (Etl)** (1906, Kaushany – 1941, Odessa), died in Shoah in 1941 *(YdV)*,
>>> husband **Peisakh Gitlin.** See **Gitlin** family.

> **Gersh (Grigoriy),**
>> daughter **Basya,**
>>> husband **Yakov Voldman,** father - **Iosif.** See **Voldman** family *(G),*
>> daughter **Tuba (Tanya),** **Yakov** and **Eynekh** are brothers,
>>> husband **Eynekh Voldman (Leonid Iosifovich).** See **Voldman** family *(G).*

> **Tsilya** (c1900 -), worked in a Book store, which was in 1950s across a Universal store, husband **Motl,** lived in Kaushany in 50s-60s. After **Tsilya** retired they moved out of Kaushany. They had 2 daughters. *(G).*

> **Isaak** (1932, Bessarabka – 1975, Kaushany, buried in Bendery),

wife **Stunya (Tatyana) Geisman** (11-Jan-1938, Kaushany – 11-Dec-1998, Migdal-
ha-Emek, Israel), married in 1957 in Kaushany, and lived there since,
daughter **Sima** (1958, Kaushany -),
husband **Iosif Barash,** see **Barash** family,
son **Grisha (Ershl)** (1962, Kaushany -),
wife **Lyubov,**
son **Mark** (1987 -),
daughter **Arina** (1990 -),
In 1991 **Stunya** *with children and grandchildren emigrated to Israel.* **Sima** *and*
Iosif *lived in Migdal-ha-Emek.*

Kumets.
Shimen,
daughter **Dvosya** (1886 -), was a cook,
husband **Khaim,**
daughter **Sura** (1928 -),
daughter **Leya** (1919) *(J-R).*

Kunicher (Cunicer).
Berko owned a haberdashery *(B24).*

Iosif owned a haberdashery *(B24),*
son **Itsik** (1909 -),
daughter **Manya** *(J-R).*

Moshko,
wife **Sura-Leya,**
daughter **Reizlya** (17-Dec-1878, Kaushany -),
son **Yankel-Shlema,**
wife **Shprintsa,**
daughter **Menya** (04-Jan-1897, Kaushany -),
son **Izrail** (11-Jun-1899, Kaushany -),
son **Gershko (Tsvi),**
wife **Rukhlya (Rakhel),**
daughter **Khana** (15-Sep-1897, Kaushany -),
son **Abram** (1904 – 1942, during evacuation from Odessa), trader,
wife **Emiliya** (1907, Bendery – 1942, murdered), father – **Israel,**
daughter **Soyba** (1934 -),
son **Efim** (1940 – 1942, murdered). *All died in Shoah in Odessa (YdV).*

Yasha,
wife **Leya (Leyka) Stanislavskaya** "lived near us" *KhK.*

Kupershlak.
Froyka (- Haifa, Israel), worked as a photographer, mother – **Etl.**
wife **Liza Vinokur** (- Kaushany), nurse. Lived in Kaushany after the war,
daughter **Rozetta** (1953 - Kaushany), graduated Russian school.
Froyka *with his daughter emigrated to Israel, lived in Haifa, buried there (G). Both*
grandmothers of **Rozetta Etl** *and* **Khanna** *died and buried in Kaushany (G).*

Latman (Lotman).
    Itsik (Yitskhok), was in Middle Class, registered in Odessa,
      wife **Ita (Yute),**
        daughter **Zelda** (5-Sep-1878, Kaushany -),
        son **Shloime** (1881, Kaushany – 4-Nov-1884, Kaushany), died from Diphtheritis,
        son **Mordko-Idel,**
          wife **Genya,**
            daughter **Malka** (4-Oct-1897, Kaushany -).

    Khenya (1870, Kaushany – 1943, murdered near Kharkov),
      husband **Nakhum Itskovich.** See **Itskovich** family.

Layner (Lainer).
    Zyoma (1924, Kishinev - 1985, Kaushany, buried in Bendery), was an economist,
      wife **Manya Letichever,** (1922, Kaushany - 1997, Kaushany, buried in Bendery), after
        the war lived in Kaushany and was an accountant *(G, RR),*
      son **Milya** (1949, Kaushany - 1992, Kaushany, buried in Bendery),
        wife **Julia,** remarried to **Fedor,** former prosecutor in Kaushany,
          two sons-twins- **Vitalii** and **Sergei** (Jan-1975), live with wife's and
            children in Saarbrücken, Germany *(RR).*

Lebedinskiy.
    Isroel, was a tinsmith *(B24).*

Lender.
    Itsik,
      wife **Rosa,**
        son **Meyer** (1907, Kaushany - 1942), hat master,
          wife **Sura,**
            daughter **Roza.**
    They lived before the war in Volontirovka. **Meyer** *was killed on the front in 1942 (YdV).*

Lerner.
    Shamsha (Ilisha). "He had a large white beard, he sold cigarettes" *(KhK)* and according
        to *B24* owned a bakery,
      son **Abram** (1896, Kaushany – 1941-42), owned a bakery, had a large hall in the yard,
        which was rented to an organization "Makkabi",
        wife **Sara Arhimovich** (1900-1978, Kishinev), **Sara's** father – **Ruvin,**
          daughter **Basya** (1927, Bendery-2014, San-Diego, buried in San-Jose, CA),
            husband **Mordekhay (Musya) Zeltser** (– 1990, Pittsburgh, PA), see **Zeltser**
              family,
          daughter **Mira** (1933 – 2007, San Diego),
          daughter **Rachel (Raya),** (-1978, Kishinev),
            husband **Aleksander Zonis,** see **Zonis** family.

    Michael
      daughter **Roza** (1906, Kaushany -).

Letichever.
    Moisey (Moshe),
      son **Berl (Berka, Boris, "mosh Potap")** (1895 – 1980, Kaushany, buried in

Bendery). He traveled from market to market with haberdashery.

    wife **Ena Shwarts** (1892 – 1986, Kaushany, buried in Bendery), father - **Aba**.
        She was from Kalarash, her father was killed in a pogrom,

      daughter **Viktoria (Vitya)** (9-May-1920, Kaushany – 10-Aug-1972, buried in Kaushany,
        and re-buried in Bendery) after the war was teacher in Kaushany Moldovan
        Elementary school *(G, RR)*,

      husband **Yakov Goldshtein** (see **Goldshtein** family),

      daughter **Manya** (1922, Kaushany-1997, Kaushany, buried in Bendery), after
        the war lived in Kaushany and was accountant *(G, RR)*,

      husband **Zyoma Layner** (1924, Kishinev-1985, Kaushany, buried in Bendery)
        was an economist (see family **Layner**),

      daughter **Tsilya** (1924, Kaushany – 2001, Saarbrücken, Germany) studied with me
        in one class of gymnasium" *(KhK)*. After the war lived in Kaushany and was an
        accountant,

      husband **Grisha Fridman** (1920, Chechelnik, Ukrane - 2014, Saarbrücken,
        Germany),

      daughter **Zhenya** (1957, Bendery) lives in Saarbrücken, Germany *(G)*,

    daughter **Khaya Kalskiy**, was buried in Kaushany,

    husband __**? Kalskiy**, see **Kalskiy** family

    son **Volodya (Velvl)** with his wife lived in Kiev,

    daughter **Mada** with family emigrated to Israel from Sambor.

Levin.

    Khaim Moshe,

      wife **Sara,**

        daughter **Serika** (1904, Kaushany – 1943 died in Shoah *(YdV)*,
        husband **Mikhel.**

Levinzon (Levenzon).

    Mendel, father – Volko (Zeev),

      wife **Perlya,**

        son **Shloime (Shlomo)** (7-Feb-1902, Kaushany -).

"We had several families with that name" *(KhK)*.

Chisil (Kisil) owned a grocery store *(B24)*,

    wife **Maria**

      son **Leontiy** (1916, Kaushany -), served in the Soviet Army, MIA since 1944 *(Mem)*.

Khana,

    husband **Shaya Ochakovskiy**, married in Kaushany 14-Nov-1914.

Levit.

    Moshko (1816 -), father – **Luzer,**

     wife **Basya** (1819 -),

      son **Mordko** (1833 -),

       wife **Dislya** (1832 -),

        daughter **Sheindel** (1856 -),

      son **Luzer (Elozor, Leyzer)** (1837 -), father – **Moshko,**

       wife **Khana,**

        daughter **Leya** (20-Feb-1866, Kaushany -),

      son **Itsik** (1841 -),

son **Penkhis** (1844 -),
son **Idel** (1849 -).

Pinkhas-Sheftel,
  wife **Mindlya,**
    daughter **Dintsya-Leya** (4-Apr-1876, Kaushany -),
    daughter **Menya-Reizlya** (23-Jul-1878, Kaushany -).

Khaim (1818 -), father – **Yankel,**
  wife **Feiga** (1820 -), father – **Yankel,**
    son **Usher** (1849, Kaushany -), was in Middle Class, registered in Bendery Kaushany
        society,
    wife **Khinka,** had 4 sons and 2 sisters. Owned a bakery in Kaushany,
      daughter **Sheiva (Sheivl, Basya-Sheiva)** (10-Sep-1874 – 1943, Dzhezgazgan),
        husband **Shloime Spivak** (10-Oct-1866, Kaushany – 1943, Dzhezgazgan), "my
          great grandparents. Both died from hunger in Dzhezgazgan, Kazakhstan"
          (KhK, YdV), see **Spivak** family,
    son **Yankel** owned a bakery store,
      wife **Feyge Klyuzman.** They had three sons:
        son **Moyshe** was killed on the front during the war,
        son **Idel** died from typhus in evacuation,
        son **Zelman (Zoka),** lived in Kishinev after the war and from 1989 in Israel,
         wife **Khova Kisinyanskiy,** lived in Migdal-ha-Emek, had two sons,
    son **Mendel (Volf-Mendel)** (6-Dec-1878, Kaushany -),
     wife **Khaika,**
      son **Benchik,**
      daughter **Sonya** (died in Israel),
      daughter **Sofiya** (1909, Kaushany -), secretary,
    son **Khaim** owned a little fabric store in Kaushany (*B24*),
      wife **Tsirl Klyuzman,** had no children,
    son **Gersh (Ershel)** (1886, Kaushany-1942, Turkmenistan), according to *B24*
        owned a tavern, inn and was a baker. Moved in 1925 to Kishinev, where he had
        a bakery at Staro-Bazarnaya street #18,
    wife **Rukhl Teper** (1889-1942, Turkmenistan). Children:
      daughter **Enna** (1912, Kaushany – 18-Apr-2004, Siettle, USA),
        husband **David Spivak** (1905, Nisporeny, Bessarabia-1972, Kishinev),
         daughter **Khinka** (1935-1992, Israel), emigrated to Israel in 1973,
          husband **Emil Kogan** (1938),
         daughter **Raya** (1944, Turkmenistan - Seattle, USA),
      son **Nyunya (Nukhim)** (17-Sep-1915, Kaushany -), studied in Jewish
        gymnasium in Kishinev, immigrated to Palestine in 1937,
       wife **Leya,** daughter **Rukhl,**
      son **David** studied in French Gymnasium, served in labor battalion and died,
       wife **Khaika,**
      daughter **Sima** (1917, Kaushany), studied in Romanian gymnasium in
        Kishinev,
       husband **Shika Avstriyskiy** served in the military and died in the war,
       husband **Iosif Altman** (1904, Orgeev - 1985, Kishinev),
      daughter **Stunya** (1920, Kaushany -), moved to Leningrad in 1946,
       husband **Izya Vaynshteyn,** died in 2000 in Bruklyn, NY,
    daughter **Pessya** (25-Apr-1876, Kaushany -),

husband **Bronshteyn** moved to USA or Argentina in 1904, divorced,
  son **Mitse,** lived in Chimishliya, after the was lived in Kishinev on Aziatskaya street,
    wife **Khova,**
      son **Monya** (- died in Israel),
  son **Meyer,** moved to Argentina in 1928-29. Had two sons,
    husband (second) **Bension (Benchik) Zindelis** (1871 -), was a widower, father – **Moshko** from Tulchin.

Abram, father – **David,**
  son **Moisey** (1914 – Nov-1944)**,** served in the Soviet military, private and was MIA since 1944 *(Mem, YdV).*

Shaya, lived before the war in Bendery,
  wife **Khaya-Feiga Gitlin** (1910, Kaushany – 1941, murdered in Shoa).

Leibelman.
  Luzer, "I remember **Luzer,** who was in the same trial with my uncle **Boris Spivak.** He got a death sentence" *(KhK).*

  Moyshe owned a grocery store *(B24).*

Leibovich (Leibovich, Lebovich, Leibovici).
  Iosif (c1870, Kaushany-1961, Bronx, NY), grain dealer, owned a grocery store *(B24),*
    wife **Shprintsa Brodskiy** (1879-1963) (Video). 3 sons, 3 daughters (one daughter died young),
      son **Moyshe** (c1906, Kaushany - 1942, Sevastopol) Served in the army and killed during the war in Sevastopol,
        wife **Rivka,**
          son **Monik** 3 years old before the war started,
      son **Markus (Mordekhai, Motel)** (June 15, 1914, Kaushany – 2009, LA),
        wife **Dora** (~1919, Poland), survived from Auschvits, got married in 1946-47, emigrated to USA in 1947-48, took parents to NY,
      son **Velvel** (c1920 -), the youngest was in the army and killed during the war,
      daughter **Marim (Miriam, Rusia)** (1912, Kaushany -), was a teacher, moved to Yassy, lived together with sister **Enna**'s family,
        husband **Isrul Gurevich,** violinist for Romania Royal Court, divorced because **Isrul** did not want to go to USSR with parents,
        husband (second) **Mozes Levin** (Video) (-2009, LA), according to B-24 lived in town of Orlovka, Kirgistan, moved to NY and later to LA,
      daughter **Enna (Genyam, Anna)** (1904, Kaushany – 1974, LA), in 1951 went to Chile, after living in Germany and Paris,
        husband **Samuel (Sami, Shmil) Berdichevskiy** (1905, Bendery – 1974, Mendoza, Argentina)**,** was a businessman in fabric, lived in Germany, Paris after the war and emigrated to Chile in 1951 *(LM),*
      daughter **Basya (Busika)** (1-Oct-1932, Yassy, Romania -), 1938 went to Bucharest, went to Kaushany for holidays,
          video: https://www.youtube.com/watch?v=nILcE2Fovqs
        husband **Solomon Shpigel** from Czernovitsh 1958 (in Chile), had three daughters,
      daughter **Olga (Olgita, Olya)** (13-Mar-1935, Yassy, Romania), PhD in Education, lived in Chile, Argentina,

video: https://www.youtube.com/watch?v=CoS25MA2hJ8
husband **Solomon Wainberg,** married in 1968 in Chile.

Efroim (- 1941, killed in Kaushany),before the war lived in Baia, Romania, during the war was in Kaushany. Was a forced laborer *(YdV).*

Liberman (Leiberman).

Elie, father – **Leib,** was a dayer, painter *(B24),* was in Middle Class, registered in Tovragin, Kovno gubernia,
> wife **Khaya,**
>> daughter **Tsipa** (1910, Kaushany -),
>> daughter **Pesya** (3-Oct-1915, Kaushany -).

Lemel,
> wife **Beila-Rukhlya,**
>> son **Arie-Leib** (6-Nov-1887, Kaushany -).

Mordekhai (Mordko), was a Rabbi in Kaushany in 19c,
> wife **Sara,**
>> son **Leib** (c1890, Kaushany – Jun-1941, killed near Kiev), mailman,
>>> wife **Khaya Reznikovskaya.**

Linskiy.

Iosif, fought in WWI, was private and MIA since 1914, father – **Yankel,**
> son **Idrul** (1919, Kaushany - served in the Soviet army and was killed in 1943 *(Mem),*
> son **Moisey** (1923, Kausahny – 30-Jan-2005), served in the military from 6-Jul-1942, private, sapper, mobilized *(Mem).*

Lipkanskiy.

Sheivakh,
> son **Srul (Israel, Shtrul)** owned a flour and products store in Kaushany *(B24),*
>> wife **Ester-Malka,** father – **Mikhel,**
>>> daughter **Dvoira** (17-Oct-1897 - 1989, Los Angeles),
>>> son **Yekhiel (Iliya)** (14-Jan-1903, Kaushany -),
>>> daughter __? (1910 - 1988, Los Angeles),
>>> son **Moyshe** (1910 - 2000, Los Angeles),
>>>> wife **Khaik**a (1921-2002, Los Angeles),
> son **Abram** owned a grocery store in Kaushany*(B24),*
>> wife **Freida,** her father – **Volko,**
>>> son **Sheivakh** (8-May-1897, Kishinev - 3-Oct-1972, Kishinev) (burial record),
>>>> wife **Sonya Eizner** (1898, Chimishlia – 1941),
>>>>> daughter **Tsilya** (1926, Kaushany-old - 1941). **Sonya** and **Tsilya** died in Shoah *(YdV),*
>>> daughter **Dintsya** (19-Dec-1902, Kaushany -),
>>> daughter **Nesya** (9-Feb-1915, Kaushany -).

Volf,
> son **David** (1891 -),
>> wife **Khona Sandler** from Bratslav uezd, Podolia, marriage on 31-Jan-1914 in Kaushany *(JG).*

Litmanovich.

    Yakov,
        wife **Kutsa Voldman**,
          daughter **Tsilya,**
          daughter **Zhanna** (1955 -), classmate of **Nona Geisman**). Emigrated to USA in
              1990s *(G)*.

    Leib,
        wife **Livsha,** lived in Kaushany in 19c, moved abroad.

Litvak.

    Gersh (1898, Kaushany – 1942, died in Shoa), merchant, parents **Shmil** and **Zelda**.
        The family lived before the war in Kaushany *(YdV)*.

Liverant.

    Toyva (Tae) was a blacksmith *(B24)*.
        son **Shika** (13-Jun-1914, Kaushany -), fought in the war, lieutenant,

    Volf, father – **Shulim,** was in Middle Class, registered in Kishinev,
        wife **Makhlya,**
          daughter **Freida** (17-Mar-18989, Kaushany -),
          son **Benyamin,**
            wife **Feiga,**
              son **Shlioma** (17-Sep-1915, Kaushany -).

Lobachevskiy.

    Mordekhai (Markus) (1887, Kiev - 1941),
        wife **Ester-Rakhel Kogan** (20-Sep-1888, Stolnicheny – 1941, Kaushany). They lived
            before the war in Kaushany. **Mordekhay** and **Ester** died in Shoah in 1941 in
            Kaushany *(YdV)*. Parents – **David Zalman** and **Sara**.
        son **David Libon** (changed surname),
        daughter **Sara,**
          husband __? **Veiner,**
        son **Emil** (1925, Kaushany – Jul-1943, served in Soviet army and was killed near
            Kursk).

Lvovskiy.

    Shlyoma, merchant, owned a business of egg and chicken production together with
            father of **Sara Gibrikh,**
        wife **Rysa,**
          daughter **Basya** (1924 -), "was my good friend, we studied in gymnasium" *(KhK)*.
           Shlyoma and Basya died in Shoah in Odessa (YdV).

    Mendel,
      son **Boris** (1877 -),
        wife **Rukhlya** (1877 -), father – **Volf,**
        daughter **Elya** (1916 -).

    Mikhel, father – **Iosko (Iosif),**
      wife **Reyzya,**
        daughter **Sura (Sara)** (30-Aug-1902, Kaushany -).

Lyubarov (Lubarov, Liubarov).
    Levi,
      wife **Gitl,**
        daughter **Fania** (1909, Bendery –1941-42, murdered in Shoa, Nikolaev), before the
            war family lived in Kaushany,
          husband **Meir Brodskiy,** see **Brodsky** family,
        daughter **Ida Tabachnik.**

Malamud (Melamed).
    Nuba owned a confectionary *(B24).*

    Volf (Yudo-Volf, Yehuda-Ze'ev),
      wife **Tuba (Taube),**
        son **Nuta** (1890, Kaushany -), baker,
          wife **Gitlya** (1898 -), father - **Itsik,** bakers,
            daughter **Brukha (Brakha)** (8-Oct-1915, Kaushany -),
            daughter **Tuba** (1933) *(J-R).*

    Zeida (Zeydel), father **Mordko,**
      wife **Khaya-Sura,**
        son Khaim (16-Mar-1899, Kaushany -),
        son **Yerikhim,** lived in Kaushany before the war, "was our neighbor, carpenter" *(KhK),*
          wife **Zisla Goldgamer,**
             son **Khaim** (1918, Kaushany -), carpenter, soldier, was missing in action.

Meir,
    son **Itsik,**
      daughter **Gitlya** (1898, Kaushany -), baker.

Moyshe,
    wife **Mindl,**
      son **Shlomo** (1873, Kaushany -), was a shoikhet- ritual slaughtrer,
        wife **Tsipora** (- 1942, Tarutino, died in Shoah *(YdV),*
          daughter **Feiga,**
      son **Asher** (1878, Kaushany – 1943, Akkerman, murdered), was a shoikhet- ritual
            slaughtrer,
        wife **Dina Milshtein,** family lived in Akkerman,
      daughter **Feiga Dunavetski.**

    Khaya (1877, Poland – 1942, during evacuation), widow, lived before the war in
            Kaushany.

Shezh,
    wife **Sura Milshtein** (1893 -), father – **Iosif,** lived in Kaushany before the war,
      daughter **Perlya** (1924 -),
      son **Khaskel** (1927 -),
      daughter **Riva** (1934 -).

Iosif,
    daughter **Sura** (1893, Kaushany -).

__?,
husband __? **Tsinkler**. See **Tsinkler** *(G)*.

Malkin (Molkin).
"I remember that family lived on a "Bud gos" –Bath street, and that they were poor
(KhK).
Bunim, and **Moshko** were men's tailors *(B24)*.

Srul, father – **Munash,**
  wife **Enta,**
    son **Munish (Munash)**, (1825 -), was a Rabbi in Kaushany in 1850s,
      wife **Malka** (1826 -),
        son **Khaim** (1845 -),
          wife **Ita,**
            daughter **Rukhl (Rakhel)** (1-Jan-1866, Kaushany -),
            daughter **Malka** (28-Feb-1876, Kaushany -),
            son **Srul-Leib** (5-Feb-1878, Kaushany -),
          daughter **Khaya** (1849 -),
          daughter **Beila** (1852 -),
        daughter **Malka** (1829 -),
        daughter **Marim** (1833 -),
        son **Lemel** (1837 -),
          wife **Keila,**
          daughter **Tsirlya** (6-Nov-1866, Kaushany -),
        son **Abram** (1841 -),
          son **Ayzik,**
            wife **Etlya,** family lived before the war in Kaushany,
              son **Beniamin** (17-Jan-1899, Kaushany -) (possible – **Bunim**), tailor,
              daughter **Golda** (1922 -), seamstress,
              daughter **Raya**(1924 -),
              daughter **Khaya** (1926 -).*(J-R)*.

Maryasin (Maryasim).
  Yankel owned a shop selling various sausages and sweets,
    son **Leyzer,**
    daughter **Riva**. "I studied with **Riva** in gymnasium, but we were not close friends.
        Leyzer also studied in gymnasium but was older. I met **Riva** at some point in Tsur-
        Shalom, Israel, but later she moved to her daughter in Tel-Aviv" *(KhK)*.

Etlya (1897), father - **Simon** *(J-R)*.

Srul (Israel),
  son **Abram** (- tragically died in 1922, Kaushany), buried in Kaushany, his stone was found not
      far from Kaushany, see section Cemeteries.
  son **Iosif (Ios-Shoel)**, owned a grocery shop *(B24)*. Died before the war
    wife **Tsipa** (- 1941, killed in Kaushany), had three children,
      daughter **Khana** (17-Apr-1902, Kaushany -),
      son **Gersh** (28-Aug-1903, Kaushany – 1941, killed in Kaushany) *(JG, TsD)*,
        wife **Roza,**
          son **Borukh** (1910 – 1977, Kishinev), owned a Ford sedan car, was servicing all over,
              including Tighina (Bendery) *(TsD)*. He was enlisted into Soviet Army, was

174

caught and put in a camp,
wife **Ester Klyuzman** (c1917, Kaushany – 2007, Los Angeles),
daughter **Perl** (– 1941, killed in Kaushany),
daughter **Tsilya,**
daughter **Ira** (named in memory of **Ides Klyuzman**), live now in Los Angeles,
daughter **Gitl** (15-Jun-1918, Kaushany - 1941, killed in Kaushany).

Mechtovich.
> **Mordko** (1915 - 1944), served in the military and was MIA since 1944. Parents – **Meir** and **Blyuma Ester Shulimovna** (Mem).

Meleger.
> **Buma** – musician,
> **Vova Buma**'s brother. Do not remember their parent's names *(G).*

Mikhailovskiy.
> **Pesya** (– Kaushany), was married for the second time.
>> Together with her husband sold ice cream in the center of Kaushany. I still remember where their kiosk and the taste of the ice cream was. *(G).* **Pesya** died and was buried at Kaushany Jewish cemetery. Had three sons
>
> son **Misha,** died at work,
>> wife **Ida Rakhales** (- Kiriyat -Yam), she worked as a nurse in Old Kaushany,
>> daughter **Raya,**
>>> husband ___? **Rosenberg**. *Ida with family of her daughter **Raya Rosenberg** emigrated to Israel. (G).*
>
> son **Shurik,** moved to Bendery, and later emigrated to Israel,
> son **Efim** (adopted), pharmacist in 1960-70s,
>> wife **Nyusya Viner** worked as pharmacists in Kaushany pharmacy.
>>> They had a son and a daughter. After they retired *the family moved to Bendery and after that emigrated (G).*

> **Raya Trakhtenberg** (**Pesya**'s sister) (see **Trakhtenberg).**

Mikhalenko.
> **Klava,** worked at the registry at Kaushany clinic in 1960-70s,
>> daughter **Elena** (1954, Kaushany -), moved to Kishinev, where worked as a judge.
>> son **Anatoliy** *(G).*

Miller.
> **Meyer** – tinsmith *(B24).*

> **Srul (Yisroel),**
>> wife **Menicha-Feiga,**
>>> son **Moshko-Volka** (22-Dec-1876, Kaushany -),
>>> daughter **Genya-Gitlya (Henye-Gitel)** (24-Jun-1878, Kaushany -).

Millerman.
> **Rivka** (1879, Kaushany – 1941, murdered in Bogdanovka), parents **Israel** and **Olti,** husband **Kopel Shoykhet,** family lived before the war in Odessa *(YdV).*

Milshteyn.

> **Asher** died in Shoah in Akkerman in 1943,
>> **Lyonya, Misha, Dina, Lopa, Raya** – family after the war lived in Kaushany.

> **Iosif,**
>> daughter **Sura** (1893 -), lived in Kaushany,
>>> husband **Shezh Melamed**, see **Melamed** family.

Mogilner. "I remember **Shlioma**. He owned a fabric store. *(B24)*.
> **Zvi (Gersh),**
>> son **Leiv (Arieh Leib Iheuda, Leon, Leib)** (1858, Kaushany – 3-Nov-1942, La Plata, Argentina), had a grocery store in Kaushany. Was in Middle Class registered in Gorushkov, Yampol uezd.
>> wife **Rukhl Khaikin** (1857, Kaushany – 6-Nov-1924, Buenos Aires),
>>> son from first marriage **Moyshe Vaisman/Waksman** (1886 – 1960s, Buenos Aires, Argentina). They had another 7 children.
>>> son **Shlioma** (1870, Kaushany - Asuncion, Paraguay) had a fabric store in Kaushany (B24). There is **Shlema Mogilner**, father -**Leib** (1883-1954, buried in Kishinev (JG). *Not sure if he is related or same as **Shlioma***.
>>> wife **Perlya,**
>>>> daughter **Beyla** (21-Nov-1915, Kaushany -),
>>>> son **Raful** (10-Jun-1884, Kaushany – 12-Aug-1937, Buenos-Aires),
>>>>> wife **Dora Krischacautzky,**
>>>>> wife (second) **Esther Groisman,**
>>>> son **Shmil** (Kishinev – Asuncion, Paraguay),
>>>> daughter **Ester** (1886 – 22-Mar-1952, Argentina),
>>>> daughter **Gietel (Catalina)** (10-Aug-1892, Bendery – 7-May-1956, Argentina),
>>>> son **Valentin** (c1900 – c1970, Buenos Aires),
>>>> daughter **Rivka (Rebeca)** (5-Jan-1897, Kaushany – 11-Jan-1963).

*The whole family emigrated to Argentina in 1912 with children but **Shlioma** who was married.*

Moldavskiy.

> **Itsko-Meyer**, was in Middle Class, registered in Tiraspol, father - **Yankel,**
>> wife **Nekha** – barber *(B24)*, father – **Shmil,**
>>> daughter **Rivka** (9-Dec-1897, Kaushany -),
>>> son **Luzor (Eliezer)** (7-Feb-1902, Kaushany -).

> **Abram-Moshko**, was in Middle Class registered in Bendery,
>> wife **Tsirlya (Ester-Tsirel),**
>>> daughter **Khaya-Rosya** (17-Aug-1876, Kaushany -).

> **Todoris** (1913, Kaushany - 1943), fought in the war, captain, died from wounds. Father – **Moisey.**

Mordkovich.

> **Leib (Yuda-Leib),** owned haberdashery shop *(B24)*. Was Merchant of 3rd Gild, father – **Idel,**
>> wife **Etlya,**
>>> son **Itskhok** (25-Jan-1899, Kaushany -).

David (David-Khaim), was in Middle Class, registered in Kishinev, father – **Meir,**
  wife **Ene (Hene),**
    son **Itsko** (29-Jul-1866, Kaushany -),
      wife **Khaya,**
        daughter **Sonya (Sara)** (13-Apr-1902, Kaushany -).

Natanzon (Natenzon).
      "There were several families with that name. I remember **Moyshe ,** but
        not his family" *(KhK).*
Moyshe (Moisey) (1885 – 1856, Lvov, Ukraine), was a peasant, father-**Shmuel (Samoil),**
    wife **Tsilya (Shprintza)** (1885 – 1950, Lvov, Ukr.), housewife, parents **Efim** and **Tabl,**
      son **Khaim (Yefim)** (1920, Kaushany – 2000, Tel Aviv, Israel), served in the soviet
          army, after the war lived in Chernovtsy, Ukraine,
      daughter **Anna (Khana)** (1926, Kaushany – 2002, Germany),
      daughter **Nyusya** (1928, Kaushany -).

Ma? (died and buried 18-Feb-1928, Kaushany), there is a fragment of inscription found near
      Kaushany, see it in the Cemetery section.

Nukhim (c1874 -), owned a fabric store *(B24)*, father – **Matvey,**
  wife **Feiga** (c1879 -), father – **Nakhman,**
    daughter **Perel** (1904 -),
      husband **Israel Volodarskiy,**
        son **Modi** (1933 -),
    daughter **Freyda** (1912 -),
      husband __**? Stanislavskiy,**
    daughter **Udlya** (1913 -), seamstress.

Motel,
  wife **Freyda,**
    son **Shmul** (1859, Kaushany – 1941, died in Shoa), trader *(YdV),*
      wife **Tauba Sobol.**

Shmul (1865, Kaushany - died in Shoah *(YdV)*, father **Mordekhay,**
  wife **Etya-Leya.**

Iosif,
  wife **Golda Kleinman,**
    son **Gersh** (8-Aug-1925, Kaushany - 29-Oct-1944, Lithuania, on front),
    daughter **Eta ,**
      husband __**? Tregerman.**

Shuka,
  wife **Ester** (1911 – 1941, murdered in Odessa),
    daughter **Rukhale** (1937, Kaushany – 1941, murdered in Odessa).

Pinkus, lived before the war in Struzheny,
  wife **Lyuba Khaikin** (1900, Kaushany – 1941, murdered), parents **Sara** and **Gersh,**
          see **Khaikin** family.

David,

son **Iosif** (1907, Kaushany -), served in the army, private and was MIA from 1944
    (Mem).
  wife **Sara (Sura)** (1902 -), father **Iosif.** They moved to Czernovtsy before the
    war,
    daughter **Nekhama** (1933 -) *(J-R)*,
son **Boris** (1916, Kaushany -), was a doctor, served in the army and was killed *(YdV)*.

__?,
  son **Leyzer,**
    daughter **Sima,**
    daughter **Nona,**
    son **Srulik, "** from our gang. **Srulik** lives now in Kirijat Yam. He already has two
        great grandchildren and always calls me to congratulate with holidays" *(KhK,
        c2000)*.
  daughter **Khona** (1902 – 1977, Izmail),
    husband **Buka (Abram) Kogan** (died in 1939-1940, Kaushany), see **Buka Kogan** family,
    husband **Leib Spivak (Khona** re-married after **Buka** died. See **Spivak** family,
  son **__?,** "**Srulik** and **Khona**'s brother, I do not remember his name. He had a daughter
    daughter **Sara,** studied with me in gymnasium. They lived not far from Kaushany, in
        a village and had a business, a grocery shop and also a large household. After the
        war **Sara** married her cousin" *(KhK)*.

Tyusha / Etel, daughter of **Shmul** (1920, Kaushany – 1998, Kiryat Nordau, Israel). She
    was a professor at Tiraspol Pedagogical Institute after the war).

Shura owned a grocery store *(B24)*.

Srul owned a dairy store on the main street.

Boris
  wife **Ester Brener**, Most likely **Ester** was buried in Kaushany Jewish cemetery *(G)*.
    daughter **Evgenia,** she was kindergarten teacher. Her mother lived with them –
        They lived in Old Kaushany. **Evgenia** had 2 sons.
    son **Iosif** (1956, Kaushany -), graduated Aviation Academy, lives in Sankt-
        Peterburg. I studied with him in Musical School *(G)*.
    son **Beniamin** (1961 -), lives in Germany.

Niselevich.
    Olga, father – **Isak.** She was French language teacher. Worked in Kaushany Russian
        school. She was cousin of **Michail Semenovich Gold.** After retirement moved
        to Bendery. She had a step-daughter – **Lyuba** *(G)*.

Noikhovich.
    Yankel (Yakov), was in Middle Class, registered in Bendery,
      wife **Shprintsa,**
      daughter **Menya** (9-Apr-1876, Kaushany -).

    David, "Family had a shoe store. Accordng to *B24* – **D. (David)** was a tanner. They had
    daughter **__?** "I studied during the 'Soviets' in 1940-41*(KhK)*.

Novogrebelskiy (Novogrobelskiy).

    Kelman (Kalman) (1890, Kushany – Odessa, murdered *YdV*), owned a confectionary
        shop *(B24)*, lived before the war in Akkerman, Merchant,
    wife **Sonya** (1897, Kaushany - Odessa, murdered *YdV*).

    Khova, *possible that Khova is Kelman's daughter,*
        husband **Ershl (Gersh) Gibrikh,** from Tiraspol, but family lived in Kaushany.
        See **Gibrikh** family.

Nukhimovich.

    Shlyoma – barber *(B24)*.

    Ikhil,
      wife **Khaika Rozentsvayg** (1865, Kaushany - died in Shoah in 1942 in Odessa *(YdV)*,
        father – **Moshe.**
      son **Meylikh** (1905, Kaushany – fought in the war, soldier, was MIA since Sep-1941,
        wife **Ekaterina.**

    Srul (Yisroel),
      wife **Baba,**
        son **Itsik** (18-Sep-1878, Kaushany -), was in Middle Class, registered in Kishinev,
          wife **Sura (Sarah),**
            daughter **Rukhlya** (9-May-1903, Kaushany -),
            daughter **Leya** (2-Jan-1915, Kaushany -).

    Nuta,
      son **Yankel,** was in Middle Class, registered in Kishinev,
        wife **Idas (Egidasi),**
          son **Abram** (8-Apr-1887, Kaushany -),
          daughter **Sura** (27-Jun-1903, Kaushany -).

Ochakovskiy.

    Srul, father - **Abram**
      wife **Mamtse** (1872, Kaushany – murdered in Shoa, *YdV*), father - **Shabse**
      son **Ruvn** (2-May-1887, Kaushany - December 20, 1971, Kishinev),
        wife **Leyka Kogan** (March 5, 1892, Kaushany – October 15, 1967, Kishinev),
          daughter of **Shabsa Kogan,**
          son **Irikhem** (12-Jul-1922, Kaushany – 18-Sep-2015, Beer-Sheva),
           wife **Dora (Dvoira) Vinokur** (May 30, 1920, Kaushany – October 17, 1985,
            Kishinev), parents **Itskhak** and **Rakhel,**
          daughter **Mara** ((December 11, 1928, Kaushany, Romania – June 7, 2020,
           Natania, Israel),
           husband **Nyuma (Nakhum) Kogan** (January 29, 1923 – September 10, 1977,
           Kishinev), married in 1952,
          son **Aleksandr (Shurik)** (1938, Kaushany -).
        daughter **Dintsa** (1910, Kaushany – murdered in Shoa, *YdV*),
        son **Ezra (Israel)** (- Dec-1941, died in evacuation, Kazakhstan),
          wife **Lyuba Khrusch** (- 1944, Alma Ata, died from starvation),
           daughter **Manya** (1922, Kaushany – Sep-1941, died in Shoa, was shot in Kaushany),
           husband **Monya Goldner.** They lived in Romanovka before the war,
          daughter **Sara** (1927, Kaushany -),

son **Mikhail Mendel** (1930, Kaushany – Sep-2022, Israel),
son **Zelman (Zalman)**
wife **Mindle,** lived in Romanovka and Kaushany before the war,
daughter **Roza** (8-Aug-1922, Kaushany – Jul-2007, Ramle, Israel),
son **Shaul** (1928, Kaushany – Oct-1993, Holon, Israel),
son **Alexandr** (18-Sep-1935, Kaushany -).
daughter **Tauba** (8-Aug-1897, Kaushany -)

Khaim,
wife **Risl Dvoirin** (1878, Kaushany – 1941, Bolgrad, died in Shoah in Bolgrad),
Parents **Leibl** and **Beila**.

Shaya, father – **Alter-Shoel,**
wife **Khana Levinzon,** married in Kaushany 14-Nov-1914.

Zamvel (Zaivel) (1906, Kaushany -), father – **David,**
wife **Riva** (1898 -), lived in Kaushany before the war, father – **Shmul,**
daughter **Fanya** (1934, Kaushany -),
son **Iosif** (1936, Kaushany -).

Odesskiy.
Gersh (Tzvi) was a shoemaker *(B24),*
wife **Khaya,**
daughter **Khava** (17-Dec-1915, Kaushany -).

Shoel,
daughter **Khaya-Zislya** (1-Jan-1876, Kaushany -),
son **Ios-Nukhim,**
wife **Etlya,**
daughter **Pesya** (4-Jan-1902, Kaushany -).

Leizer, private in the Russian Army,
wife **Golda,**
son **Shovel-Aron** (23-Feb-1887, Kaushany -).

Moshko, was a dress maker, father **Itsko.**

Srul, father – **Miron (Meir),**
son **Mordko** (1907), was a nurse, served in the army, was killed *(Mem).*

Sura(1870), father **Itsik** *(J-R).*

Opachevskiy (Opachesky).
Berl (Berko) (1899 -), was one the owners of a fabric store, where worked **Lyova
Spivak. Berl** was sent to GULAG in 1940-41, because he was rich, died
on a way" *(KhK),*
wife **Rahil (Rukhlya),** women's clothing seamstress *(B24).*

Yankel (Yakov),
wife **Ester-Khaya,**

son **Itsik-Reful (Yitskhok-Refoel)** (5-Jun-1878 -), twin,
son **Volko (Zeev)** (5-Jun-1878 -), twin.

Yankel, father **Srul** *(1906 Voter's list),*
  wife **Tsipa,**
    daughter **Bune** (26-May-1887, Kaushany -),
    daughter **Shprintsa** (29-Jan-1899, Kaushany -), twin,
    son **Iosif** (29-Jan-1899, Kaushany -), twin.

Leyzer *(1907 Voter's list),*
  son **Volf** (1887, - Kuba),
    wife **Khana** (04-Nov-1890 – 24-Apr-1973, Kishinev), father - **Yankel,**
      son **Khaim** (1920, Kaushany -),
      daughter **Mariyasa** (1924, Kaushany -),
     son **Ovshey** (- Kaushany, ?), grave in Kishinev points that Ovshey died and buried in
                Kaushany.
  son **Itsik** (1892, Kaushany -),
    wife **Sitsva** (1897, Kaushany -), father **Favel,**
      daughter **Tsilya** (1927 -),
      daughter **Tuba** (1920, Kaushany -), seamstress *(J-R).*

      "Two brothers and a sister **Mariyasa** were in the family. I knew well her, but she was
      younger than me and we did not belong to the same group" *(KhK).*

Khaim *(1907 Voter's list),*
  wife **Ester** (1897 -), father – **Khaim,**
    son **Tsay (Tsayek)** (1886 -), lived in Kaushany,
      wife **Udlya** (1890), father - **David,**
        daughter **Golda**(1924 -) *(J-R),*
  son **Elik** (1897 -),
    wife __?,
      son **Boris (Borukh)** (5-Mar-1927, Kaushany -), fought in the war, was Senior
                Lieutenant Engineer, demobilized after the war.

Golda, father – **Ruvin,**
  husband **Shulim Averbukh** (see **Averbukh** family**).**

Toyve (Tolya) (1920-30s – Beer-Sheva)
  wife **Sonya Epelman** (- , Beer-Sheva), after they married moved to Bendery.
        Two children: **Misha, Lenya.** Emigrated to Israel, **Lenya** lives in Beer-Sheva,
        where **Sonya** and **Toyve** were buried *(G).*
Tsilya, Toyve's sister (1938). Also emigrated to Israel with her son *(G).*

__?,
  wife **Tanya Soltanovich** (sister of **Semen Soltanovich).**

Velvel (1860s, Kaushany - ?),
  wife **Miriam Braunshtein** (1860-), father – **Sroel,**
    daughter **Frima (Fanny) Schecter** (1882, Kaushany -),
      husband **Harry Schecter** (born **Friedman,** adopted by **Schecter** family),
        son **Yankel,**

son **Reuven,**
daughter **Ethel,**
daughter **Sadie,**
daughter **Ida.**

Osnis (Osnas).

Iosif, "I remember **Iosif,** he owned a fabric store on the main street on the corner of
"Birzha". One son studied in Belgium, and after the war was a doctor in Kishinev
Hospital #2 *(KhK).*
son **Shulim** (1-Mar-1909, Kaushany -), fought in the war, was Major of the Medical
Service, demobilized after the war.

Abraham,
wife **Shifra,**
daughter **Khana** (1927, Kaushany -).

Ovis.

Yakov,
wife **Etel** (1906, Kaushany – 10-Sep-1941), lived before the war in Tarakliya, died in
Shoah in 1941 in Ukraine *(YdV).*

Pechyonyy.

Zeylik (1905, Bendery – 1941, served in Soviet Army and died in Odessa *YdV*), parents
Volf and **Sofiya,**
wife **Roza Vaysbeyn,**
daughter **Sofiya.** The family lived before the war in Kaushany.

Perchis.

Shlyoma owned store selling flour and flour products *(B24).*

Perelman.

Peisakh, father – **Iosif,** was in Middle Class, registered in Bendery,
wife **Genya-Sheindlya,**
daughter **Malka** (25-Oct-1899 -),
daughter **Perlya (Perl)** (16-Apr-1903 -).

Khaim (1907, Kaushany -),
wife **Riva** (1908 -),
daughter **Shloma** (1936 -)*(J-R).*

David,
daughter **Frida,** lived in Kaushany, during the war evacuated to Uzbekistan *(Y-V).*

--? elderly parents of **Izya Perelman** (1935), native of Kaushany.
Seems they were buried at the Jewish cemetery in Kaushany (G).
son **Izya** (1935, Kaushany-1970-80?, Kishinev) – engineer. Lived with family in
Kaushany, not far from Russian school, on the road to Christian cemetery.
wife **Ester** (1932, Kishinev), graduated Kishinev Medical Institute, worked as
neuropathologist in Kaushany region hospital. Father – **Aron.**
son **Boris** (1957, Kaushany -),
son **Igor** (1959, Kaushany -),

182

son **Nyusik** (1928) was a friend with my father **Usher Geisman, (**G**)**,

son **Misha** (1946) – dentist, lived in Kishinev and in the beginning of 1970s, emigrated
to Israel.

*Izya Perelman died in Kishinev and buried there. Family moved to Kishinev in
the beginning of 1970s. **Ester** emigrated to Israel with sons in the beginning of 1990s.
They lived in Ashdod (G).*

Pfeyfer.

Iosif (1913, Kaushany – 1943, served in the Soviet Army and was killed), parents **Dinne**
and **Pepe** *(YdV)*. The family lived in Kaushany before the war.

Pinkovskiy.

Genya (1893 -), father **Srul**,
husband **Yakov**, family lived in Kaushany before the war,
son **Pinkus** (1925 -),
daughter **Zhenya** (1922 -)*(J-R)*.

Pogoriler.

Moshko-Nakhman, father – **Duvid,**
wife __? (likely she passed before 1914, and **Moshko-Nakhman** re-married,
wife **Matya Fershteyter,** married 24-Aug-1914 in Kaushany,
son **Zelman,** was in Middle Class, registered in Grigoriopol, father – **Moshe-
Nakhman,**
wife **Rukhlya,** father – **Gershko (Hersh),**
son **Khaim** (25-Jul-1911, Kaushany -).

Khaim (1869, Kaushany – 1934, Romania, Bessarabia), owned a grocery shop *(B24),*
wife **Khona Kogan** (1883, Tarutino – Aug-1942, Saratov),
daughter **Klara Khaya** (7-Mar-1907, Kaushany – 2-Jan-1981, Czernovtsy, Ukraine),
husband **Shloime Vasserman**. Lived before the war in Kishinev,
son **Efim,**
daughter **Sheindl** (10-Dec-1912, Kaushany – 26-Apr-1976, Kishinev),
husband **Aleksandr Shnayder**. Lived before the war in Kishinev.

Polin.

Leyzer owned a hat studio *(B24),*
son **Shmil,**
daughter **Donya (Dvosya)** (11-Apr-1918, Kaushany – 12-Apr-1967, Chimishliya) *(JG),*
husband __? **Reznik.**

Polskiy.

Fishil,
wife **Ester,**
son **Froim** (25-Feb-1878, Kaushany -),
son **Duvid** (1866 – 1941, killed in Kaushany), owned a fabric store *(B24)*, was in
Middle Class, registered in Kishinev. **Duvid** was burned alive by locals.
wife **Khaya (Taba?),**
son **Leib** (11-May-1903, Kaushany -),
son **Matus** (1906, Kaushany -), fought in the war, soldier, was MIA from 1941 (Mem).
daughter **Rakhel** (1913, Kaushany - 1941, killed in Kaushany), murdered by locals,
daughter **Ester** (1916, Kaushany – 1941, killed in Kaushany), murdered by locals) *(YdV).*

Pomos.

> **Gedal,** father – **Mark.** He was one who in 1949 lived in Kaushany and was representative from Jewish community of Kaushany when the community and synagogue got closed. See section "The end of formal Jewish Community, 1949, 25 November, Kaushany".

Prelutskiy.

> **Leib** owned an inn with tavern *(B24)*.

> **Khaim,** father – **Ikhiel** *(JG)*.

Pressman (Presman).

> **Raya** owned a tavern *(B24)*.

> **Iosif** owned a lamber storage/shop *(B24)*,
>> son **Zanvel** (1896, Kaushany -), carpenter,
>>> wife **Nekha** (1901 -), father - **Kagas**,
>>>> son **Gedali** (1924 -), carpenter *(J-R)*.

> **Ikhiel**, father – **David**
>> **Zolman** (1913, Kaushany -), fought in the war, private, was MIA,
>> **Tovie** (1919, Kaushany -), fought in the war, private, was MIA.

Pretik.

> **Grigoriy,**
>> wife **Lida** – arrived to Kaushany after the war, worked in the veterinary services in Kaushany region,
>> son **Igor** (1958, Kaushany -),
>> daughter **Zhanna**.
> *All emigrated to Israel in the beginning of 1990s (G).*

Rabinovich.

> **Srul (Yisroel),** was in Middle Class registered in Bendery, Kaushany society,
>> wife **Mariam (Mayki),**
>>> daughter **Khaya-Sura** (29-Feb-1876, Kaushany -),
>>> son **Naftuli-Gerts** (20-May-1887, Kaushany -).

> **Iosif,** father – **Itsko,**
>> wife **Sosya-Dvoira**, father – **Itsko-Leib,**
>>> son **Khaim** (21-Apr-1897, Kaushany -),
>>> daughter **Vitya** (21-Sep-1902, Kaushany -),
>>> son **Leib** (27-Jul-1911, Kaushany -).

> **Zaydel-Gersh,** was in Middle Class, registered in Kishinev, father – **Shulim,**
>> wife **Beila**, father – **Berko,**
>>> son **Berko** (13-Jan-1897, Kaushany -),
>>> daughter **Liya** (24-Feb-1899, Kaushany -),
>>> daughter **Feiga** (2-Mar-1903, Kaushany -).

> **Motl,** "We have **Motl**, who owned the only theater/cinema hall in Kaushany and rented it to touring artists and showed movies. He had two daughters.

daughter **Sima,**
daughter **Manya,** but I do not know anything about them." *(KhK).*
> *It was also another **Rabinovich,** who lent money for interest to people like my grandfather **Shloime** (KhK).*

Mordko (22-Aug-1880, Kaushany -), possibly this is **Motl.** Parents **Itsko** and **Asna.**

Ilona owned a tavern *(B24).*

Moshko owned haberdashery *(B24), (1934, court document).*

Shmil lived on main street *(1934, court document).*
son **Simkha** (1908, Kaushany -), served in Soviet Army and was MIA since 1944, (Mem).

Rapaport.
Sarra and her husband, lived in Kaushany in 1960s. **Sarra** was an accountant.
son **Feliks** (1944 -), lives in Florida, USA.
Moved to Bendery and in beginning of 1990s to Israel. (G).

Rashkovskiy.
Gedaliya owned a bakery, which was near the gymnasium,
daughter **Basya,**
daughter **Fanya (Feiga)** (1917 -), was an accountant,
son **Nisl** *(J-R).*

Sidal (1888), father **Nukhim** *(J-R).*

Raskin.
Mikhail,
son **David** (1912, Kaushany -), fought in the war, private *(Mem),*
wife **Ester,** father – **Abram.**

Ratsin (Ratzen).
Pinya (1876) owned a lamber store *(B24),* carpenter, was in Middle Class, registered in Melnitsa, Kovel uezd, father – **Mendel,**
wife **Blyuma** (1872), father - **David,**
son **Mendel** (10-May-1903, Kaushany -),
daughter **Khaya** (1918) *(J-R).*

Moyshe, father - **Mikhel,** was in Middle Class, registered in Melnitsa, Kovel uezd,
wife **Rivka,**
son **Ioyna** (19-Aug-1902, Kaushany -).

Reydich (Reidici).
Usher (1888 – 1967, Kaushany, re-buried in Bendery), father – **Moisey,**
wife **Leya** (1881 – 1967, Kaushany, re-buried in Bendery), father – **Isak,**
son **Michail (Moisei)** (- Germany), worked in a store in Zaim, close to Kaushany village. Before the war **Michail** with parents lived in Tarakliya.
wife **Angelina** (1923 - Germany), housewife. Arrived to Kaushany at the end of 1950s. They were friends of my parents. *(G),*
son **Vladimir** (1954, Kaushany -),
son **Misha** (~1956, Kaushany -),

son **Boris** (~1958, Kaushany -).
Emigrated to Germany in 1990s. (G).

Reznikov.
>**Froim,**
>>son **Moyshe** (1913, Kaushany -), served in the military and was MIA since 1941,
>>wife **Sh**.
>>daughter **Genya** *(Mem)*.

Rivkin.
>**Mikhel,** was in Middle Class, registered in Kishinev, father – **Moshko,**
>>wife **Sura-Feiga,** father – **Yankel,**
>>>son **Iosif** (27-May-1897, Kaushany -).

>**David** (1916, Kaushany -), owned a farm, **David** died in Shoah in 1944 *(YdV)*,
>>wife **Ester**. They lived before the war in Petrovka.

Royzman.
>**Gersh** (1862 -), father **Iosif,** before the war family lived in Kaushany,
>>wife **Charna** (1874 -), father - **Srul,**
>>>daughter **Khana** (1906 -) *(J-R)*,
>>>daughter **Mintsa** (1909 -), cashier,
>>>daughter **Riva** (1909 -).

>**Rimma** (1909 -), father - **Berl** *(J-R)*.

Rozenberg (Roizenbarg).
>**Gersh (Tsvi),**
>>wife **Udel (Hodel),**
>>>son **Toshka (Khaim)** (19-Jan-1866, Kaushany -).

>**Milya** "my good friend and he is also a father-in-law of my nephew" *(KhK)*.

Rozenfeld.
>**Barukh (Boris)** (1885 -), blacksmith *(B24)*. Father – **Mark,**
>>wife **Reveka** (1887 -), father – **Naum,**
>>>son **Semen** (1914 -),
>>>daughter **Betya** (1912 -), teacher, family lived in Kaushany before the war,
>>>>husband **Mark Belman,**
>>>>>son **Leva** (1941 -),
>>>daughter **Anna** (1916 -), they lived in Kaushany before the war,
>>>>husband **Semen Dubosarskiy** (1914 -), father – **Moisey,**
>>>>>daughter **Tatiana** (1841 -).

>**Mordko** (possible father of **Barukh** above) owned a grocery store *(B24)*.

>**Fishel-Aron** (1901), father - **Leib,** accountant *(J-R)*.

Rozentsvayg.
>**Khaika** (1865, Kaushany – 1942, MIA near Odessa), father – **Moshe,**

husband **Ikhil Nukhimovich.** See **Nukhimovich.**

Rukhverger (Rokhverger, Ruchwarger).
    Bentsion,
        wife **Khana** (1900, Kaushany – murdered in Transnistria),
           son **Srulik** (1924,   Kaushany - murdered in Transnistria),
           daughter **Ester** (1922, Kaushany - murdered in Transnistria),
           daughter **Ida**. *Khana, Srulik, and Ester died in Shoah in Transnistria (YdV).*

Scharevskiy.
    Isakhar owned an inn, tavern *(B24)*.

Serebryannik (Serebrennik).
    Shmil owned an inn with tavern *(B24)*,
        son **Mikhail** (1910, Kaushany -), fought in the war, private *(Mem)*.

    Moyshe-Ber (Moshe-Dov), father - **Ikhil** *(Video)*,
        wife **Soyba,**
           daughter **Liba** (11-Sep-1902, Kaushany -).

Sevriver.
    Semen, math teacher in Russian school in 1950s, father – **Grigoriy,**
        wife **Sarra** (- 2020, Rehovot, Israel)**,** doctor therapist in Kaushany regional hospital.
           Graduated from Kishinev Medical institute and was send to work in Kaushany.
           Father – **Lev.**
        son **Lev** (1955, Kaushany -), graduated Kishinev University,
        son **Efim** (1959, Kaushany -),
    In the beginning of 1970s family moved to Kishinev, and after that emigrated to Israel. **Semen** *and* **Lev** *lives in Israel,* **Efim** *in USA (G).*

Shafir (Shafer).
    Itsik (Tsuk) owned a grocery store *(B24)*. Father – **Gersh.**
        son **Fishel** (1912, Kaushany -), fought in the war, private, was MIA since 1943,
           wife **Sonya**, father – **Samuil,**
        son **Mendel** (1916, Kaushany -), fought in the war, private, was MIA since 1943.

    Efim,
        wife **Sofiya** (1916 -),
           daughter **Raya** (1941 -).

Sherman (Shirman).
    Vigdor, father – **Azril,**
        wife **Ester,**
           daughter **Khaya** (27-Feb-1899, Kaushany -).

    Moshko was men's tailor *(B24)*.

    Iosko (Iosef) (1902, Kaushany – 1941, Kaushany), had a belt/lether shop *(B24)*,
        Merchant.
        wife **Tsiviya Khayat** (1905, Dubossary – 1941, Kaushany), parents – **Etl** and **Leizer,**
           son **Khaim** (1932, Kaushany – 1941, Kaushany).

*Iosko, Tsiviya and **Khaim** died in Shoah in 1941 in Kaushany (YdV).*

Shesterman.

> **Shimon** son of **Abram,** Melamed, had a class of 24 students in 1858 in Cheder in Kaushany. See Appendix D. There were several families with that surname in the middle of 19c *(JG)*.

Shikhman.

> **Gersh** (1914, Kaushany -), lived in Kotovsk, Odessa oblast, was arrested in 1957, and in 1960 case was dismissed *(VT)*.

Shinkar.

> **Sokher (Sukhor, Isakhar)** owned a confectionary store *(B24)*. Father - **Gersh (Tzvi).**
> wife **Gitlya,**
>> daughter __? (2-Aug-1899, Kaushany -),
>> daughter **Tsipa** (27-Feb-1902, Kaushany -).

Shitman.

> **Zelman** (1906, Bendery - 1941), trader, father - **Godl**, family lived before the war in Kaushany, **Zelman** fought in the war and was killed on the front near Odessa in 1941 *(YdV)*.

Shmulovich (Shmulevich).

> **Iosko (Iosif)** owned a tavern *(B24)*, was in Middle Class, registered in Mayaki, Podolia, father – **Yankel-Itsko,**
> wife **Yenta-Rukhlya,** father – **Aron,**
>> son **Samuel** (2-Jul-1903, Kaushany -), fought in the war and was an MIA since 1944,
>> daughter **Dusya,** "**Dusya** lived in Kishinev after the war at Kagulskaya street #27 (we lived at #35)" *(KhK)*.

Shpolyanskiy.

> **Yakov** (12-Oct-1955, Leovo, Moldova -), married in 1978,
> wife **Anna (Nonna) Geisman** (1955, Bendery), lived in Kaushany with parents until 1973. Studied at Kishinev University,
>> son **Vladmir** (10-Mar-1979, Kaushany -), graduated University in Ariel, Israel,
>> wife **Olga Heifits** (3-Apr-1980, Moscow -). Three children.
> *Emigrated to Israel in 1991 from Kishinev. (G).*

Shteyn (Stain).

> **Mnosh ben Moyshe,** was private in WWI and wounded in November of 1914.

> **Gilel (Hilel),** Middle Class, registered in Litin, Podolia gubernia, father – **Meir,**
> wife **Malka,**
>> son **Menakhem-Mendel (Menashe)** (30-Sep-1887, Kaushany -),
>> daughter **Tsivya** (3-Apr-1897, Kaushany -),
>> daughter **Basya** (5-Jan-1899, Kaushany -).

> **Menashe,** son of **Moyshe** was private in WWI, and wounded on 4-Nov-1914.

> **Pincas** (Iasi -), during the war was in Kaushany, and was in forced laborer.

Riva (Rivka) (1900, Kaushany – 1958, Storozhynets, Bukovina), father – **Lazar, Eliezer.**

Anna, housewife, and great needlewoman,
  husband **Lyusik**, worker. Lived in Kaushany from 1950s,
    daughter **Mola** (!952 -) worked in library,
    daughter **Sofa** (1955 -) was my classmate,
    son **Roman** (1959 -).
      *In 1972 family emigrated to Israel and lived in Kirijat Gata. **Sofa** got married and moved*
      *to USA, **Mola** got married in Norway. **Roman** is in Israel (G).*

Shufman.
  Nesanel,
    wife **Makhlya,**
      son **Khanina** (16-Oct-1876, Kaushany -),
      daughter **Dvoira** (10-May-1887, Kaushany -).

  Shulim, father – **David,**
    wife **Pesya,**
      daughter **Rivka** (2-Jan-1899, Kaushany -).

  Anna owned a grocery store *(B24).*

Shults (Shultz).
  Yankel was from Tarutino. He had three daughters:
    daughter **Anna**,
    daughter **Leyka**,
    daughter **Zina**, who was a secretary in the Primarie of Kaushany (Town hall).

Shuman.
  Peysya (1921 -), father **Motl** *(J-R).* Before the war lived in Kaushany.

Shvarts (Shvartz).
  Israel (1902 -), father – **Berko,**
    wife **Dvoira** (1911 -), father **Iosif,**
      son **Beresh** (1937 -) *(J-R).*

Shvartsman.
  Gersh (Zeev),
    wife **Sura-Rivka,**
      daughter **Ester** (22-Sep-1876, Kaushany -),
      son **Iosl (Yoisef)** (29-Jun-1878, Kaushany -).

  Shmul ben Gersh, was private and wounded in WWI in September of 1914.

  Mordko (Mordekhai), father – **Khaim,**
    wife **Tsipa,**
      daughter **Dina** (10-Sep-1902, Kaushany -),
      son **Froim (Efraim)** (10-Sep-1902, Kaushany -).

"It was a girl **Gita,** two years younger than me and her mother once asked me to bring **Gita** to Elementary School from home and back. After the war I saw her once. She married and lived in Romanovka, not far from Kishinev" *(KhK).*

Menasim (Menashe) (Kaushany -), had a fabric store *(B24).*
  wife **Henia Naikhovich** (Kaushany -),
    son **Iosif.**

Motel was a butcher. *(B24).*

Khaim,
  son **Gersh** owned a grocery store. *(JG-1897. Voters1906-07).*

Mark,
  son **Gersh** (1891, Kaushany -), worker,
    wife **Perli** (1897, Kaushany -), father – **Gersh,**
      son **Daniil** (1925, Kaushany -),
      daughter **Bronya** (1931, Kaushany -).

Menashe (1883, Kaushany -), father – **Berko,**
  wife **Shprintza** (1888, Kaushany -), father – **Leyzer,**
    daughter **Tzilya** (1917, Kaushany -).

Iosif (1907, Kaushany -), cooper, **Iosif** fought in the war and was killed on the front in 1941 *(YdV),*
  wife **Tsilya**, had one child.

Bentsion,
  wife **Basya,**
    daughter **Roza** (1902, Tarutino – 1941, died in Shoah, *YdV),*
      husband **Moyshe Kogan** (1892 -), lived in Kaushany before the war.
        See **Moyshe Kogan** family above.

Sichuga (Sychiga).
  Simkha, shoomaker *(B24),* father – **Mendel,**
    wife **Sima Grinberg, family** owned a Tea store,
      son **Nusn (Nyuska, Natan)** (1924, Kaushany – 1942, died on the front of the war),
        wife **Fanya Koen,** had two daughters,
      daughter **Raisa,**
        husband __**? Granik,**
      son **Mendel** (1916, Kaushany – 1942, MIA), shoemaker, died in Shoah in 1942.
        "lived not far from us. There were many children in the poor family. During the Soviets they were better. They owned a Tea store. *(KhK).*

Slepoy.
  Yakov,
    wife **Betya,**
    daughter **Rukhl,** lived in Kaushany before the war.

Iosef (14-Jan-1899 – 1-Jun-1974, Romanovka), they lived before the war in Romanovka,
      father – **David,**

wife **Khaya Epelboim** (Kaushany – 1941, killed in Ukraine, in bombardment *YdV)*,
son **David (** - 1941, killed in Ukraine, in bombardment *YdV)*,
son **Gidaliy,**
daughter **Inda** (1925 -).

Slesarenko.

Maksim,

wife **Alla** – both teachers of Kaushany Evening school. Arrived to Kaushany in the
beginning of 1960s from Zaim (close village to Kaushany). Later moved to Bendery.
daughter – **Dina** *(G)*.

Sobol.

Gersh, according to *(B24)* he had a grocery store. Was in Middle Class, registered in
Dubossary. Father - **Khaim-Leyzer**.
wife **Dobrish,**
daughter **Khaika** (1897, Kaushany – Jun-1941, Odessa, murdered *YdV*),
daughter **Molka** (1898, Kaushany - died in Shoah in 1941 *(YdV)*.

Moyshe-Duvid, was in Middle Class, registered in Dubossary, father - **Srul-
Shlema,**
wife **Tsipora,**
son **Yakov** (27-Mar-1902, Kaushany -),
son **Ber (Dov Boris)** (2-Jul-1907, Kaushany – 1944, killed during military service),
wife **Matilda Goldenberg,**
son **Israel.**

Soltanovich (Saltanovich).

Leyka owned a grocery store *(B24)*.

Khaim (Khaim-Gerts) (14-Feb-1878, Kaushany -), owned a water mill *(B24)*,
Parents **Shoel** and **Tsirlya**.

Arkadiy (Kaushany -), lived before the war in Kaushany. He had a wife and a child.
Arkadiy died in Shoah *(YdV)*.

Aron (1910, Kaushany -), fought in the war, private, was MIA, father – **Arukh**.
wife **Sura**.

Yankel,
wife **Livshe,**
daughter **Etl** (1885, Kaushany - 1941 died in Shoah in Odessa *(YdV)*,
husband **Peisakh Goligorskiy**, see family **Goligorskiy,**
daughter **Sheine-Liya** (7-Feb-1887, Kaushany -).

Yasha (Yankel) (Bendery -), in the beginning of 1930s went to Palestine to build happy
life, fought in Spain International Brigades, nickname was **Krasnov**. Died in Israel.
wife **Mara Kachkis** (1922 -), secretary,
daughter **Sofa,**
son **Artur.**

Isaak (1898, Kushany -), was a store director, father – **Shmul**,
   wife **Tuba** (1899 -), father - **Shmul** *(J-R)*.

Moyshe (1886, Kaushany – 1942, died of starvation),
   wife **Shprintsa** (1891 – 1965, Tiraspol), father – **Sender,**
     son **Leva** (- Akko, Israel), worked in trade. In the middle of 1970s moved to
       Bendery and after that emigrated to Israel.
      wife **Manya (Meni) Spivak** (- Akko, Israel), they did not have children.
        Lived in Starye (Old) Kaushany. **Meni** was a good housewife, a great cook.
       They lived in Akko, buried there. They were nice and kind people (G).
     daughter **Zina,**
      husband **Sema (Shlomo) Korenberg** lived in Old Kaushany, Zina's mother
       Shprintsa lived with them and moved to Tiraspol in the beginning of 1960s and
       in 1970s emigrated to Israel.
     son **Semen** (1924, Kaushany - Bendery) worked on bread factory,
      wife **Fira Grinberg** (1915, Talmazy - Israel), father – **Boris**, worked in trade,
       married in 1950,
       daughter **Betya Shkolnik** (1951, Kaushany -), worked in KinderCare center,
        emigrated from Kaushany in 1991,
       son **Misha (Moisey)** (1955, Kaushany -), worked as welder, now retired, lives in
        Kaushany,
     daughter **Tanya,**
      husband __? **Opachevskiy.**

Spektor.
   Abram was men's taylor (*B24*).

   David owned a tavern.

   Tema (1886 –), lived before the war in Kaushany, father – **Gdaliy.**

   Leyzer. Relocated to Kishinev before the war, died during evacuation *(YdV)*,
    wife **Ester Leya Beitenbroit** (1904, Kaushany – 1941, during evacuation).

Zelik,
   son **Motya** (1908 -), barber,
    wife **Khaika** (1905 -),
     son **Zelik** (1930 -),
   daughter **Golda** (1908 -).

Spivak.
   Volko (Vulf) (c1730 -),
    son **Shulim** (1765 – 1846),
     wife **Basya** (1770 – after 1854),
      son **Mendel** (1815 -),
       wife **Malka** (1817 -), father – **Berko,**
  |---   son **Iosif (Ioska, Iosl)** (1841, Kaushany – died before 1921),
  | daughter **Khaya** (1840 -),
  | son **Shulim** (1849 -),
  | wife **Khaya,**
  | son **Srul-David** (23-Jun-1870, Kaushany -).

Iosif (Ioska, Iosl) (1841, Kaushany – died before 1921),

  wife **Khaika**, had 4 sons and a sister,

    son **Shlyoma (Shloime)** (10-Oct-1866, Kaushany – 1943, Djezgasgan, Kazakhstan) owned a tavern *(B24)*, "in 1932 that business did not exist. At that time, he was a very small trader – getting a small credit in the morning, buying grain from farmers, and selling at the market" *(KhK).*

    wife **Sheiva (Sheivl, Basya-Sheiva) Levit** (10-Sep-1874, Kaushany - 1943, Kazakhstan). Both died from hunger in 1943 in Dzhezgasgan, Kazachstan *(YdV).* They had six children.

      son **Yankel** (1887, Kaushany -),

        wife **Sonya Gokhberg** (Tarutino – 1970, Chernovtsy), no children,

      son **Leib (Lyova)** (1898, Kaushany – 31-Mar-1964, Ismail),

        wife **Fanya Khaimovich** (1896, Tarutino – 1940, Kaushany),

        wife (second) **Khona Kogan (Natanzon),** Married in 1941, Kaushany,

         son **Iosif** (1921, Tarutino, died in 1932, Galatz),

         daughter **Khinka** (1923, Tarutino – 6-Feb-2020, Tzur-Shalom, Israel),

          husband **Abram Kogan** (7-Sep-1924, Kaushany – 9-Mar-1991am., Tzur-Shalom, Israel), see **Abram Kogan** family.

         son **Izya(Isaak)** (9-May-1928, Galatz, Romania – 29-May-2012, Seattle),

          wife **Nellya Kovarsky** (1-May-1932, Minsk -), two children: **Iosif** and **Alla**,

      son **Moisey** (17-Jan-1899- died in childhood),

      daughter **Ester** (2-Jun-1904, Kaushany – 1941, Guriev),

        husband **Boris Shafir**, lived in Petrovka, not far from Kaushany. **Ester** died during evacuation in Guriev,

      daughter **Betya** (30-Oct-1909, Kaushany – 13-May-1994, Nataniya, Israel),

        husband **Litman Roytshteyn** (1-May-1911 – 1-Jun-2002, Natania). In 1939 they lived in a village called Tomala near Chimishliya,

        daughter **Fanya** (27-Apr-1941, Kaushany -),

         husband **Lenya** died in Israel. **Fanya** lives in Tel Aviv,

        son **Grisha** (1946, Kishinev - 2003, Nataniya, Israel),

      son **Boris (Berl)** (2-Jul-1913 - 1975),

        wife **Ester Vinitskaya** (- 1992, Israel),

        daughter **Khanyusya** (1945), husband **Misha Voldman,** live in Kirijat Yam.

    son **Berl (Berku)** (8-Dec-1870 -) worked at **Moyshe Erlikh** bank,

      wife **Idora** (1872-died after 1924),

      second wife **Stunya**, two daughters and a son,

        daughter **Ester** (25-Apr-1901, Kaushany - 1989, Israel), was married and soon divorced. She was a housewife. Did not speak well Russian. Mostly spoke Yiddish. She lived with her younger sister – **Soybel Spivak.**

        husband __? **Bargolovskiy**. Lived in Kaushany the whole life (except during the war). They did not have children.

        son **Shmil (Shumli)** (2-Dec-1909 -),

        wife **Beile Spivak** his cousin, daughter of **Ershl Spivak,**

         Shmil and Beile were first cousins, and they were not allowed to get married. They asked for and received permission from King Karl 2.

        daughter **Stunya** (1933, Kaushany), lived in Bendery, and in 1970 emigrated to Israel, lived in Acco, Israel,

        daughter **Soybel** (3-Apr-1910 - , Kaushany), was engaged to a person from Old Kaushany, but the war started, and he disappeared. She was a seamstress. Lived in Kaushany with her older sister **Ester**. Died and buried in Kaushany *(G).*

son **Gutman** (1871, Kaushany – Aug, 1941, Mozdok, Caucasus). moved to Bendery
      in 1907,
  wife **Sofiya (Sisel, Sosel)** (1869, Khotin, Bessarabia – Aug-1941, Mozdok, Caucasus).
      Both died in Shoah *(YdV)* in town of Mozdok, North Caucasus.   They had four
      sons and a daughter.
    son **Abram** (7-Oct-1896, Kaushany – 22-Jun-1960),
     wife **Ida** (1896, Kirkaeshty- 1989, Bendery), three sons: **Boris, Isaak** and **Samuil,**
    son **Mendel** (23-Aug-1899, Kaushany -),
     wife **Dora,**
    son **Leib** (3-Mar-1902, Kaushany - 1988, Israel),
     wife **Dvoira Glikman** (1905-2001), daughter **Roza** (1936, Romanovka),
    son **Moyshe** (1904, Kaushany – 1941),
     wife **Tsipa,**
      daughter **Polina** (1922-1941). **Moyshe** and **Polina** died during evacuation.
    daughter **Basya** (1910, Kaushany- 1941),
     husband **Leib Tulchinskiy,** son **Monya.** All three were killed by Nazis in
      Bendery in 1941 *(YdV).*
  son **Ershl (Gersh)** (1870, Kaushany - 1941), carpenter,
   wife **Pessya,**
   wife (second) **Kriva (Stunya).** Six daughters and two sons:
   daughter **Prive** (October 30, 1895 – 1976, Israel), was married before the war,
      and husband was killed on the front of the war,
   daughter **Ester-Malka** (1896, Kaushany – Feb-1978),
    husband **Ikhil Geisman,** (1896, Kaushany – June 30, 1967, Bendery), see
      family **Geisman,**
   son **Shmil (Shumli)** (15-Sep-1897, Kaushany – 1994, Israel), after the war **Shmil**
      returned to Kaushany,
    wife **Khana (Khona) Geisman** (12-Sep-1898 - died during the war or right
      after. **Shmil** married second time,
    wife (second) **Fira,**
     son **Nyunya** (1926, Kaushany - 2003, Akko, Israel), worked in a military plant,
      wife **Liza,** lived after the war in Bendery, moved to Israel in 1973,
     daughter **Tuba (Tanya)** (1932, Kaushany -),
      husband **Shulik Itskovich** (- Dec-2005, Israel), moved to Israel in 1970s,
     daughter **Stunya** (1935 -) *(J-R).*
   daughter **Dvoira (Deborah)** (28-Oct-1899, Kaushany – died young), seamstress,
   daughter **Beyla** (35-Feb-1902, Kaushany -), seamstress,
    husband **Shmil Spivak,** her cousin, see above,
   daughter **Elka** (17-Jan-1904 – 1975, Israel), she was not married,
   daughter **Mina (Mene, Manya)** (December 11, 1908 -), seamstress
    husband **Leva Saltanovich,** did not have children. She was a housewife, moved
      to Bendery and later emigrated to Israel, Akko, where they both buried.
   son **Avrum (Abram)** (1-Jun-1909 – 1944, fought in the war, private, was MIA,
      Mem), carpenter before the war.
    wife **Sura,** sister of **Liza,** wife of **Nyunya Spivak,** see above *(Mem).*
  daughter **Frida,**
   husband **Toyva Teper,** had ten children, see **Teper** family.

Mendel (1876 -) it is possible that this family is related to Spivaks above, but the
    relationship was not established.
  wife **Roza** (1876 -) , six children: **Naftaliua** (1906), **Moyshe** (1908), **Feiga** (1910),

Sura (1913), **Shulim** (1916) and **Yankel** (1919).

Srulevich.

    Iosif (- died before 1914, Kaushany), he was a cattle trader,
      wife **Sheiva** (1837 – Feb-1941, Kaushany). Lived in Kaushany, Monzyr, possible
                Tarutino, Galatz (Romania). They had 12 children, 4 of them died young.
        children **Shlima, Sofia** and **Yakov** emigrated to USA in 1905-1906.
        son **Srul** (- c1940), lived in Odessa before 1917, left for Shanghai in 1918.
         son **Morris**. *In 1940 sent last letter to family in Kaushany after his father died.*
        son **Gedaliya** (oldest son),
        daughter **Golda** (- 1937, Kaushany), married,
          husband **Khaim Khaimovich** (c1865-1933, Galatz, Romania),
             See **Khaimovich** family.
        *In 2007 I met descendants of **Shlima** and **Sofia** living in US for the first time in 100*
        *years! After that grandson of **Shlima**, **Jeff Katz** visited my mother **Khinka** granddaughter*
        *of **Golda** in Israel. Read Jeff's stories in Chapter 5. (Yefim Kogan).*

    Roza (1896 – 26-Aug-1932, Kishinev), was buried in Kishinev Jewish cemetery and it is
        written on the tombstone that she was from Kaushany, father – **Moisey**,
    husband __? **Averbukh.**

Stanislavskiy.

    Gersh "owned a lamber shop *(B24)*, family rented house at **Shloime** Spivak's house
        before 1932" *(KhK)*,
      daughter **Leya (Leyka)** "lived near us" *(KhK)*,
        husband **Yasha Kunicher,**
      daughter **Sara,**
      son **Lyova.**

    Yakov,
      wife **Rublya** (1873 -), father – **Obo (Aba?),**
        daughter **Dora** (1910 -),
        daughter **Anna** (1912 -).

    Shlyoma was a shoemaker *(B24)*, father – **Abram (Avraham),**
      wife **Ester,** father – **David,**
        son **Shmul** (27-Feb-1897, Kaushany -),
        daughter **Elka Tsikman (Cikman),**
        daughter **Roza** (1905, Kaushany – 1943, Odessa, murdered),
         husband **Shlomo Kalitskiy,**
           daughter **Leya** (1920), all died in Shoah*(YdV),*
        son **Israel (Azriil)** (20-Jan-1903, Kaushany – Aug-1941, Odessa, murdered, *YdV*),
           shoe maker,
          wife **Esfir (Fira) Leyzgold** (1905(8), Kaushany – 1941, Odessa, murdered, *YdV*),
             parents – **Berl** and **Leya,**
           daughter **Mara** (1930, Kaushany – Aug-1941, Odessa, murdered, *YdV*),
           daughter **Basya** (1937, Kaushany – 1943, Odessa, murdered, *YdV*). All lived
             before the war in Kaushany.

Sukharlev.

    Mendel, had children **Srul, Favel, Mortko,**
      son **Srul (Isrul)** (Kaushany - Kaushany),
        wife **Miriam Vaysenberg** (Poland - Kaushany), originally from Poland,
          daughter **Rukhl** (- 1941 died in the war),
          daughter **Keyla** (3-Aug-1920, Kaushany – 26-Jul-1985, Bendery),
          daughter **Feiga** (9-Jun-1924, Kaushany – 6-Mar-2010, NY),
          daughter **Anna** (15-Apr-1925, Kaushany – 13-Jul-2018, NY),
          daughter **Yahod** (22-Apr-1928, Kaushany-),
      son **Mordko (Mordekhai), Mordko** was in Middle Class, registered in Tiraspol,
        wife **Yares,** father - **Yankel-Moshko,**
          son **Rahmil-Mendel** (27-Mar-1878, Kaushany -),
          daughter **Freyda-Maryasya** (15-Dec-1887, Kaushany -),
          daughter **Feiga** (19-Feb-1897, Kaushany -),
          daughter **Livsha** (14-May-1899, Kaushany -),
      son **Favel** (1878 - 1943),
        wife **Masya,** had 5 children:
          son **Abram** (19-Dec-1919, Kaushany – 19-Apr-1989, Bendery),
          daughter **Feiga** (, Kaushany -),
          daughter **Sonya** (, Kaushany -),
          son **Khaim** (, Kaushany -),
          son **Alik** (, Kaushany -).

    Usher Zelik (10-Oct-1876, Bendery – 1958, Philadelphia) was in Middle Class, reg. in Tiraspol. His parents – **Abram Gersh** and **Keylya.** 23-Nov-1929 arrived to Philadelphia, USA) with children **Abe, Chasya, Mania** and **Velvel**), other children in 1929 remained in Kaushany, Bessarabia, Romania).
        In 1930 changed last name to **Simmons.** *It is not clear how Usher and Mendel, Srul related*
    wife **Feiga** (- 1913),
    wife (second)**Khaika Vitcovits** (1894,Volodotolov, Russia – 1-May-1934, Kaushany),
    wife (third) **Ida,**
      daughter **Livsha** (31-May-1902 - 1995),
        husband **Nissel Krimberg** (- 1985),
          daughter **Sura,**
            husband **Gregory,**
      son **Abe (Abraham) Gersh Simmens** (1-May-1904, Kaushany – 24-Oct-1965, Philadelphia), baker,
        wife **Fannie** (26-Nov-1903 – 28-Jan-1987). They got married in Kaushany and then moved to Philadelphia. Had four children: **Betty, Clair, Yossy** and **Harvey,**
      son **Motel** (1907 – 1915),
      daughter **Osna** (15-Jun-1909 - 1997),
        husband **Michel Stepansky** (1907 – 1971),
      daughter **Chasia** (1-Jan-1912 – 1943, Bendery),
      daughter **Mania (Molly)** (3-Dec-1914 - 1971),
        husband **Morris Greenbaum,**
      son **Velvel (Volf) (Volf, William)** (1-Mar-1918 -), lived in Philadelphia,
        wife **Bea Frank**, children **Herbert** and **Sam**, served in WWII,
      daughter **Kekha (Clara)** (Aug-1920 -),
        husband **Bob Adelman** (1916 – 2008),

daughter **Rukhl (Rose)** (10-Dec-1922 -),
  husband **Samuel Luber,**
daughter **Chana** (23-Nov-1925 -),
son **Herman,**
  wife **Shirley Kershbaum,**
son **Peisa (Paul)** (23-Jan-1928 -), lived in Philadelphia and died in Florida,
  wife **Elaine** (- 1989, Florida).

Svedlik. "I remember that they had a small shop selling newspaper, stationery and paper" *(KhK).*
  Bunya owned a tavern *(B24).*

Struk and **Sheiva** owned a grocery store *(B24).*

Abram,
  wife **Tsipa**,
    daughter **Sima** (1918 , Kaushany – 1941, murdered in Shoa *YdV*),
      husband **Gersh Gitlin.** They lived in Lambrovka before the war.

Moshko was a student at Cheder in 1858 in Kaushany with melamed
  Shesterman Shimon. See Appendix D.

Yankel-Gersh (Yakov-Tsvi), owned a grocery shop, father - **Shmul**
  wife **Ester-Zislya,**
    daughter **Khaya-Sura** (6-Nov-1878, Kaushany -),
    son **Yakov** (23-Aug-1897, Kaushany -).

Tabachnik.
  Khaim (1894 -),
    wife **Chaya Sura (Klara, Tabla?) Lyubarov** (- 1928), father **Moysey.** Family owned
        a confectionery and haberdashery in the center, near "Birzha" and sold
        water and ice cream *(KhK+ B24),*
    son **Motl (Milya)** (1921 – 1942, Rostov), served in the army and got killed in
        1942 *(YdV),*
    son **Shmuel** (1921 - "served, as I remember, in pilots' battalion during the war, where
        many of our boys died in 1941-42" *(KhK),*
    son **Grisha (Ershel)** (1927 -).

Filya (Rafail) (1920, Kaushany), immigrated to Israel *(Video).*

Gullya (1924 -), father **Ekhshev** *(J-R).*

__?,
  wife __? worked in Kaushany in procurement office,
    daughter **Nina** (1958, Kaushany -), now lives in Eylat, Israel.

Tabak. Was a doctor with that surname in Kaushany in 1930s *(KhK).*

Talis.
  Matul owned a steam mill *(B24).*

  Dvoira (1905 -),

husband **David**,
   son **Shula** (1933 -) *(J-R)*.

Mordko (Mordekhai),
  wife **Khaya-Sura,**
    son **Srul-Yankel** (18-Aug-1887, Kaushany -), twin,
    son **Vigder-Leib** (18-Aug-1887, Kaushany -), twin.

Osip-Matus, was in Middle Class, registered in Kishinev, father – **Itsko**,
  wife **Iska-Malka,**
    son **Leyzor** (6-Jan-1899, Kaushany -).

Abram,
  wife **Gitya** (1884 -), father – **Berko**. Family lived in Kaushany before the war *(YdV)*,
    son **Berko** (1918 -), was a saddler,
    son **Iosif** (1923 -),
    daughter **Tsilya** (1926 -).

Talisman.
    Khaika, lived in Talmaz, father – **David**,
   husband (second) **Misha,**
    daughter **Riva** (1934 -),
    daughter **Fanya,**
    daughter **Polina** (1857, Kaushany -),
      husband **Abram Stekolshchik.**

Talmatskiy.
    Rakhmil was a tinsmith, according to *B24* – roofer,
    son **Iosif** (1914 -), tinsmith, was one of the leaders of communists in *Kaushany (from Pilat I.N, book "From the History of Jews in Moldavia"),*
   wife **Valya Stiopkina,**
  son __? was a cantor in synagogue.
"They had several children, but I knew only one - **Iosif** (1914), tinsmith, who was in prison in Doftana, Romania together with a friend **Aron Dvoirin** for five years for communist matters. After the war, he married Moldovan **Valya Styopkina,** I studied with her in elementary school. I also remember **Iosif**'s brother, who was a khazan and very nicely sang in a synagogue during Jewish holidays. Their mother said that **Valya** is the best daughter-in-law" *(KhK)*.

Teper.
    Toyva,
  wife **Frida Spivak**, they had 10 children,
    son **Lyova** (1897 - 1989, Kishinev), lived in Kaushany before the war,
     wife **Klara** (1898 - 1980, Ladispoli, Italy, during emigration from USSR,
      daughter **Zhana** (1925, Galats, Romania – 1999, Rotchester, NY),
       husband **Fima Reytikh** (1921, Kishinev – 2004, Rotchester, NY)   ,
    son **Yankel** worked in a bakery in Kaushany, made bagels,
     wife **Etl Lifshits**, son **Lyova** (oldest), moved to Canada,
      son **Yura**, wife **Lyuba**, lived in Moscow, Australia, children **Ida, Lilya,**
      daughter **Frida** (1923-24, Kaushany – 1980s, Kishinev),
       husband **Shura Litvin**, emigrated to Beer-Sheva, son **Lyonya,**
     son **Lyonya,**

son **Tolya,** immigrated to Israel,

son **Sasha** (1941), wife **Lida,** lived in Moscow, immigrated to Los Angeles,

son **Roma** lives in Los Angeles,

daughter **Rukhl** (1889 – Feb-1942, Turkmenistan),

husband **Ershel Levit** (1886 – Jan-1942, Turkmenistan), see **Levit** family,

daughter **Pesse,** "**Pesse** lived in a village of Tarakliya. I remember her from 1936-37, she died during the war" *(KhK).*

daughter **Malka,**

husband **Ruven Khotinskiy,**

daughter **Frida** (1924, Zaim), lived in Zaim and Lambrovka, not far from Kaushany. Married to a Polish Jew and went with him to Belgium after the war.

daughter **Khana,**

daughter **Basya,**

daughter **Zelda,**

son **Mendel** owned a bakery *(B24).* They lived after the war in Bendery,

daughter **Elka,**

son **Elik** (1906, Kaushany- 1980, Israel), sold fish before the war,

wife **Tuba Lifshits,** son **Leova** (1939), wife **Polina,** live in Toronto.

Topor.

Gersh-Leib (Gershon) (1882, Kaushany – 1943, near Stalingrad), hat-master, died in Shoah in 1943 near Stalingrad under bombardment, father - **Ruvin,**

wife **Bat-Sheva Bilerkina,** parents **Zelman** and **Raya** (1877 -),

son **Benyamin** (1925 -).

Tovbin.

Ion (1912, Kaushany – 1941) fought in the war and was was MIA since 1941, lived in Akkerman before the war, father - **Isaak.**

Itsko (1921 -), fought in the war and died in 1944 (Mem). Father – **Berko.**

Trakhtenberg.

Leyzer, "I remember **Leyzer.** He went with his horse wagon to the villages buying eggs. One day he was killed, and his horses brought him home *(in 1930s).* The whole town was shaken. *(KhK).*

son **Abram.** "**Abram** was involved in a process for communist propaganda together with my uncle **Boris** in 1933 and was jailed for 4 months "*(KhK),*

wife **Golda Bersudskaya** (died young),

wife (second) __? lived in Haifa,

son **Alex** lives in Philadelphia,

son **Mekhel,**

wife **Milka Roitshtein,** sister of **Litman,** husband of my mother's aunt **Betya** *(KhK),*

son ? "who was involved in the case of the hijacking a plane by Jewish students, in order to go to Israel. He was jailed in the 70s. After he was released, he moved to Israel for a short time, later USA. **Mekhel** died a long time ago, **Milka** lived for some time with her son in USA, but later returned to Israel" *(KhK).*

Monya (1890, Kaushany – murdered in Transnistria), trader,

wife **Manya** (1895, Kaushany -), both died in Shoah in Transnistria *(YdV).*

Kheskel (1901, Kaushany – 1941-42, killed in military service near Stalingrad), parents **Perl** and **Abram** *(YdV)*,
wife **Rakhel Vaysman**,
son **Abram**.
Khaim (1890 -), father – **Mikhail,**
wife **Roza** (1904), father - **Volf**, seamstress, family lived in Kaushany before the war,
son **Solomon** (1927, Kaushany -),
son **Boris** (1930, Kaushany -) *(J-R)*.

Raya lived in Kaushany. She was a sister of **Pesya Mikhailovskaya**. **Raya** had two sons: **Sema** (was killed) and **Borya** *(G)*.

Treyger.
Abram was a men's tailor *(B24)*. Was in Middle Class, registered in Soly, Vilna Gubernia, father – **Itsko (Yitzkhak),**
wife **Reyzlya,**
daughter **Shlima** (3-Jan-1915, Kaushany -),
daughter **Ranya** (1923 -), lived in Kaushany before the war.

Ershel, baker,
wife **Riva,** lived in Kaushany, seamstress,
son **Filipp** lives in Russia,
daughter **Sima** lives in USA.

Shurik, mechanic,
wife **Lilya,** worked in commerce. Emigrated to Israel in 1990s. Lived in Petah-Tikva. Two sons: one lives in Kishinev, second – in Israel *(G)*.

Tsapovskiy.
Aleksandr – engineer-mechanic,
wife **Ella,** doctor ophthalmologist in Kaushany region Hospital. Came to Kaushany in the beginning of 1960s to work. father – **Peter,**
daughter **Lilya.** "Family emigrated to Israel in the beginning of 1990s. **Ella** was a terrific doctor, specialist. Even in old age found a job in Israel, what was not easy in 1990s. She died in Israel. They lived in Ashdod" *(G)*.
brother of **Aleksandr __?,** worked as engineer,
wife __? was a doctor laboratory assistant,
son **Marik** (1951-52?) studied in Russian school. He graduated with honors *(G)*.

Tsiekh.
Mendel studied in the same class with **Lev Bruter**, class in Kaushany middle school *(Video)*.

Tsimbler.
Mendl, relocated to Kishinev before the war,
wife **Udl** (1877, Kaushany – 1941, died in Shoa *YdV*).

Tsinkler.
Isak – moved to Kaushany after the war from village Opach, not far from Kaushany. Was a tailor. *(G),*
Isak's brother _?,
wife _? **Melamed**. Came to Kaushany from Opach *(G)*.

Tsurkan.
  __?, was a doctor in Kaushany hospital.

Tulchinskiy.
  "I remember that they had a store" *(KhK).*
  Shmil owned a grocery store *(B24).* Father – **Motel,**
    son **Borya** studied with me in Gymnasium *(KhK).*

  Abram (c1890 -), was a blacksmith,
    wife **Khana,**
      son **Mordekhay** (1935, Kaushany – murdered in Shoa, Kitskany).

  Boyaz,
    daughter **Maria** (1903 -),
      husband **Izrail** (1900 -), father – **Shmul.**

  Khava (1876 – 1941, murdered), merchant, parents **Dov** and **Rivka,**
    husband **Peisakh Kogan,** lived in Kaushany before the war, **Peisakh** was my great
        grandfather (Yefim K.)**,** see **Kogan** families.

Turkenich.
  Yefim (1924, Kaushany – 1942, killed in combat, buried in village Michurino), parents
        Aron and Polya, lived before the war in a German colony Leiptsig, Bessarabia (now
        Odessa oblast) *(YdV).* **Yefim** had a brother who survived.

Vaksman.
  Idel,
    wife **Pesya,**
      son **Perets** (29-Nov-1871, Kaushany -).

  Srul (-1983, Bendery),
    wife **Sarra** (- Israel). Lived in Kaushany after the war until the middle of 1970s,
      daughter **Anna** (~1948), married in Bendery. Graduated Kaushany Russian school,
      son **Sema** (1955), studied in Kaushany school,
      son **Dodik.**
  From Bendery family emigrated to Israel in 1990s (G).

Vasserman (Wise, Wasserman).
  Abraham,
    wife **Sureh Rivka Toben** (second marriage). (- c1909). Family owned a
        confectionery shop. They sold milk, cheese and ice cream, baked goods, and candies.
      son **Leyzor,**
        wife **Khaya-Rukhlya,**
          daughter **Mariya** (30-Apr-1899, Kaushany -),
      daughter **Feige Hinda** (1891 -),
        husband __?,
      son **Joseph (Joe),** was first one to come to USA from the family,
      son **David.**

  Shloime, lived before the war in Kishinev,

wife **Klara Khaya Pogoriler** (7-Mar-1907, Kaushany – 2-Jan-1981, Czernovtsy, Ukraine),
>> son **Efim.**

Vatashevskiy (Vitashevskiy).
>> **Zise,**
>>> wife **Tsipora,**
>>>> son **Bentsion** (1900, Kaushany – 1942, Stalingrad, an MIA, *YdV)*, shoemaker, parents **Zus** and **Tsipora**, family lived in Kaushany before the war,
>>>>> wife **Brana (Bronya) Zemelman** (1905 -), father – **Aron,**
>>>>>> daughter **Mikhlya** (1924 -),
>>>>>> daughter **Kilya (Kalya)** (1933 -),
>>>>> son **Leyzer** (1913 -),
>>>>>> wife **Nesya (1914 -), father – Elik.**

Vaynberg (Vanberg, Vainberg, Vannberg).
>> **Pinkhas,** was citizen of Moldova principality, later it became part of Romania,
>>> wife **Ester Marya,**
>>>> son **Iosif** (1874, Kaushany -),
>>>>> son **Zelman** (1909, Kaushany -),
>>>>> daughter **Roza** (1913 -),
>>>> daughter **Malka** (24-Mar-1876, Kaushany -),
>>>> daughter **Rukhlya (Rakhel)** 31-Jan-1878, Kaushany -).

> **Solba** (1888 -), father – **Lev.**

> **Itsko (Itzkhak),** was citizen of Romania, father – **Nuta,**
>> wife **Genya-Rukhlya,** father – **Moshko,**
>>> son **Shloime** (14-May-1897, Kaushany -),
>>> son **Gersh (Tzvi)** (29-Apr-1902 -).

> **Yankel,**
>> wife **Khana** (1916 -), tailor, family lived in Kaushany before the war, father – **Khaim,**
>> daughter **Dora** (1941 -).

> **Grigoriy** was chief physician of Kaushany Veterinary hospital (1950-60s),
>> wife **Lyubov,**
>>> daughter **Lina** (c1948-49, Kaushany -),
>>> daughter **Lora** (c1951, Kaushany -).
>>> *Family moved from Kaushany at the end of 1970s, and later emigrated to USA(G).*

> **Ida** (1931 -), father **Semen**, Russian Language teacher in school,
>> husband **Grigoriy**, engineer,
>>> son **Sasha** (1955 -) – math teacher,
>>> daughter **Anya** (1958 -) – biology teacher.
>>> *Family moved to Bendery, and emigrated to Israel, live in Ashdot (G).*

Vaysbeyn.
>> **Roza,** husband **Zeylik Pechyonyy,** see **Pechyonyy** family.

Vaysenberg.

Ida (Kaushany -), parents **Leyka (Liza)** and **Shimke**. Ida in 2008-9 moved to Germany
to live with her granddaughter.

Vayser.

Duvid glazier *(B24)*.

Vaysfeld.

Etya, father – **David,** after the war lived in Kaushany and was a French Language
teacher in Russian school #3 *(G)*.

Shoilyk,
wife **Sarra**. Lived in Kaushany and died in old ages. They had 3 daughters *(G)*.

Abram (Arkadiy) (– 2012, Bendery) grow up in Kaushany, studied in Russian school,
worked in a service center, moved to Bendery, died in 2012,
wife **Bilana,** moved to Israel with grown up daughters *(G)*.

Vaysman.

Itsek (Iche) owned a tavern *(B24)*. "He was a friend of **Leva Spivak**, my father.
They worked together as accountants at Egg-Chicken plant after the war" *(KhK)*.

Matus (Motes, Matel), was selling paint *(B24).*, father – **Iosko (Iosif),**
wife **Gudlya (Hadel),**
daughter **Ester** (19-Sep-1902, Kaushany -).

Moshko,
wife **Rukhlya,**
son **Moshko** (19-Aug-1878, Kaushany -),
*Moshko and his brother **Khaim** were students in Cheder class of 1858 in Kaushany,* see
Appendix D.
Etl (Kaushany - 1941, near Astrakhan, died from starvation), tailor, mother - **Genesse**
husband **Mendel (Monya) Garshtein** (1908, Kaushany-1941, died from bombardment),
see **Garshtein** family.

Dudle.

Haike.

Veytsman.

Shlema owned a tavern, inn *(B24)*.

Viner.

Nyusya. worked as pharmacists in Kaushany pharmacy,
husband **Efim Mikhailovskiy**. See **Mikhailovskiy** family.

Dvoira,
husband **Nasanel Goldfarb** (1888, Kaushany – killed in Shoa), trader, *(YdV)*.
See **Goldfarb** family.

Vinitskiy.

David "was a father of my aunt **Ester**, wife of Uncle **Boris Spivak,** he owned a
blacksmith shop. *(KhK)*,
daughter **Ester** (- 1992, Israel),
husband **Boris (Berl) Spivak** (2-Jul-1913-1975), see **Boris Spivak** family,
daughter **Pesya,**
daughter **Enta.**

Shmerel (1882 -), father – **Srul-Ios**, from Kriulayny,
wife **Charna Volodarskaya** (1891 -), married 27-May-1914 in Kaushany, father –
Ovshey son of **Leib,**
daughter **Enta** (1917 -).

Vinokur.

Srul (Yisroel), was in Middle Class, registered in Bendery, Kaushany society,
wife **Tsipa,**
son **Bentsion** (2-Jul-1876, Kaushany -),
son **Itsik** (23-Jul-1878, Kaushany -).

Meyer,
daughter **Lelya** (1921 -), lived in Kaushany before the war.

Khanna, died and buried in Kaushany.
daughter **Liza,** died and buried in Kaushany
husband **Froyka Kupershlak.** See family **Kupershlak.**

Itskhak,
wife **Rakhel,**
daughter **Dora (Dvoira)** (May 30, 1920, Kaushany – October 17, 1985, Kishinev),
husband **Irikhem Ochakovskiy** (Kaushany – 2015, Beer-Sheva), see **Ochakovskiy**
family.

Vitkovskiy.

Yakov (1914, Kaushany – was in the military, died during defense of Sevastopol *(YdV)*,
parents **Elik** and **Ester,**
wife **Sura.**

Voldman.

Iosif,
son **Yakov** arrived to Kaushany in the beginning of 1950s from Romanovka
(Bessarabka), was director of Service plant, and later manager of procurement
Office,
wife **Basya Kuchuk** was an accountant, father – **Grigoriy,**
daughter **Lilya.** Emigrated in 1990s to USA *(G)*,
son **Eynekh (Leonid).** Came to Kaushany from Romanovka (Bassarabka), worked in
trade,
wife **Tuba (Tanya) Kuchuk**, housewife. Had two daughters:
daughter **Fanya** (1948 -),
daughter **Shura** (1951 -). Emigrated to USA in 1990s *(G)*.

Kutsa,

husband – **Yakov Litmanovich.** See **Litmanovich** family. *(G).*

Volodarskiy.

    Ovshey (Yehoshua) (26-Mar-1897, Kaushany -), father – **Leib,**

    wife **Menya-Rakhlya,** had five sons and a daughter. **Ovshiy** owned a tavern, inn *(B24),*

        father – **Abram,**

      son **Moyshe** (1883-1959, Kishinev),

        wife **Khaika** (1885 – 1953, Kazakhstan), had four sons:

          son **Iosif** (1909-2004, Los Angeles). emigrated in USA, LA in 1991,

            wife **Tsilya** (26-Aug-1911 – 6-Mar-1992, Kishinev),

          son **Abram** (27-Mar-1915, Kaushany -1953, Kazakhstan), from twins. He was
            arrested in 1945 by NKVD and sent to GULAG *(VT).*

          son **David** (27-Mar-1915, Kaushany - 2005, Los Angeles), from twins, emigrated
            in USA, LA in 1980,

            wife **Shaindl Lipkansky (**1910_-1988, Los Angeles),

          son **Mekhel** (1918, Kaushany-2009, Los Angeles), emigrated to USA, LA in
            1991,

            wife **Mira Shaposhnikova** (1927-2018, Los Angeles),

            "I knew **Moyshe** personally. They had a small grocery shop after the bridge. One
            of several rich families (Video). As I remember correctly **Moyshe** was deported in
            1940, when the Soviets came" *(KhK).* "In 1941 **Moyshe, Chaika.** their son
            Mekhel were sent into exile in Actyubinsk oblast, Kazakhstan. The family returned
            to Kishinev in 1956 *(Yasha V. and JG).*

      daughter **Charna,**

        husband **Shmerel Vinitskiy,** married 27-May-1914, Kaushany. *(JG).* See
            Vinitskiy family.

      daughter **Ester? (Khaika),**

        husband **Moyshe (Mendel) Kopanskiy,** see **Kopanskiy f**amily,

      son **Aron** (8-Nov-1902, Kaushany – 27-May-1981, Kishinev),

        wife **Elka**, died in Kishinev,

          daughter **Raya**, died in Kishinev,

            *"After the war **Aron** worked with your father for many years."* *(KhK).*

      son **Kolman** (30-Jan-1887 – 12-Feb-1966, Kishinev),

        wife **Masya**, died in Kishinev,

        daughter **Roza Dvoirin (Mitelman),**

          husband **Aron Dvoirin** (see **Dvoirin** family).

          *"I remember Roza Dvoirin, her husband Aron Dvoirin. They were my close
            Friends". (KhK)*

        daughter **Raya,**

        son **Leonid**, died in Los Angeles,

      son **Raful** emigrated/escaped to Argentina in c1920,

      son **Srul (Israil)** (26-Mar-1897, Kaushany – 5-Feb-1965, Kishinev) *(JG),*

        daughter **Raechka** 14-Dec-1937 – 29-Dec-1941),

        son **Monya**. Died in Israel.

Yatom.

    Mordekhai (Reb Motl), from Bendery,

      wife **Miriam,**

        son **Iosif** (1902, Peschanka, Podolia – 1944, killed in Kaushany, murdered), Rabbi in
          Kaushany from 1928.

        wife __**?,** *(Bendery Yizkor book).*

Zaborov.
> **Shmil** (1905 – 1944), father - **Duvid-Khaim,** fought in war and was MIA since 1944 (Mem),
> wife **Molka,** father – **Leontiy.**

Zaltsman.
> **Isaak**, accountant,
>> wife **Betya,**
>>> daughter **Faya** (1955, Kaushany -), "my classmate, family came to Kaushany after
>>> the war" *(G).*
>>> daughter __?.
> *Family moved to Bendery at the end of 1960s (G).*

Zalzgend.
> **Khana** (1910 -), father - **Leib** *(J-R).*

Zaslavskiy.
> **David,**
>> wife **Beila,** father – **Yakov,**
>>> son **Mikhail** (1922, Kaushany - 1943) fought in war, MIA since 1943 *(Mem).*

Zeltser (Zelcer, Zeltzer).
> **Leib Aharon,** owned small hardware store, and groceries *(JG),* father – **Ikhil,**
>> wife **Malka,** was a blacksmith, *B24.* Had 8 sons and 3 daughters,
>>> daughter **Bunya** (1897, Kaushany – 1943, Namangan, Uzbekistan during
>>> evacuation),
>>>> husband **Volf Kofman** (1892 -), accountant, father **Itsik,** see **Kofman** family,
>>> son **Iosif** (1901, Kaushany – killed in 1942, Kishinev), head of a bank, **Iosif** murdered
>>> in Shoah in 1942 *(YdV),*
>>>> wife **Dora (Dvora).** Lived in Galatz, but during the war they were in Kishinev,
>>>>> daughter **Dina** (1924, Kaushany - 1942, killed in Shoa, *YdV),*
>>> son **Ikhil** (12-Dec-1903, Kaushany – killed 1941, Kaushany) *(JG, YdV),* Ironmonger,
>>> son **Raful,**
>>>> daughter **Malvina (Molka) Levit,**
>>>>> son **Semyon (Senya)** (1951), graduated school #34, Kishinev in 1968,
>>>>> lives in Seattle, WA,
>>> son **Shloime,** had daughter **Dora (or Dvora),** her son **Leonid** lives in Massachusetts.
>>> son **Shoil** was communist sympathizers, died in NY,
>>>> son **Yasha,** lives in Richmond, VA, has a daughter **Francis,**
>>> son **Shmil** (Kaushany - died young, about 40 years old in 1940 from tuberculosis,
>>> Kishinev),
>>>> son **Mordekhai (Musya)** (- 1990, Pittsburg, PA),
>>>>> wife **Basya Lerner** (1927, Bendery - 2014, San-Diego, buried in San-Jose, CA),
>>> son **Zainvel (Seinvel)** (1908, Kaushany – 1942, Odessa), was a communist
>>> sympathizer, was killed in Shoa,
>>> son **Falik** (1915, Kaushany -), was zealous communist and was imprisoned in
>>> Doftana, Romania, fought against Germans, lost one arm, and was a war veteran
>>> under Soviets,
>>>> second wife **Charna Kofman,** daughter of **Bunya** below, had 2 children **Boris** and
>>>> **Tanya.** Live in Israel.
>>> daughter **Tabel (Taba, Tuba) Friling** (1917, Kaushany -). Had one son. Evacuated

during the war to Namangan, Uzbekistan.
daughter **Roza** (1906, Kaushany -) **,** had no children, during the war was evacuated
to Uzbekistan.

Abram – was one of the communist leaders in Kaushany *(from the book of Pilat I.N.*
*"History of Jews in Moldova"). Not sure how **Abram** is related to other Zelter*
families?

Zemelman (Zamelman).
Leiba (1879 -), "owned a tavern, inn., lived in Kaushany before the war, father
Vladimir,
son **Ayksh** (1918 -), weaver *(J-R),*
daughter **Sara** (1923 -).

Aron (Aharon),
wife **Feiga,**
son **Leib** (1882, Kaushany – Jul-1942, Fergana, died during evacuation), farmer,
wife **Reizl Zaslavskaya,**
daughter **Miriam Kislyanskaya,** moved to Israel,
son **Avrum** (- 1998-99, Hulon, Israel**),** "I remember him very well, he was
always a humorist at the table. He also was the one who always toasted on
Passover – 'Next Year in Jerusalem'" *(KhK).*
wife **Mara (Mariem) Kogan** (3-Apr-1920, Kaushany – died, Israel), parents
Yankel and **Beila,**
son **Rivn,**
daughters **Dolya, Khana** and **Riva. Riva** immigrated to Palestine in 1930s,
son **Yankel** (1892, Kaushany – 24-Jul-1944, Tashkent obl.), father – **Abram,**
wife **Dvoira Venberg** (1901 -)**,** father – **Shaim,**
daughter **Doyla (Deyla)** (1924, Kaushany -),
daughter **Makhlya** (1926, Kaushany -),
daughter **Brana (Bronya)** (1905 -),
husband **Bentsion Vatashevskiy** (1900, Kaushany – 1942, Stalingrad, was an MIA,
YdV), shoemaker, parents **Zus** and **Tsipora,** family lived in Kaushany
before the war. See **Vatashevskiy** family.

Roza (1892 -), lived in Kaushany before the war, father - **Muney** *(J-R).*

Moshko owned a tavern *(B24).*

Zilberleib.
Berko, *Information from JG records, thanks to **Dmitry R.***
wife **Perlya** (1810 -),
son **Srul-Gersh** (1829-30 -) was a farmer in Balashevka, Tiraspol uezd, Kherson
gub. *(JG-1858).* After 1858 the family moved to Kaushany and was relisted from
farmers to Middle Class *(JG-1864).*
wife **Nesya** (1828 -),
son **Moyshe-Ber** (1848 -),
son **Avrum** (1851 -),
daughter **Feiga** (1855 -),
daughter **Enta** (1857 -),
son **Yankel** (1832 -),

wife **Velya** (1835 -),
son **Beynes (Beinish)** (1841, Kaushany -),
daughter **Malka** (1843, Kaushany -).

Zilberman (Zylberman).
Yakov-Iosif, was citizen of Turkey,
wife **Zlata,**
son **Sender** (10-Nov-1878, Kaushany -),
son **Noyach** (5-Oct-1887, Kaushany -).

Avrum,
wife **Sara** (1905, Kaushany – 1941, Kleastitz, died in Shoa, *YdV*), lived before the war
in a village, Klyastitz, near Tarutino.

Shabsa, before the war lived in Kaushany,
son **Semen** (1913 -), confectioner *(J-R)*,
daughter **Dine** (1919 -)
daughter **Ite** (1925 -).

Zilbershteyn.
Leiba was a butcher *(B24)*.

Zisman.
Zelman, "I remember **Zelman** well. He was a relative of my grandfather **Shloime.**
According to *B24* he owned a fabric store, but in the middle of 30s the store was
gone." *(KhK).*
wife **Mirel (Mirlya),**
son **Srul,**
wife **Elka,** father – **Iosko,**
son **Leib** (1-Jan-1897, Kaushany -),
son **Yakov** (9-Mar-1899, Kaushany -),
son **Syoma (Shlioma, Shlomo)** (17-Jan-1915, Kaushany -),
son **Pinya** (1908, Kaushany – 8-Jul-1944), fought in the war, sergeant and was killed
in 1944 *(Mem),*
daughter __?.

Zismanovich.
Srul, nickname «Katyr», owned a haberdashery shop, *(KhK).*

Moshe (Moisey) (1886 -), father **Khaim,**
wife **Manzi (Miriyam, Mindel)** (1885 -), father – **Abram.**
daughter **Dvoira** (1917 -),
daughter **Rukhlya** (1920 -), seamstresses,
daughter **Perla** (1924 -),
son **Zeev (Volf)** (1911, Kaushany – 1942, fought in the war, private, was killed in
fighting near Stalingrad), *(YdV, J-R).*
wife **Bella,**
daughter **Ester.**

Zolotov.
Ilona owned a grocery store *(B24)*.

Yankel, father – **Khaim**. Found in Duma Voter list in 1906-1907. *(JG)*.

Zonis.
    Leib,
      wife **Pesya-Rivka,**
        son **Usher-Zeilik** (21-Jan-1878, Kaushany -).

    Samuil, moved to London and disappeared,
      daughter **Beila Goldshtein** (Romanovka -),
      step-son __? in 1960s moved to Kaushany,
      step-daughter __? in 1960s moved to Kaushany.

    Aleksander,
      wife **Rachel (Raya) Lerner,**
        son **Semen (Sam)** (Kaushany - 2015, Israel). He was a physics teacher in
          Mathematical School #34 in Kishinev in 1960-1970s. He was my teacher *(Yefim K.)*.
      wife **Lyusya.**

    Yudko (1852 -), son of **Fishel** was student at Cheder in 1858 in Kaushany with
      melamed **Shesterman Shimon.** See Appendix D.

Total of **259 different surnames, 202** surnames were in the original version.

Total of **1016 families, 532** families were in the original version.

Total of **2957** Jews, **1243** Jews were in the original version.

Bibliography

Map of the Carpathians, Roumania and Part of Balkans. (1916). Albany, NY: Cartographer G. Peltier.

(1940-1941). *Land and Property documents.* Kishinev: Moldova Republic Archive.

Final Report of the International Commission on the Holocaust in Romania. (2004). Bucharest, Romania.

Holocaust on the territory of U.S.S.R. (2011). Moscow: ROSSPAN.

Jewish Documentary Sources in Saint Petersburg Archives. (2011). Saint Petersburg, Russia: Mir.

Broghauz, & Efron. (1908-1913). *Jewish Encyclopedia.* St. Petersburg, Russia.

Dubnov, S. (2002, reprint). *Newest History of the Jews, 3 volums.* Msocow.

Ed. Michael Berenbaum and Fred Skolnik. (2007). *Encyclopaedia Judaica.* Detroit: Macmillan.

Eliach, Y. (1998). *There once was a world. A 900-Year Chronicle of the Shtetl of Eishyshok.* Boston, New York, London: Little Brown and Company.

Kantemir, D. (1714, Latin, 1973, Russian). *Descriptio Moldaviae (Biblioteka Academiae Mosqvitanae Scientiarum.* Kishinev.

King, C. (1999). *The Moldovans. Romania, Russia, and the Politics of Culture.* Standford, CA: Hoover Institute Press.

Kogan, Y. (2021). *Family Album, Volumes 1, 2. Eight edition.* Boston, MA.

Magocsi, P. R., & Matthews, G. J. (1993). *Historical atlas of East Central Europe.* Seattle: University of Washington Press.

Mitrasca, M. (2002). *Moldova: A Romanian Province Under Russian Rule.* New York: Algora Publishing.

Nesterov, T. (2002). *Patrimonial cultural al judetului Tighina.* Kishinev.

Pilat, I. (1990). *Iz istorii evreev v Moldove (From the History of Jews in Moldova).* Kishinev: Society of Jewish culture.

Russian Jewish Encyclopedia. www.rujen.ru. (n.d.).

Schulsohn, S. J. (n.d.). *Immigration and Settlement of the Jews in Bukovina.* Retrieved from JewishGen: http://www.jewishgen.org/yizkor/bukowinabook/buk1_001.html

Tamari, M. (1975). *Kehilat Benderi: sefer zikaron.* Tel-Aviv.

The YIVO Encyclopedia of Jews in Eastern Europe, Bessarabia. (n.d.). New York: YIVO.

Sapozhnikov, I. (2016). *Causeni in the second half of the XVIIIc.: Kurum Giray Khan palace and other structures.* Kherson University, Kherson, #3 (6)

www.ingramcontent.com/pod-product-compliance
Lightning Source LLC
Chambersburg PA
CBHW082009150426
42814CB00005BA/274